THREE WORLDS, ONE VOYAGE

Cruising to Antarctica *(and trying to get home)*
during the Coronavirus Pandemic

A Travel Memoir by

DON JORGENSEN

HUMAN FACTOR PRESS
TUCSON, AZ

ISBN: 978-0-578-77024-6
Printed in the United States of America
Human Factor Press, Tucson, AZ

Book design by TeaBerryCreative.com
Front cover photo by the author

"ALL JOURNEYS HAVE SECRET DESTINATIONS
OF WHICH THE TRAVELER IS UNAWARE."
—*Martin Buber*

TABLE OF CONTENTS

To Kathy,
For sharing the greatest journey of all.

ONE

WELCOME TO ARGENTINA

"If that's all that happens, no problem."

SATURDAY, MARCH 7, 2020

My cellphone buzzed as I stepped off the plane.

"What is it?" Kathy asked as I blinked at the morning light filtering through the wall-to-ceiling windows of the strange terminal. I nodded toward the left and leaned against a wall away from the rush of fellow airplane escapees and scanned the brief text.

"It's from American. I think we have a problem."

The text from American Airlines alerted me that one of our bags had been stuck on a conveyor belt in Los Angeles. They promised to send it on the next flight. I knew there was only one flight a day from LA to Buenos Aires because we had just walked off it. It was 8:00am. The next one would not arrive for another 24 hours. We would not be here when it arrived. We would be 300 miles away. And only in that location for 48 hours.

The silver lining was the four-hour layover we faced before we had to catch a domestic airline flight to Ushuaia, the small port town perched near the southern tip of Argentina from which our 12-day Antarctica cruise would depart. I hoped that four hours would be sufficient to arrange for our wayward suitcase to follow our trail on two different airlines and across three different terminals and arrive in Ushuaia before we set sail on Monday.

We had left Tucson 20 hours earlier and now traipsed bleary-eyed through the Buenos Aires terminal after the overnight flight. I had entered that 'overtired but not sleepy' twilight zone of international travel. Kathy and I hiked down an endless hallway past waiting gates areas full of excited flyers. We descended the escalators to the baggage carousels to learn which of our two bags arrived and which was the unlucky loser of this little lottery. I hoped that Kathy's suitcase would appear rather than mine since it would be far easier for me to make the last-minute clothing purchases for this trip. Twenty minutes later my dry, scratchy eyes had scanned and re-scanned dozens of suitcases circling by.

A familiar blue bag emerged from the black hole into the light, a familiar million miler tag printed for "Donald G. Jorgensen" dangling from the handle.

Darn. My suitcase had made the trip; Kathy's bag remained stranded, cold, and alone at LAX. The missing suitcase contained all of Kathy's cold weather—really cold weather—clothing. Since she had packed multiple layers for temperatures ranging from zero to a new Ice Age, we now faced the possibility of a last-minute speed shopping extravaganza at three times the price.

I eased away from the grinding baggage claim carousel to

stand against a small row of bolted-together chairs and called the number on the back of my American Airlines card. I knew that since 'my' AA was not a partner airline with the other AA— Aerolineas Argentinas—the delinquent suitcase might not be automatically transferred. I had to make certain that the suitcase would arrive in Buenos Aires tomorrow morning, be taken off one plane, carried from the international terminal to the small domestic terminal, placed on a plane belonging to a different airline, and reach Ushuaia on the only flight arriving before our departure on Monday. I ran through each step in my head. I knew it could be done, but I was standing in an unfamiliar airport in an unfamiliar country. I pictured Kathy's suitcase exiled to airport limbo, aka the island of misfit bags, upon arrival in Buenos Aires. I was concerned. I felt some trepidation; not a great way to start a vacation. Worse, I hated the feeling of helplessness knowing that I had zero control over the outcome. I knew that I needed help.

I wasted the next fifteen minutes stuck in a frustrating telephone conversation with "Jenny," a polite client service representative who spoke halting English with a very heavy yet unidentifiable accent. She slowly and carefully explained to me—twice—what I already knew. The bag would arrive in Buenos Aires on the same flight tomorrow morning. She could not give me any information or assurance beyond that. Jenny and the help desk were no help.

This was not a surprise to anyone who travels a lot. I would not call myself a road warrior, but I do average about 15-20 trips each year, mostly around the US and Canada. And I really do not like to check bags. But I love to travel. Most trips result from rewarding work as a behavioral health surveyor or as a private consultant for behavioral health programs.* The consultancy pays much better, but the surveyor work provides value by helping organizations improve their operations and service outcomes. I also try to mix in one or two international trips per year for social service or pleasure, which feeds my childhood desire to see the worlds across the oceans. I had toyed with the thought of making this trip for many years, never certain that I would have the chance. Thanks to several fortunate events of recent years (described later in the book) we were on our way to Antarctica, my seventh continent.

I recall the scene in 'Up in the Air' where George Clooney's character pulls out his huge stack of travel affinity cards to breeze through a hotel check-in. I could relate. Fortunately, spending that much time on the road does provide more than just travel benefits. Kathy swears that my solo excursions also enhance marriage longevity. If I have not left my home office for six or seven weeks, I am likely to get a sideways look at dinner followed by a suggestion. Like on Jeopardy (an all-time favorite) it comes in the form of a question: "Don't you have a trip coming up soon?" I think that she is on to something. We have been married now for over 39 years.

Absence does make the heart grow fonder, but just for three or four days. Longer trips get lonely, and I have sampled enough Hilton breakfast buffets to last a lifetime.

While I had been trapped on the phone listening to the American Airlines person repeating over and over why she could

---

* I have been honored to work for over 28 years as a surveyor and trainer for CARF, an international accreditation commission.

only guarantee that our bag would travel from "LAX to EZE" in time but could not guarantee that it would find its way to "USH," Kathy had wandered off in search of a American Airlines baggage desk and an English-speaking agent. She knew that our limited travel Spanish might not be up to the task. Just a few steps down the hall from the baggage carousel she spotted a tall, impressive looking gentleman wearing an official-looking airport badge. She stopped and smiled up at him. Accompanied by expressive hand gestures honed by thirty years of working with the deaf she asked, "Hola, can you help with a bag?"

He returned her smile. "Sorry, no habla ingles." Then he motioned further down the hallway to where a small number of passengers loitered around a distant grouping of desks. Kathy hoped that he was directing her toward the baggage claim office. She took off in that direction.

I lost sight of her. After ending my call with the no-help desk I headed to where I had last seen her. Fast-walking past the end of the baggage area, the money changers, and ATMs I spied her blond head leaning over a short set of counters at the end of the long, bright hallway. I stepped up next to her. She grabbed my arm with a relieved exhale and introduced me to Maria, a stocky, dark-haired baggage agent wearing an American Airlines insignia on her collar. Switching effortlessly between English and Spanish Maria worked her headset phone and computer console in a polite, no-nonsense tone as she arranged for our bag to be transferred between airlines delivered at 6pm the next evening (Sunday) to Ushuaia in time for our Monday cruise. Her fingers flew across her keyboard until she located the right codes and transfer numbers. She flashed a triumphant smile and promised to contact the other airline herself. Then she handed me a card on which she had written her phone number and told me to call her with any questions. She assured us one final time that Kathy and her bag would be reunited. I had no doubt she would make it happen. Muchas gracias, Maria.

We retraced our steps through the now deserted baggage area and navigated through the customs gauntlet with our single suitcase and overstuffed backpacks. We pushed open the doors into the sticky air and bright, late morning sun. I hefted the backpack from one shoulder to another, trying to let the slight breeze dry my extra-wicking t-shirt that stuck to my back under the lightweight dark blue and completely wrinkled, 'wrinkle-free' Columbia travel shirt.

After 20 hours of airplanes and terminals I did appreciate the fresh air that accompanied our ten-minute hike over to the well-worn, domestic terminal squeezed in between the large international center and a dusty, multi-story parking structure still under construction. We checked in for our next flight, were directed to a second window where we paid a surprise $30 fee to check a single bag, and then shuffled past a bored security agent to arrive at our gate area. We walked to the end of the cramped, six-gate annex and claimed a small two-seat table by a window on the runway side of a small snack bar. I ordered a couple of surprisingly decent ham, cheese, and pickle sandwiches and two diet sodas. We spent the next two hours sitting in that half-stupor familiar to international travelers everywhere.

We did take a few minutes to discuss Plan B. We would spend the next day checking out the local clothing stores in Ushuaia. If the errant bag failed to arrive tomorrow evening, then we would race out to replace everything on Monday morning. I looked at Kathy and said, "Really, if that is the only problem that happens to us on this trip, then no problem!"

Spoiler alert...more happened.

One stop and four hours later we descended from the clouds onto a small piece of land barely large enough for the single runway jutting into the Beagle Channel. A windy, rainy Ushuaia greeted us. We grabbed the obedient suitcase and exited the small, modern terminal. The diminutive cabbie popped the trunk and reached for my bag while Kathy raced off after her thick blue scarf, snatched off her neck by a chilling gust. After she retrieved her scarf we hopped in and the cabbie drove us down the hill and around a rotary at the entrance to the city. Giant white block letters spelling out 'USHUAIA' welcomed us to the edge of a picturesque harbor filled with a handful of fancy yachts on one end and a large mix of working fishing boats tied to weather worn docks or anchored a few yards offshore.

To our left we took in a stunning gray-green mountain vista topped by snowy peaks indented by glaciers past and present. We turned away from the harbor and drove four blocks up to the door of the Hotel Alto Andino, a five-story boutique hotel perched along the top of a steep hill in the center of town. Ushuaia is a smaller-than-it-looked burg of 55,000 on the Beagle Channel marking the edge of Tierra del Fuego. The bay is home to a much larger-than-it-looked fishing fleet that extended beyond one end of the harbor. The small passenger port with its long concrete dock jutting from the foot of the hill below the center of town serves as the departure point for nearly all Antarctica vessels, including the National Geographic Explorer, Crystal Cruise, Azamara and Oceanwide cruise ships. When we first entered our hotel room, we dropped our bags and moved to the window. We scanned the harbor from our fourth-floor overlook. Kathy pointed out what looked like a fishing boat. It seemed far too small to be cruise ship.

"Is that ours?" she asked.

"I hope not." I said.

I pulled out a small pair of binoculars from my backpack and squinted at the name on the stern. Yes, it was the m/v Plancius. Wow, I thought. The larger vessels dwarfed the tiny 116 passenger expedition ship. It looked like a kid at the adult table. I handed the binoculars to Kathy.

"It appears that we will be crossing the Drake in an oversized bathtub toy," I said.

I picked up the travel brochure that I had grabbed during check-in. Ushuaia's bay was dotted with colorful private sailing vessels and colorless working boats. The duty-free port benefits not just from the seasonal Antarctic tourism but also hosts a sizeable crab fishery and surprisingly, a growing electronics industry. Ushuaia—literally "bay that penetrates to the west" in the indigenous Yamana / Yagan tongue—perches on a stretch of land between the Beagle Channel waters and the rugged spine of the South American Andes, where the Atlantic and Pacific Oceans meet. As could be expected from such an exposed setting, the weather is often unpredictable. The late afternoon winds that day were blustery, but the temperature was pleasantly mild.

Upon arrival I had asked for Margie Tomenko's room number. Margie was the volunteer guide for our Sierra Club travel group. We met her on our only previous Club sponsored travel outing in 2018 when she led a group of 16, including eight Tucson friends, on a fascinating trek across parts of Ireland. We enjoyed a unique view of the island's history and geography that included great historical sights, walking the famine trail, multiple hikes and cycling amidst spectacular scenery. Here at the Hotel Andino, Margie's room happened to be right next to ours. Kathy knocked on the door to say hello. We were greeted by a friendly Californian named Kate Froman, a smiling, seventyish woman with short gray hair. She introduced herself as a fellow Sierra Clubber and Margie's roommate for the trip. She told us that Margie's flight had been delayed.

We invited Kate to join us for dinner. She immediately recommended a restaurant that she had sampled the day before, so we exited the hotel and walked down the street for a block before turning right and easing our way down two blocks of uneven steps, broken pavement and muddy walkways to the main drag. We turned left and walked three blocks along the wider, well-lit sidewalk of the main street to a busy, glass-walled local establishment on the corner. We were quickly escorted to a comfortable table along one of the street-side clear walls, where we flopped down and waited patiently—well, exhaustedly—for our overworked waiter to arrive.

Kate entertained us with tales of her experiences as a solo traveler from California, and as we watched full meals pass by on their way to nearby tables the three of us swapped stories of previous Sierra Club trips. Kate recounted her most recent voyage with Margie to the Galapagos, complete with a rocking ship and rolling tortoises that she enjoyed immensely. By the time our orders had finally been taken and our dinners eventually arrived—perhaps flown in from Chile—we had described each trip in full detail. My meal of Argentinian pasta and Kathy's seafood stew were a treat and nearly worth the wait, since the long evening allowed ample time to gain a new friend.

Our dinner talk turned to the March events that we would miss back at home. The Tucson Festival of Books was one of my favorite spring weekends every year and, of course, we would miss March Madness, an obsession common to all from Arizona Wildcat country. I had also passed up a speaking invitation at an annual Tucson-based national conference. All in all, still a 'no-brainer' decision compared to exploring the bottom of the world.

We moved to current events, carefully expressing our opinions regarding the political crises currently roiling in the U.S. Kate quickly made her political leanings clear; we were kindred spirits. Not surprising, really, since as fellow Sierra Club members our political views tend to align closely in many areas and none of us were fans of the current president or his corrupt administration. I am rarely shy about discussing politics in public. I did hope this trip would provide a brief, welcome respite from the constant battle to reclaim our nation from the current hate-tinged extremism and corruption fostered by the current White House occupant, his cronies, and sycophants in Congress.

We barely talked at all about the Coronavirus. Two days before we left Tucson the current occupant of the White House reported that *"The United States…has, as of now, only 129 cases…and 11 deaths. We are working very hard to keep these numbers as low as possible."* And just yesterday, March 6th that same individual wore a personal campaign hat during an official presidential visit to the CDC and proclaimed, *"I think we're doing a really good job in this country at keeping it down…a tremendous job at keeping it down."*

Full disclosure: I hold this individual in such low regard that

I will not besmirch this book with his name. Since the impact of US government actions in response to the pandemic made a significant impact on our voyage, I must refer to the president or his administration occasionally in this book. Several identifiers were considered, but as I am no longer a practicing therapist nor an attorney, I chose not to refer to him as the sociopath, the narcissist, wannabe dictator or unindicted co-conspirator. He-who-must-not-be-named will henceforth be referred to simply as #45, as in forty-fifth president. Feel free to insert your own appellation.

On that night we spoke only in passing about the mild threat posed by the coronavirus, yet during the next ten days every single one of the events I lamented missing would be canceled. We would miss nothing. The encroaching pandemic remained a world away, but for now ignorance was bliss.

Kate revealed that even a once-in-a-lifetime visit to Antarctica was not enough. A second excursion awaiting her immediately following the cruise. Upon our return to Ushuaia she would return to the hotel for two days before meeting up with a different travel group for a Patagonian hiking adventure. Rather than lugging a second large suitcase and duffel with cooler clothing and all of her hiking gear, Kate had decided after talking with fellow post-cruise travelers and an accommodating hotel staff to store her extra bags at the hotel while on the 12-day cruise. It seemed like a good idea at the time.

Two hours later after our 'quick bite to eat' we trudged back through the late twilight up the hill to the hotel. Before we left the restaurant, I did grant full absolution to the very slow waiter when he insisted that I take one of their chocolate marshmallow brownies back to the hotel for a late-night snack. That was my initial introduction to the addictive sweets of Argentina, which no doubt helped me enjoy a rare full night's sleep in an actual bed.

Earlier at dinner I had shared with Kathy and Kate how much I looked forward to the extra cruise benefit—a twelve day escape from the constant barrage of politics on TV, in the newspapers (I read about four a day—I know, old school), online and in every conversation with friends. I tend to immerse myself. This is a critical election year, so I am staying active with two local campaigns, supporting a statewide campaign, and appearing periodically on a two local political talk shows—a veritable talking (radio) head. I declared that this trip would be a welcome break from all that. Politics could not reach us in Antarctica, right?

Boy, did I get that wrong.

I had one other goal in mind that I did not share at dinner. I needed to make a change in my life. The routine into which I had settled over the past five years no longer worked for me. I hoped that I could figure it out along the way. I had twelve days.

TWO

EXPLORING USHUAIA

"Who turned out the lights?"

SUNDAY, MARCH 8, 2020

We emerged from our hotel room freshly re-animated as we bounded up three flights of stairs to a small buffet in the top floor breakfast room. Kathy grabbed her usual coffee, water, one poached egg and dried fruit as I sampled the hot tea, fresh fruit, and a cake of coconut and caramel.

Along with their love of chocolate Argentinians seem quite fond of caramel—baked, injected or spread into everything. I remember a Rotary Club service trip that we made to Brazil a few years ago, where I discovered that Brazilians displayed an equal obsession with cheese and had found a myriad of ways to include cheese in nearly every dish. Also not a bad thing—I even enjoyed the weird banana-cheese breakfast concoction served to us each morning. Now, if we could get these two countries to collaborate, then perhaps they could create another fabled pairing like bacon and eggs or peanut butter and jelly (though I prefer marshmallow, i.e. the fluffernutter.) Cheese and caramel? Perhaps not.

Kathy and I sat at a four-person table next to one of the large windows with a panoramic view of the city and bay as we planned our day. The weather report called for a chance of rain and blustery winds, and the light gray skies made no promises.

We were impressed with the hotel. Our room was just a bit nicer and a big larger than expected, and the hotel staff exuded friendly competence. After breakfast I walked down the five short flights of stairs to the front desk. I pulled out my phone and called the airline to confirm the arrival of the missing suitcase, but I was struggling to understand the fast-talking Aerolineas Argentinas employee on the other end. I grimaced over the counter to Angela, the front desk manager, and shrugged. She smiled and took the phone from my hand. I could not follow the rapid-fire conversation, but she ended the call and handed my phone back with a nod. She relayed the airline worker's promise that the bag would arrive on the 6:20pm flight. I thanked Angela profusely. My faith in customer service was restored.

Seven members of our Sierra Club contingent were heading off to go hiking in the nearby Tierra del Fuego National Park. I had politely declined their invitation at breakfast. Another member, Meg Weesner, had also invited us to join her for a small boat cruise on the Beagle Channel, but I replied that we preferred to spend the day exploring the town on foot. After a day and a half of sitting in airplanes and airports I needed to get out and move, and I was not the one with restless legs. Kathy was going nuts. Neither of us fancied a day-long muddy hike in bad weather, and we always loved exploring a new city on foot. Today was our best opportunity to enjoy a stroll around Ushuaia and perhaps our only chance to pick up any gifts or souvenirs. Last I heard, the penguin colonies of the Antarctic did not operate any open-air markets or tourist bazaars.

We hiked down the two blocks of uneven steps, broken pavement, and narrow sidewalks to the main drag. Looking both ways we noticed that every intersection within sight had been blocked off. We turned left toward a pulsing beat and a distant sea of colors. Five minutes later we waded into a two-block long menagerie of brightly colored shorts, tees, and tank tops. Women outnumbered the men three-to-one, but all were stretching and bouncing in rhythm with the pulsing loudspeakers stacked six feet high. I looked up at the banner stretched across the road above the rainbow balloon arch. Welcome to the Global Women's Day 5K.

"Oh man, I should run back to the hotel for my running shoes." I mused aloud.

Kathy smiled patiently as she pointed out a minor detail. "You have no running clothes."

She said no to watching me run the streets of Ushuaia in fleece tights and a t-shirt. Cooler heads prevailed.

We hung around for the start of the race. Two energetic twenty-somethings jumped on a big stage erected in the middle of the street to aerobicize the growing mob of runners (the ones checking their wrist monitors and shoelaces) and walkers (the ones taking selfies with their lattes.) The music grew louder. The leaders belted out exhortations as everyone mirrored their gyrations. We soon gave up on seeing an actual race and headed into the stiffening breeze toward the harbor. The darkening sky and sputtering rain accompanied us toward the east end of town. Ten minutes later we hiked up another hill to the Museo Maritimo, a former Argentinian prison. The prison complex formed a K-shaped structure with five 'arms' that had been transformed into centers for historical presentations and art exhibitions highlighting the past and present Ushuaia. Like the British founding of New South Wales in Australia as a penal colony in the late 1700s, Ushuaia was established as a prison colony for convicts and political prisoners sent from the rest of Argentina to this remote outpost. I handed over our modest admission fees to a stern-faced volunteer in the repurposed sally port and she directed us to two connected rooms displaying glass boxes containing models of former exploration ships from the region. We moved quickly past the initial exhibits toward the main attraction; two stories of period-restored prison cells. We spent the next hour crisscrossing our way along the cell blocks, stepping into each to view multi-media exhibits of murderers, swindlers, political and civil rights leaders, each housed side-by-side in brutal conditions.

We passed through the faded metal doorway at the far end of the hall and crossed a large, open main hub of the complex. We selected the 'spoke' to our right and entered my favorite wing of the museum, a series of historical exhibits featuring centuries of daring Antarctic explorations. Over the years I have devoured tales of Antarctic adventures so it was a pleasure to see them all detailed in one place, from the U.S. Exploring Expedition of 1838–1842 to the mixed triumph and tragedies of Shackleton, Amundsen and Scott. I recommend Nathaniel Philbrick's book on the former. It is a fascinating true story from one of my favorite authors.

I lost track of time as I moved from cell to cell marveling at the multitude of artifacts, period pictures and restored documents.

By the time I finished my circuit Kathy had long since exited to discover her own favorite cellblock: a refurbished hallway hosting the local art museum. The clean bright walls featured paintings, sculptures and multi-media pieces from local area residents and native artists from the region. I stood patiently on sore feet—I guess benches would have ruined the aesthetic—as Kathy fully examined each work, appreciating the style and effort in excruciating detail.

"What do you think of this one?" She would ask, inspecting a multi-media conglomeration of paint, bird feathers and fabric.

"It's OK," I would respond, to be polite.

"Why don't you like it?"

I have been married long enough to heed the flashing red lights triggered by that question.

I learned long ago that comments like "It looks good to me" or "I don't care for it" proved insufficiently insightful and comments like "it looks like the cows in that painting gave up and went home" were not appreciated.

"Tell me why YOU like it." I said. The red lights turned green.

Another hour slipped by. I was getting a little grumpy. Time for a break and something to eat. Kathy says this is a trait that daughter Jana and I share—like an early warning system that one ignores at their peril, she says. Before heading back to the streets in search of lunch though, we wandered back across the hub and stepped into the tiny museum gift shop. The cozy shop displayed a surprisingly well-stocked selection of clothing and art pieces, along with the usual souvenir magnets, pens, and key chains. Our bulging suitcases could fit little else, so Kathy settled for a small selection of post cards. As she thumbed through the card racks,

I snatched an item from a basket below a register near the doorway. I made a quick swipe with my credit card to purchase a 2020 Christmas ornament—a hand painted penguin that I snuck into my backpack. During our early travel years I would always bring home a surprise ornament unique to the local region. Sometimes we picked it out together, or sometimes we would find them on our own and surprise each other. Each December we overload on warm, funny, and embarrassing memories of places and people as we decorate the Christmas tree.

We exited the museum under dry gray skies and headed back down the hill to the east end of Ushuaia's main street. Av. San Martín was lined by a colorful, bustling mix of souvenir shops, restaurants, clothing stores, and travel centers. We soon discovered a pleasant tea and sandwich shop on one corner nearly hidden by leafy trees.

We split a warm grilled cheese and tomato sandwich served by a pleasant young woman who introduced herself as the shop's owner and lone employee. She returned with Kathy's hot coffee. My carefully brewed artisan craft tea arrived three days later.

Refueled and refreshed, we stepped out of the shop as a light rain resumed. The sudden coolness remined me that I needed to add one more long-sleeve t-shirt as another base layer for the icy climes. We came upon a bustling local shop selling everything from travel guides to good quality cold weather accessories and souvenir t-shirts, sweatshirts, hats, and gloves. I found a heavy dark blue t-shirt with 'Ushuaia' on the front within a subtle design.

Kathy grabbed a woolen hat with a bright pom-pom on it. It looked good on her. I told her that she would be easy to find in a snowbank. She hesitated. She thought that perhaps she should check out a few other stores on Monday, but I invoked one of our top ten rules of travel. *Unless you are certain of finding the same item or a better deal nearby, do not wait. If you see it and you like it, Buy It.* Stuff happens. Plans change, itineraries are altered, and you may never see that store or that item again. Spoiler alert: We never did see that store again, but those items now reside in our Tucson closets.

Still heading west on the Av. San Martin sidewalk, we stepped around two of the healthiest stray dogs I have ever seen sprawled unconcerned in front of the southernmost Hard Rock Café on the planet. I maintain a habit of checking out every 'HRC' I encounter across the globe. When Jana was 15 the three of us enjoyed two whirlwind days exploring London before embarking on a celebratory 12-day cruise to Scandinavia and Russia to celebrate the sale of my first business. During our double-decker hop-on/hop-off tour through town (yes, we went 'full tourist') we spied the original Hard Rock Cafe. We hopped off. After a surprising good lunch Jana received her first Hard Rock t-shirt. She loved it, so it became a treat for me to bring one home from each major city I visited. This time was different. We walked up the steps into the little store to the left of the café and walked out five minutes later with a rockin' onesie for our beautiful, four-month old grandson Ryan—Jana's new baby boy. The tradition continues.

We re-entered the flow of busy sidewalk tourists. The constant breeze suddenly smelled sweeter. Just across the street an aromatic chocolate shop beckoned. A thirtyish dark-haired Argentinian welcomed us into her narrow store lined with glass cases on the right and three small tables on the left. The proud proprietor repaid our enthusiasm by insisting that I sample an Argentinian favorite, the Alfadores, a cookie-like treat that resembles a Ring-Ding—like a Hostess Ding Dong for you non-New Englanders—except with caramel in the center. I ate two of them to increase the validity of my rating. Excellent. I bought four for the road and planned a further taste test in Buenos Aires in two weeks. Back at the hotel I surprised Kate with one of the Alfadores. She gushed with equal delight at the chocolaty goodness.

Our longtime travel agent Linda (more on her later) suggested that we add a two-night visit to Buenos Aires at the end of the trip. Linda's suggestions are usually spot-on, so I agreed without hesitation.

One example occurred back in June of 2005. We had scheduled a ten-day family tour of Italy, after which we boarded a train from Florence to Salzburg and dropped Jana off for a six-week summer session in Austria. Her school, The University of Portland, operated a dorm and programs in Salzburg where she could take classes during the week and explore Europe every weekend, of which she took full advantage. I am happy NOT to have all the details of her excursions.

Linda suggested that Kathy and I could save money by extending our trip an extra three days. And go where? I asked, after we would spend three days overloading on everything Mozart amongst the old streets and museums of Salzburg.

She asked, "Why don't you go to Prague?" The city had never been on my radar, but we said OK. We had a great time. Prague was a newly vibrant, adolescent-like city mixing centuries of kings, cathedrals, wars and oppression with imaginative new architecture and a new energy on the streets. It was the icing on the cake of our summer excursion.

So, when Linda suggested spending extra time in Buenos Aires, we both loved the idea. After spending 12 nights on a small ship I knew that we would enjoy stretching our legs on a guided walking tour around the capital city, dancing to the tango (Kathy didn't know that yet) and sampling much more of the local cuisine. Sadly, Buenos Aires remains unmarked on the world travel map hanging on my office wall. There is, however, a new pin on that map that neither of us expected to add.

We hustled back to the Andino for a quick rest-and-refresh. Upon our return I had asked Angela to arrange for a cab. The taxi pulled up in front of the hotel right at six o'clock. We headed for the airport with fingers crossed to await the arrival of Kathy's bag. We did not want to spend the morning on a furious shopping spree back along Av. San Martin. Our taxi driver wound his way through the back streets of town around several blocked-off intersections. Pounding drums and blaring music filled the air, but we could not spot the source. We glanced down each empty street. Nothing. As we made the last turn up the hill toward the airport, we caught a glimpse of the for our circuitous route—a boisterous Global Woman's Day march filling the streets to support women's rights and freedom from sexual abuse. We did not mind the delay after all.

I paid the driver. I heard a droning from above and looked up to spot a single plane on final approach. We jogged into a nearly empty airport terminal. Kathy marched up to an older, heavy set gate agent resting his elbow on the Aerolineas Argentinas desk. The droopy-faced veteran employee did not appear overly concerned when she explained the situation. I checked the monitor and announced that the plane had just landed. He nodded and picked up the desk phone, motioning us toward the small greeting area in the main hallway between the baggage claim and the main terminal doors. We stood and watched each passenger emerge from the frosted glass doors and head out the exit, bags in hand as they passed by. No agent emerged with Kathy's black suitcase.

Two times Kathy started toward the baggage claim doors to sneak past an exiting passenger, despite the red "Secure Area—Entrance Prohibited" sign above the frosted doors. I grabbed her arm. I had spotted security guards inside, and I did not recall that getting arrested on her first full day in Argentina was listed on the itinerary.

The rush ended. The hall quieted. No agent, no bag.

I hustled back to the desk.

"Has anyone checked for our bag?"

"Yes sir, there was no bag."

I implored the agent to check again. He sighed loudly, picked up the phone and made another call. He shrugged. Five minutes later a uniformed baggage attendant casually strolled up the hallway and over to the desk, wheeling Kathy's bag behind him. I exhaled deeply, said a quick thank you and handed him a small tip. A tearful reunion between a woman and her belongings ensued. Crisis averted.

Back at the hotel Kathy took a few minutes to reconnect with each item in her errant suitcase. I turned on the TV and flipped through the meager selection of channels to find only soccer (sorry, futbol) and Spanish language talk shows, but not a single CNN or BBC news show. Kathy disappeared for twenty minutes before re-emerging with 'fixed' hair and fresh clothes. We headed out the door, turned right and eased down the hill in search of another good local dinner spot.

The heavy bass drum and lively guitars echoed between Av. San Martin and the harbor below. Three blocks down we spotted the women's rights marchers on a small street side square a short distance from the harbor. Women danced and men clapped in time with the blaring beat of the portable speakers. We debated joining the celebration. Our heads said yes; our stomachs said no.

We turned back up the hill to our right and hiked another block. That afternoon we had passed a sidewalk window displaying tanks of live lobsters. To the right an open doorway led to an inviting room of a dozen tables, only one-quarter filled. A sign above the doorway read Resto El Faro. The comfortable-but-not-too-fancy furnishings and wait staff looked exactly right. We received a warm greeting from a waiter who led us to a table for two alongside a wall adorned with local harbor photos. Freshly cooked lobsters paraded past us to nearby tables as we perused the menu. Neither of us were in the mood for lobster specialties, so we each selected a locally caught favorite. Ten minutes later I dug into my fresh caprese appetizer—and all the lights blinked out. The restaurant became almost completely dark, the only remaining light filtering in from the front window. Our waiter rushed out to the street. He returned and announced to the curious diners that a complete blackout had hit the entire area. Then he shrugged and smiled. The restaurant staff did not miss a beat. Lighted candles were doubled at each table. Thanks to their gas stoves and easy hospitality our evening was transformed into a romantic candlelit dinner.

An hour later our meal concluded with wide grins and wider waistlines. I paid the bill by flashlight. We waved goodbye and walked out the door into the approaching darkness. We took pity on a chocolate shop owner holding her door open to catch any stray customers in the fading light. Kathy went for her go-to favorite, a rum truffle, while I sampled the local entry for world's best peanut butter cup. It tasted satisfyingly pleasant, but no one comes close to the reigning champion. (That would be the Rocky Mountain Chocolate Factory. Trust me on this. Pack up the babies and grab the old ladies and go try one.)

We said goodnight to the proprietress and trudged back up the two blocks of steep concrete steps and around the corner to our hotel. As we passed from the street through the double glass doors all the lights of the city blinked back on.

THREE

GOODBYE WORLD

"U.S. citizens...should not travel by cruise ship."

MONDAY, MARCH 9: CRUISE DAY 1

POSITION:	5°53'S / 067°42'W
WIND:	E 4-5 KNOTS
WEATHER:	CLEAR
AIR TEMPERATURE:	+10 C

Eighteen mature adults—judging by age, not attitude—gathered in the breakfast room annex on the fifth floor for our first official Sierra Club tour group meeting. Three of us lingered on the outdoor balcony to soak in the panoramic views of the city and bay on this clear, crisp morning.

Our contingent was comprised of seven couples and four single women from a cross-section of states, including Arizona,

California, Florida, Iowa, Illinois, Pennsylvania, New Hampshire, and Minnesota. In the center of the sunlit room, waving to get everyone's attention stood Margie Tomenko, a short, dark-haired bundle of energy from Sacramento. Before retirement Margie managed a variety of people and technical projects for the state of California. Her positive, caring demeanor that we first encountered two years ago in Ireland made her the perfect volunteer Sierra Club trip leader, now on her second trip to Antarctica. During a conversation while traveling between villages on the Irish west coast I had learned that she was scheduled to lead this trip. An excursion to the 'last continent' had always been on my list of future destinations. I do not call it a bucket list though; I do not care for that term. My list never stops growing. It is not a 'before I die' list; it is a 'never stop living' list. Kathy often comments that I am most relaxed and happy when traveling. She is not wrong.

A childhood story: I have always wanted to 'get away' but not always for the best reasons. From the age of 10 until I left home for college at 17 every time we moved to a new town or a new house, I would make a new plan to escape. I never thought of it as running away.

I would pick a destination and check planes and rail schedules, figure out the cost and how much money I would need to save. Most kids got paper routes to earn money for baseball gloves or candy; I did it for train fare. Growing up in an alcoholic home does not lend itself to normal thinking. Growing up in a Coast Guard family also meant that we moved between houses, towns or states every twelve to eighteen months, so I made lots of plans. I found out later that my father had requested a few of those transfers to stay one step ahead of trouble. Now that I think about it, that may be a reason I have done so much consultation work in strategic planning and conflict management. Good early training.

By the time I was graduated from high school (one year early, which allowed me to leave home respectably sooner) I had already lived in at least 13 homes and had attended 12 schools.

The happy ending: My father enjoyed sobriety for the last 25 years of his life, even earning recognition as one of the founders of the renowned Navy Alcoholism Treatment Program in the 1970s. He and I developed a close relationship as adults and together with my mother established Jorgensen Healthcare Associates and the Tucson-based Kachina Center for Addiction Recovery in the 90's.

Having seen so much of the United States as a kid I only wanted to see more as an adult. I wanted to experience everything—new places, people, culture, foods, all of it. I had the bug. A few years ago I grabbed the opportunity to conduct a survey in Montana, making it my fiftieth state visited. Traveling for work or for fun—with Kathy or solo—I have now spent time in 40 countries. (No, airport transits do not count.) Argentina made it 41. Setting foot on Antarctica just four days from now would hit another milestone—continent number seven. Check that. Dragging Kathy along was the real accomplishment since it was NOT on her list. Too far, too cold, too much ocean. But still she agreed to join me. Why? She knew that bunking solo was not an option for me on this trip—everyone had to share a cabin.

I am not the "roommate" type. I had not had a roommate since college and bunking with a stranger was not an option for me. I could not ask any of my close friends or brother—this was not a quick trip to Vegas. It was certainly not cheap. You had to really want to go to Antarctica. They did not. Kathy knew how much the trip meant to me. She volunteered to come along, shrugging at the time while muttering "Well, I do love penguins." And me, clearly. Wife of the Year.

Margie kicked off the meeting as we exchanged introductions and reviewed the schedule for the day: Deliver bags to the Oceanwide transfer station, enjoy a Sierra Club-sponsored lunch, and meet at 3:30pm at the port entrance to begin the boarding process. She passed out a second set of medical forms and special activity preferences to fill out. We opted for kayaking and overnight camping on the Antarctic snow. I think Kathy began shivering right then. Margie also passed around personally made-up gift bags of chocolates, Sierra Club branded rescue whistles, luggage tags and mini flashlights. A genuinely nice move—everyone likes free stuff.

No one thinks about the $14,000 worth of trip and clothing costs it took to get here. It is free stuff! But it was also a thoughtful gesture on Margie's part, and not the last one that we would appreciate in the weeks to come. This will sound like an ad, but I have to say that using the Sierra Club as a conduit for these excursions has proven to be more enjoyable, less stressful, and more cost competitive than a do-it-yourself excursion. Thanks to guides like Margie we have become fans.

Five minutes after the meeting ended, we piled a small mountain of suitcases in center of the small lobby. Three taxis pulled up outside to transport our pile of bags to the Oceanwide Cruise building. Jim from Illinois and I squeezed into one of the cabs to accompany Margie to the bag check-in. The Oceanwide team greeted us with smiles and clipboards as we hefted the collection of large suitcases, duffel bags and stuffed totes through the doorway. The cruise team smoothly tagged and positioned each bag in its proper boarding place. I nodded to the crew and we waved off the cabs, electing to walk the ten blocks back to the hotel under the mild sun. At noon, our group reassembled at the same restaurant where we had enjoyed dinner with Kate two nights earlier. I grabbed an open seat next Jason and Kathy, a friendly couple of married auto engineers from Ann Arbor. Sitting across from me waved a bright, bubbly woman named Judy, a recently retired Iowa school counselor with an infectious laugh. No surprise that she and Kathy hit it off immediately as they swapped tales of dealing with teen angst and attitudes for over two decades. After an unhurried lunch of huge meals—Judy's single slice of pizza covered her entire plate—Kathy and I raced out to enjoy a last chance to grab another t-shirt, a few small gifts, a perfectly fitting 'Antarctica' baseball cap and, of course, more chocolates for the trip. And not just any chocolates. Kathy could simply not pass by the dozen tiny penguin-shaped chocolate creations she spied in yet another gourmet sweet shop window. Friends and family members will no doubt rejoice. Oh, and we searched through three different corner stores for one more item: an extremely large bottle of hand sanitizer. At the time we simply considered it a normal precaution for a cruise. Had we known its true value I would have bought ten. Prices were relatively cheap in Ushuaia, which was surprising for the only town at 'el fin del mundo,' as was advertised on nearly every mug and sweatshirt in sight.

We window-shopped a bit longer before meandering down to the passenger port entry at 3:15pm. The dock agents played hurry up and wait for another half-hour until finally directing us through security with full bag and body checks. We headed along the wide concrete dock and took our place in the single boarding line along the starboard side of ship. Our soon-to-be temporary residence seemed tiny compared to the 800 passenger Azamara ship sitting ahead of the Plancius' bow, shrinking further still under the shadow of the massive Celebrity Cruise vessel tied up across the dock.

I exchanged casual greetings with the mix of veteran cruisers and newbies. Nervous excitement filled the diesel-tinged air. Kathy, per usual, gathered life stories from everyone within reach, no doubt learning the names of all their children and grandchildren within the first five minutes. Members of the expedition crew walked the line to greet and chat as the ship's doctor and two assisting crew members waited at a long table set up by the gangway to check our temperature and hand out personalized key cards.

Standing next to the sturdy ship I was still struck by the relatively small size of this trans-oceanic vessel, designed to stand up to roaring oceans and frozen bays. Once on board I discovered that the m/v Plancius was built in 1976 as an oceanographic research vessel for the Royal Dutch Navy.

Originally named "Hr. Ms. Tydeman," The ship sailed for the Dutch Navy until June 2004, then sat in port until eventually purchased by Oceanwide Expeditions. The vessel was completely rebuilt in 2009 as a vessel with the capacity to carry 116 passengers and 46 crew members on Arctic and Antarctic cruises.

According to the Oceanwide Expeditions website, *The Plancius "offers a restaurant/lecture room on deck 3 and a spacious observation lounge (with bar) on deck 5 with large windows, offering full panorama view. M/v "Plancius" has large open deck spaces (with full walk-around possibilities on deck 4), giving excellent opportunities to enjoy the scenery and wildlife. She is furthermore equipped with 10 Mark V zodiacs, including 40 HP 4-stroke outboard engines and 2 gangways on the starboard side, guaranteeing a swift zodiac operation. M/v "Plancius" is comfortable and nicely decorated, but is not a luxury vessel. Our voyages in the Arctic and Antarctic regions are primarily defined by an exploratory educational travel programme, spending as much time ashore as possible.*

Plancius fully meets our demands to achieve this. The vessel is equipped with a diesel-electric propulsion system which reduces the noise and vibration of the vessel considerably. The 3 diesel engines generate 1.230 horse-power each, giving the vessel a speed of 10—12 knots. The vessel is ice-strengthened and was specially built for oceanographic voyages. M/v "Plancius" is manned by an international crew of 37 (18 nautical crew and 19 hotel crew), 8 expedition staff (1 expedition leader, 1 assistant expedition leader and 6 guides/lecturers), and 1 doctor."

My turn came to step up to the check-in table. I said hello to a young-looking, friendly, no-nonsense woman from Amsterdam. She introduced herself as Nelleke, the ship's doctor. *Note: I seem to refer to all doctors as "young-looking" now. Oh-oh.* Dr. Nelleke carefully scanned my pre-submitted health survey answers. The most significant survey question asked, *"Have you spent any time in China during the previous two months?* I had marked NO and smiled at this query. I had been scheduled to speak in Guangzhou just three months earlier, but due to the fallout from #45's trade tantrums the nation of China denied the host organization permission to bring our team of speakers on healthcare outcomes to their country as they had the previous year.

Now it appeared that I may have lucked out on two fronts. According to several reports, the coronavirus likely began its scourge during the period that I would have been in China. And now, although it remained too lightly regarded by the inept US government in early March, it had begun its march across the planet.

Like most everyone we had followed the recent news of the Diamond Princess debacle. It had certainly put all cruise ship passengers on notice, yet US leaders had insisted on downplaying the threat. Government officials repeatedly compared it to a bad case of flu even after receiving first reports in December 2019 from the World Health Organization, who called it an "unknown viral pneumonia." On January 22, #45 claimed *"We have it totally under control. It's one person coming in from China, and we have it under control. It's going to be just fine."* By January 29, 2020 there were over 2000 cases of coronavirus worldwide.

After receiving a clean bill of health from Nelleke I shuffled through the remaining gauntlet of final passport and document reviews and endured the happy-passengers-boarding pictures as we proceeded up the gangway.

I smiled at Kathy as we stepped onto the deck of our temporary new home, safely removed—or so we thought—from the trials and tribulations of the real world. Two men dressed in crisp white shirts welcomed us aboard. They introduced themselves as Alex, the ship's Hotel Manager and Dragan, the Restaurant Manager. Those titles sound funny on any cruise ship, but especially on this compact vessel. I learned later how their roles incorporated functions well beyond their nametags, and I had an entertaining encounter with Dragan during a simulated drill on day 13.

Alex directed us to a cabin on the third deck where our bags sat outside the door awaiting our arrival. Our traveling entourage were all grouped along the same corridor. Meg and Judy were settling in the cabin to our right; Terry and LaRae from Minnesota waved from inside the door to our left. We stepped into our own cabin. It looked compact but surprisingly comfortable.

"It's certainly not the Windjammer," I observed. Kathy let out a short laugh.

For my fiftieth birthday we had booked a Maine Windjammer cruise (another 'life list' item) during a summer visit to New England. The region remains our favorite vacation destination. Not only had I grown up in the northeast, but Kathy had spent ten years in Vermont and New Hampshire before moving west. That summer we sailed for three days on the "Mercantile" out of Camden, a three-masted schooner that carried only 29 passengers. The Mercantile's so-called cabin allowed room for only one person to stand upright in front of a small double bunk jammed under the portside deck. If you lifted your head too quickly medical attention was required. Still, I highly recommend that cruise if you might enjoy a day-long schooner race, grilled fresh lobsters on deck and sailing among beautiful coastal Maine islands. I did.

Our cabin on the Plancius included a single porthole featuring a cramped view of the starboard side ocean, partially obstructed by the gangway crane. Oh well. Cabin 306 also contained a small two section closet, a bathroom with a small sink, toilet and shower stall, separate bunks with suitcase space underneath, a small desk area, a wall mounted TV, a shared nightstand and plenty of grab bars at critical spots throughout the cabin and bathroom.

Clothes and gear were hung, folded, repacked, or strewn about artfully before we headed down the short hallway to our left and up two short flights to the observation lounge on deck number 5. The observation lounge served as the meeting room, lecture hall, reading room, muster area, game area, snack room and bar. It became the center of activity for the entire cruise.

First Officer Miia, a tall blonde late-thirtyish Dutchwoman, led the fully assembled group through the mandatory SOLAS (Safety of Life at Sea) Safety and Lifeboat Drills. I struggled into a huge blocky orange life jacket and joined the line waddling down the hall to an outside hatch, stepping through and marching up and down three short metal stairways past the lifeboat stations to re-assemble on the rear deck. The mini-sub shaped lifeboats reminded me of the one in which Tom Hanks was held hostage in the movie 'Captain Phillips.'

I strained to hear Dragan shout out the final instructions for abandoning ship. He was interrupted by the assault from two blasts of the ship's horn. Ushuaia faded into the distance as we sailed (sounds better than "propellered") out of the Beagle Channel toward the deeper, colder waters of the Southern Ocean.

Hotel Manager Alex, a stocky eastern European gentleman in his mid-forties took the microphone to welcome us to our floating abode, and to drum into our minds the lessons of life onboard.

Lesson #1: Do not fall overboard. Use the rails and handholds. The rule was 'one hand for you; one hand for the ship.'

Lesson #2: Do not lose a hand. You would not want one of the heavy fire doors between hallways to slam closed on an extremity.

Lesson #3: Hand sanitizers appeared on walls or pedestals throughout the ship. Use them. *Note: EVERYONE used them. Often.*

Alex led the parade of orange vests back to the lounge where a slightly weathered, lean, and wiry Scotsman in his early 40s waited at the front of the room. Iain Rudkin introduced himself as our expedition leader and master of ceremonies for all daily briefings. After a career designing cancer drugs for a living, Iain's adventurous nature led him to Antarctica. He 'overwintered' three times on Antarctic research stations for the British Antarctic Survey, spent more than 10 summer seasons on the ice, and had led expeditions in some of the remotest parts of the continent. (Two weeks later during the frantic search for a friendly port we learned that Iain's first baby was due to arrive any day.)

Iain introduced each of the Expedition Team members who would guide us in and around Antarctica—more on them later. He then brought forth Plancius Captain Artur Iakovlev, a native of Russia (a fact worth knowing on trivia night) who welcomed us with a traditional bon voyage toast.

At seven-thirty Alex's voice on the intercom called us to dinner. We made the short walk from our cabin down the hallway, past the stairwell and the hotel information counter to the dining room, which spanned the entire width of the ship near the stern. After a quick squirt from one of the ubiquitous wall-mounted hand sanitizers we headed to one side of the bright and comfortable room. Passengers immediately gravitated to their preferred seating areas. Our traveling group favored the starboard side where four long tables were bolted to the deck perpendicular to the large oval windows. Two padded split bench seats placed on each side of the table allowed seating for 8 per table. Three oval tables of eight were anchored along the center axis of the dining room. The same arrangement of tables and seating was favored by the younger crowd on the port side. Tampa residents Bill and Dotty beat us to the windowside seats of the first long table, as they did most nights, so we grabbed seats next to them and across from Margie and Meg.

I already knew Meg Weesner. She is a bright and lively sharp-eyed fellow Tucsonan whom I had encountered at various district Rotary events. Her healthy head of long gray hair made her easy to spot in any group. I had run into her at a district conference last spring and mentioned my planned visit to Antarctica. Her eyes lit up. By the next day she had grabbed the final spot. I did not know at the time that Meg was the local Sierra Club chapter president and quite familiar with their process and menu of guided trips. I did know that Meg was also a retired National Park Service ranger. She had transferred to Tucson years earlier for an assignment at Saguaro National Park on the east side of town. I was most familiar with the park as the site of the annual 8-mile Labor Day Run, one of the toughest runs of the year. The race starts before sunrise and features tough, steep hills and longer inclines that begin quick-baking under the rising desert sun. I have run it—well, survived it—four times. The unique Sonoran Desert vistas were worth the pain.

Dinner was served. Two amazing attendants named Charlotte and Kim showed off their expertise at balancing 4 or 5 plates on one arm while gliding through the crowd and over the pitching and rolling carpeted deck. This was Cirque de Soleil level skill on display. Charlotte quickly secured her place as my favorite. Despite covering three or four tables full of diners she quickly memorized my preferences and never failed to deliver, no matter which seat I had grabbed. My morning hot tea, afternoon Coke Light and evening sparkling water appeared by my side nearly as soon as I sat down. The sodas were not free, so she would smoothly whip out her laser-eyed device for a quick swipe of my keycard and a light *"Thank you Mister Don"* before skimming away.

I do not recall who first brought up the topic, but discussion quickly turned to fears and expectations of surviving the infamous Drake Passage. Over 600 miles wide, the Drake Passage connects the Atlantic and Pacific oceans between Cape Horn (the southernmost point of South America) and the South Shetland Islands, situated about 100 miles north of the Antarctic Peninsula. The passage defines the zone of climatic transition separating the cool, humid, subpolar conditions of Tierra del Fuego and the frigid, polar regions of Antarctica.

We each recounted visions of YouTube videos and movies depicting the crossing as one long nausea fest amidst heaving waves, driving rain and hurricane-force winds. Kathy submitted the film *Is That You, Bernadette?* for 'worst nightmare' scenario.

You have got to love Oceanwide Expeditions own description of the Drake "rite of" Passage:

> Positioned between the southern tail of South America and the Antarctic Peninsula's north-sweeping arm is a lively little waterway known as the Drake Passage.

> *The* Drake is considered by many polar travelers to be the gateway to the Antarctic, while others view it as the necessary rite of passage everyone must experience before enjoying the boundless natural wonders of Antarctica.

In the Drake Passage, layers of cold seawater from the south and relatively warm seawater from the north collide to form powerful eddies. These eddies, when combined with the strong winds and sometimes violent storms common to this area, can make the Drake Passage richly earn its reputation as one of Earth's roughest waterways. But don't let this intimidate you.

It takes the average cruise ship about 48 hours to sail from one end of the Drake Passage to the other. This depends on the exact embarkation and destination point, of course, but the conditions of the Drake are also highly relevant.

If you're prone to seasickness, it's a good idea to see your doctor before you sail the Drake Passage. And even if you're the type who laughs at rollercoasters, there's a good chance the Drake's weather is going to test that cast-iron stomach of yours.

As we talked, I felt the rocking and rolling intensify. We had exited the Beagle Channel and hit the open water. Even though the Drake Passage was relatively calm for our two-day crossing, every booming wave reminded me that our small ship was a toy boat in an excessively big bathtub. Unlike those Vegas-sized floating hotels masquerading as giant cruise ships, the Plancius did not have those large underwater stabilizer wings that extend from each side of the ship to limit the impact of every large swell or rogue wave. The ship's side-to-side movement remained a constant presence in both calm waters and roiling seas.

We entered the infamous southern sea around midnight. By now most passengers had downed their Dramamine or slapped on one of the ubiquitous scopolamine patches behind an ear. Long years of experience with my head hung over a gunwale or kneeling before a ship's toilet had taught me that such pedestrian medications were useless against my usually ironclad—kidding, more like swiss cheese—stomach.

Dramamine did as much good for me as downing a tic-tac. Same for scopolamine patches. Meclizine, a slightly stronger drug quelled the internal uproar on airplanes when needed but was no match for a roiling sea.

A few years earlier during a Panama Canal cruise with Jana and Brendan (one of my all-time favorite family excursions) we endured a day on board an 800-passenger cruise ship with a mysterious broken vacuum line in one unknown hallway. "No one please use the toilets for the next 4 hours" was not a welcome announcement. To pile on the discomfort the captain had increased the ship's speed to 17 knots through rough Caribbean waters to make up for a delayed departure. I passed 'miserable' after the first hour. While staggering between an outside lounge chair and a restroom I overheard a crew member comment that the medical office would open at 4pm. By 3 o'clock I was leaning against the wall outside the door. The lone nurse took pity on my pathetically pale visage and led me into the single exam room. The doctor questioned me briefly and disclosed that he did have a stronger drug, but it required an injection—in the posterior region, naturally—and he would have to bill my insurance for it. I responded by pulling my pants down.

"What are you waiting for?" I nodded.

Ten minutes later I returned to the land of the living.

I had found my miracle drug—promethazine. Kathy and I had

visited our home physicians prior to our Antarctic journey and arrived armed with the magic potion—now thankfully available in pill form. We were ready. Nevertheless, I was still grateful for the hand grips in the bathroom, and the raised edges on each bunk now made perfect sense as we rolled from side-to-side or top-to-bottom through the night. But the drug worked. Not only did it perform its magic once again, but after two days I acquired my sea legs (another first) and rarely had need for the wonder pill. Take that, Drake. Our first night at sea was a breeze.

I was healthy and happy, anticipating an exciting two weeks exploring a rarely viewed world of wonders. Back in the old world, unbeknownst to any of us, the following notice had appeared on the U.S. State Department's website:

US STATE DEPT RELEASE:

March 8, 2020

Passengers on Cruise Ships

U.S. citizens, particularly travelers with underlying health conditions, should not travel by cruise ship. CDC notes increased risk of infection of COVID-19 in a cruise ship environment.

In order to curb the spread of COVID-19, many countries have implemented strict screening procedures that have denied port entry rights to ships and prevented passengers from disembarking. In some cases, local authorities have permitted disembarkation but subjected passengers to local quarantine procedures.

While the U.S. government has evacuated some cruise ship passengers in recent weeks, repatriation flights should not be relied upon as an option for U.S. citizens under the potential risk of quarantine by local authorities.

As we sailed south, blissfully unaware, the number of COVID-19 cases in the United States had reached 423… and counting.

FOUR

CROSSING THE DRAKE LAKE

"Will we see penguins?"

TUESDAY, MARCH 10: CRUISE DAY 2

POSITION:	56°49.1'S / 065°30.2'W
WIND:	W 3
WEATHER:	SLIGHT OVERCAST
AIR TEMPERATURE:	+7C

"Good morning, everyone, good morning!"

Iain's jaunty tone burst from the ship-wide speakers at 7:00 am that morning, and each day thereafter. He would deliver the current weather forecast, share important updates, describe the ship's current location, and review the schedule of activities planned for that day. More than anything, Iain's update helped us to keep track of the calendar, as actual days and dates were soon replaced by designations like kayak day, camping day, or big storm day.

No storms, winds, or heavy waves in sight on that morning. I asked each crew member I encountered if they had ever seen this section of the ocean so calm. Most shook their heads and laughed. Miia referred to it as "The Drake Lake." The temperature hovered around a mild 40 degrees all day long, or "5-7C." I needed to re-familiarize myself with Celsius conversions. I recalled the quick tip I had picked up somewhere: For a rough Fahrenheit estimate, just double the Celsius number and add 30.

By the time Iain's voice woke the late risers I had already spent a half-hour circling the outside decks. I stopped on the upper bow deck, inhaling slow, deep breaths of fresh, salty sea air.

Who needs meditation? This is what my body craves. My neck and shoulders loosened; I could feel the tightness and stress leaving my system. I grew up in New England on the Atlantic side of Cape Cod and I think that is where I incorporated those sense memories for life. Kathy emerged from the steel doorway. She smiled as she breathed it in.

"It's very nice," she agreed.

But I know it does not hit her the same way. I know that she feels invigorated by the morning desert air at home, but she knows that even after 40 years of living in the foothills of Tucson I would trade it in an instant for an oceanside home—if we could bring all of our friends with us. That is partly why I try to spend time at our little condo on Puget Sound as often as possible, which is never often enough. (Boohoo, poor me. I know.)

The stretch of ocean glimmering before us had been labeled by sailors of old as the 'Furious Fifties' and the 'deadly forties of the Southern Ocean,' but they were hardly living up to their fearsome reputation. I felt a bit cheated. We were not exactly earning our stripes by riding the roller-coaster of thundering waves and fearsome winds of the Drake. Neptune slept, said one crew member. Perhaps we were tempting fate? We did have a return trip ahead.

Before leaving home we had signed up on the Oceanwide online portal for two of the three specific supplemental activities offered during the trip—all free. After breakfast we returned to the lounge to hear each activity guide deliver a detailed Basecamp Activity Briefing. Mal Haskins led off by describing the Mountaineering options, which ranged from easy novice walks to advanced climbing for the experts on board. Adam Harner, a lithe, slightly balding kayaking coach, and university lecturer from Wales, covered the steps required to 'kit' out and prepare for the 2-person sea kayak tour. Rustyn Mesdag, a former Seattleite who lives and works in Chile leading tours in Patagonia, stepped forward next. He reminded all of us who had volunteered to spend a night camping on the Antarctic continent that each of the four overnight forays would take place—or not—depending on the weather or other factors. I did not quite catch what 'other factors' referred to, but I would come to learn its meaning a few nights later. Kathy and I had signed up for the kayaking and the camping adventures before leaving home. The idea of camping overnight on a frozen Antarctic snowfield seemed a bit sketchy at first, but we changed our minds after watching a few more YouTube videos of previous Plancius excursions. It looked like fun and would certainly make for a memorable once-in-a-lifetime story, so why not?

Rustyn described a typical overnight camp: Zodiacs would transport us to a semi-flat, snow -covered piece of land pre-selected by the crew and as far away as possible from hidden crevasses, rocks, and penguins. We would pick our spot, 'simply' dig a trench to block the wind, lie down inside a sleeping bag over and under four or five layers of extra warm coverings and stare up at the southern stars. Rustyn reminded us to bring a flashlight and avoid liquids beforehand, since relieving oneself on pristine Antarctic snow was forbidden and an icy midnight trek to the small camp porta-potty was not an inviting proposition. When the 4am wakeup call sounded we would pack up, load up, and motor back to the ship before breakfast. Only four nights would be available, with each outing limited to 30 campers per night. No make-ups were guaranteed if an outing was canceled due to extreme weather or marauding penguins. We signed up for the first night. Kathy admitted to feeling a nervous excitement, so I thought it best to take the first opportunity rather than increase the anxiety for an extra two or three days.

We had passed on the Mountaineering activity. The original description targeted folks with some experience at climbing and roping. I tried climbing once in college with a friend. Jeff was a six-foot, four-inch experienced climber; I am 5'9". It did not go well, especially when he yelled down something like:

"Just use the same footholds and handholds as me."

"My arms don't stretch that far," I think I said, adding in a few extra words for emphasis.

Still, the mountaineering activity looked like fun, and when Mal explained that several of the treks were designed as "no experience necessary" glacier walks we reconsidered. Like most of the guides Mal revealed an impressive backstory.

A stocky native New Zealander, Mal Haskins exuded the easygoing friendliness of a Kiwi coupled with the expert knowledge and competence of an active mountain search-and-rescue expert,

46

which is how he spent winters back home. He piloted our zodiac on several excursions and proved to be an engaging, smart, and energetic guide on both sea and land.

I checked the mountaineering sign-up sheet on the wall immediately after the meeting, but all the slots had been quickly filled. Later I asked Meg and another newbie climber about their trek. Both said they enjoyed the easy walks and the demonstrations (e.g. falling onto a crevasse) but said that the views from higher up were not that different. Sounded like fun, but every trip activity delivered such fascinating experiences that neither Kathy nor I felt deprived of excitement.

"Over here!"

A shout erupted from across the lounge. The calm ocean and clear skies delivered our first sighting of south seas whales as two curved, brownish backsides emerged from the waves along the port side. They seemed much smaller that the majestic black and white Orcas we often spotted around the San Juan Islands northwest of Seattle. These creatures looked more like oversize porpoises.

Pippa, another expedition guide, identified them as minke whales, the smallest of the baleen whales, weighing 'only' five to ten tons. She explained that minke whales are naturally inquisitive and often approach passing ships. They generally travel alone, so spying a pair of them was an unusual sight in the Southern Ocean. Pippa Low, a native of Scotland sporting curly black hair, served as the assistant expedition leader. Pippa's stocky physique attested to her status as a former Scottish national rugby team member. She exhibited a less ebullient personality than Iain, though she appeared quite competent. Serious but friendly, the stress of leadership appeared to weigh more heavily on her shoulders, especially later when the voyage presented unexpected challenges.

The afternoon agenda introduced the first of daily 20 to 40-minute presentations from each of the expedition staff subject experts. Rustyn kicked it off with fascinating talk about the little-known Antarctica Treaty.

The Antarctic Treaty originated during an unusual period of Cold War-era cooperation. In the mid-1950s, a group of scientists convinced the United Nations to institute an event to promote cooperation in the sciences. To this end, the UN designated July 1957 to December 1958 the "International Geophysical Year."

During this 18 month "year" (apparently time is fluid among this group) scientists from 12 nations worked successfully together in Antarctica. One result was the drafting of the Antarctic Treaty in Washington in 1959, which recognized that *"it is in the interest of all mankind that Antarctica shall continue forever to be used exclusively for peaceful purposes and shall not become the scene or object of international discord..."*

The original 12 signees included the governments of Argentina, Australia, Belgium, Chile, the French Republic, Japan, New Zealand, Norway, the Union of South Africa, The Union of Soviet Socialist Republics, the United Kingdom of Great Britain and Northern Ireland, and the United States of America.

Since 1959 an additional 41 countries have signed on to the Treaty. Key articles from the Treaty included:

- *Antarctica shall be used for peaceful purposes only; any military measures, with the exception of use of military assets for scientific research or any other peaceful purpose, are prohibited.*

- *Freedom of scientific investigation in Antarctica and cooperation shall continue.*
- *Plans for scientific programs and the observations and results thereof shall be freely exchanged; scientists may be exchanged between expeditions.*
- *All national claims are held static from the date of signature.*
- *Nuclear explosions and disposal of radioactive waste are prohibited in Antarctica.*
- *The provision of the Treaty applies to the area south of 60° South latitude.*
- *Any Contracting Party may appoint observers. They shall have complete freedom of access at any time to any area of Antarctica, with the right to inspect any other nation's buildings, installations, equipment, ships, or aircraft or to carry out aerial observations.*

All in all, a great treaty with a horrible publicist. It remains to this day an impressive example of strategic common-sense among nations. Well, perhaps not that common.

The onboard seminars were always well attended. I do not think this occurred just because of the limited entertainment options available, but more likely due to the self-selected presence of an educated, naturally curious group of avid travelers and bright, engaging presenters.

The intercom interrupted our applause for Rustyn with another exciting announcement: Lunch time.

The conversation at our table turned for the first time to the saga of the Diamond Princess, the 2600+ passenger cruise ship that had been quarantined at a port in Japan due to the corona-virus. Over 700 passengers and crew tested positive on that ship and 13 died. No one expressed any real concern about the virus showing up on the Plancius. Kate brought up past shipboard out-breaks like Legionnaires disease and several of us listed our own previous cruise experiences. None of the frequent cruisers at that table—Bill, Dottie, Margie, Kathy, or I—had ever sailed on such an unlucky ship.

"I could imagine it," I said. Kathy and I described three nights the previous October on one of those weekend "booze cruises" on a 2000 passenger Carnival ship from Long Beach to Mexico. I had signed up to attend our district Rotary conference, which required an eight-hour drive from Tucson to southern California to board the boat on a Friday afternoon. Our group had arranged to conduct a service project for a local school while docked in Ensenada. Kathy and I had hoped to lend a hand, but instead we paid an unexpected Sunday morning visit to an extremely accom-modating ophthalmologist. Not the first time Kathy altered an international trip for a medical emergency, but the crisis was soon resolved and we made it back to the ship in time for departure. As a result, other than a handful of meetings with a small coterie of service-minded Rotarians we spent three nights surrounded by bachelorette parties, family reunions, loud, crowded, buffets and alcohol-fueled dance extravaganzas. Any virus would have had a field day on that ship.

The Diamond Princess also demonstrated once again how quickly and easily a potent virus could escape any nation's bor-ders. We knew that the number of Americans testing positive for the coronavirus had increased, but government officials blamed the outbreak on the fact that the U.S. passengers were all seated on the same bus and on the same airplane home.

News updates were hard to come by, and to be honest I preferred to remain detached from 'the real world' for a few days. I did not know that the very next day, March 11, the World Health Organization would declare Covid-19, the disease caused by the coronavirus, a pandemic. No U.S. official had yet uttered the word 'pandemic' as far as we knew. In fact, back home in the U.S. after a meeting with Republican senators #45 said, *"We're prepared, and we're doing a great job with it. And it will go away. Just stay calm. It will go away."*

By the end of the day there were 959 confirmed cases and 28 deaths reported in the U.S. Still, it would be more than week before that global wave impacted our ship.

After lunch passengers roamed the sun splashed decks or relaxed in the lounge on one of the comfortable padded benches or swivel chairs anchored around small round tables, reading in blissful solitude or at cards, board games or small group socializing. A 4-stool bar awaited customers in the back corner to the right of the open double door entrance. The small bar opened at 4pm daily for happy hour, and younger bar-lurkers cheered whenever host bartender Raquel would arrive a few minutes early. Raquel was a petite, dark-haired young woman from the Philippines, and like her fellow countrywoman Charlotte she quickly learned everyone's preferences as she kept beer, wine and soft drinks flowing.

I have no idea how such a small ship could carry such a large stock of beverages, but even during our later 'voyage to nowhere' the service never stopped. I guess they knew their customers. The real reason Kathy and I—and everyone else—gravitated to the lounge around this time was to await the fresh daily treat from ship's resident baker. Popular items like the big chocolate chip cookies or banana bread disappeared quickly. The lemon cakes seemed to linger on the platter late into the evening.

I looked around the room that afternoon for any of my Sierra Club compadres. I squeezed in between Kathy and Margie on one of the benches just as the speakers blared: "*Good Afternoon, everybody, good afternoon, we will begin the daily recap in fifteen minutes.*"

Iain's Daily Recap presented an up-to-the-minute weather forecast, colorful slides, and videos from the day's excursions along with a quick status update covering the following day's destinations and adventures. He was always sure to add a line like 'subject to change depending on the weather, ice flows, penguins, etc.' Other expedition staff members shared key moments and surprise pictures before the microphone was handed over to the afternoon's featured speaker.

The four large TV monitors came to life as Dorette, the ship's no-nonsense, fiftyish Dutch media and photo expert presented a colorful video highlighting our embarkation process and the journey first days at sea. She had created it on her iPhone. Impressive.

Rustyn captivated everyone with a truly awe-inspiring talk about seasickness. Just kidding. To summarize; "Go see Doctor Nelleke and GET A PATCH!" Great timing, but the seas were still mild as 7:30 arrived and Alex beckoned us to dinner. We lined up to lather on the hand-sanitizer and reclaimed our usual seats for another three-course repast and a leisurely conversation.

The southern stars captivated Kathy and I as we walked our dinner off under a star-filled sky. Circumnavigating the ship by foot resembled a challenge course. Success required exiting the fifth deck lounge through one of the heavy watertight steel doors (a good workout on windy days) out onto the bow. I recalled the oft-repeated announcement from day one: "Remember, one hand for you, one hand for the ship." I grabbed the handrail and descended on one of the two short sets of stairs to the forward deck area where the anchors and bow machinery sat. Ten more steps brought us to a small circular crow's nest at the point of the ship. A handful of couples lined up to pose in front of the pole beneath the blue flag with the white-lettered 'Oceanwide Expeditions' logo—a popular photo spot.

We climbed two levels to deck six, ambling clockwise along the narrow starboard walkway toward the stern. Navigating around the safety equipment and gauges required stretching up and over through another steel door, then stepping down one stairway and up another to proceed past the two lifeboats attached on either side just before the stern. We paused to watch the frothy white wake merge with the black sea, hypnotized by the ship's movement combined with the swooshing water flowing by. After enjoying the sensation and solitude a few minutes longer we turned and retraced our steps. A set of stairs lead to the highest level of the ship, which featured the largest square footage of outdoor space on board. We stopped in the center of the deck bracketed by eight benches, four along on each side facing out to sea. The view toward the bow was interrupted by the windowed rear wall of the ship's bridge. Small covered platforms extended from the bridge featured open doorways on the port and starboard wings for easy access. Kathy and I moved to the railing and gazed upward into the unfamiliar black and white canvas. I regretted not studying a star chart before we left, and my starscape phone app was too dim to view in near darkness. A slight design flaw, you think?

Nevertheless, we endeavored to identify a few of the brilliant clusters and constellations. I stood amazed by the brightest expanse of the Milky Way that I had ever seen. I pointed out the Southern Cross to Kathy; she spotted Orion before I did.

We guessed at a few more star configurations, and if we did not know the name of a particular grouping, I would make one up. "That's the constellation Prius." The astronomer named it for his car so every time he saw it, he would remember to change the oil." I thought of the 'old guy' birthday card where the grandfather points to a tiny peninsula. "See that piece of land sticking out over there? That's called a stick-out." Lots of bright 'stick outs' in the sky that night.

Our first full day at sea was in the books. The Drake Passage was a pussycat. The tally so far: Don 1, Drake 0. I wondered if tomorrow would even the score.

<hr />

FIVE

SAILING TO THE BOTTOM OF THE WORLD

"Remember the 5-meter rule."

WEDNESDAY, MARCH 11: CRUISE DAY 3

POSITION:	60°01.9'S / 063°37.6'W
WIND:	NNW 1
WEATHER:	CLEAR SKY
AIR TEMPERATURE:	+2C

"You have cancer." Hearing those words at the age of 22 changes your perspective on the nature of mortality. The next thing I remember hearing from a doctor at the University of Arizona Student Health Center was "I have good news and bad news." Seriously, he said that. I remained stuck on the word 'cancer.' I do recall that he whipped out a mortality chart, so I think that his good news comment meant that I would probably not die, but I am not sure. A successful surgery did rid my body of the malignant melanoma, but at the cost of a big chunk taken out of my chest. So much for my career as an underwear model.

Why did that image come to mind as I stood admiring a beautiful sunrise on a deep blue rolling sea? Because I have been betrayed by my body too many times in the past to let down my guard just yet. But on that morning, I felt great. No hint of queasiness or stomach discomfort, even though the motion of the small expedition ship matched the rocking during my previous no good, very bad day on the Panama Canal trip. It was far too early to declare victory. I vowed to treat my stomach gingerly all day. A hidden pun there—I always carry a little fresh ginger when flying in case I need to settle my system. That first event at 22 was a life-changing one, so I am slow to trust any good fortune in health or life. (Yes, also a character trait not unfamiliar to adult children of alcoholics.)

I work to stay in shape and as anyone over 40 knows, it takes more and more effort just to stay even. My parents both passed away near the age I was fast approaching, so it is hard to let my guard down, especially when physical scares arise in me or anyone I love. A few years earlier Jana had a basal cell cancer removed with no visible damage thanks to Moh's surgery. (Well done, Dr. Moh). This procedure is somewhat de rigueur for long time Sonoran Desert dwellers, so I had little concern when I needed to undergo the same surgery not long ago. Kathy has had a few recent glaucoma scares as well, but so far so good. As a friend of mine once observed, 'getting old is not for the timid.'

Just a few months before the cruise I heard one of those dreaded words from a doctor again during a routine eye exam: "You have a retinal melanoma." Are you kidding me?

I was referred to a diabolically engaging retina specialist (Him: "I love this stuff.") He conducted an ultrasound test on my eye, which consisted of placing a lubricated device—about the size of a mini-flashlight—on my eyeball and rolling it around. Great way to spend a morning. So far there is no noticeable evidence of the disease and no progression, but now I get to visit another doctor twice a year.

OK, enough about my physical condition, I sound like the old fart at a bad dinner party. Sorry about that. Getting old might not be for the timid but talking about it should only be inflicted on other old people or friends who say things like "This tastes awful—try it."

I stayed on deck until the call to breakfast, soaking up the invigorating sea air and solitude. I vowed to start every day this way unless high winds or occasional storm threatened to blow me over the side. I finished my cup of the free flowing and surprisingly good hot chocolate that I had grabbed from the 24-hour 'coffee and' machine in the lounge. Usually the self-service set-up carries a nasty tinge of coffee remnants in the other beverages, and I do not care for that odious liquid.*

After breakfast Iain welcomed us to his first presentation of the day: the official IAATO briefing. That is the acronym for

---

* I promised Kathy that I would avoid using the word "hate" in this book. OK, then I also 'strongly object' to beets, cantaloupe, so-called reality shows and #45's human rights policies.

the International Association of Antarctica Tour Operators, a 100+ voluntary member organization founded in 1991 to advocate and promote the practice of safe and environmentally responsible private-sector travel to the Antarctic. IAATO members adhere to a set of rules and guidelines for the care and preservation of the Antarctic environment—the largest wilderness area in world. The association has established regulations and restrictions that members agree to follow when leading tours in and around the continent. Regulations address the numbers of people allowed ashore at any time; staff-to-passenger ratios; site-specific and activity guidelines; wildlife watching; pre- and post-visit activity reporting; passenger, crew and staff briefings; previous Antarctic experience for tour staff; contingency and emergency medical evacuation plans; and more.

We paid the greatest attention to the 5-meter wildlife rule. Iain advised us to stay that far away from penguins, and to keep a 10-meter distance between us and any penguin in the process of molting. If a penguin walks closer to you, however, that is their choice. We were asked to stay out of their well-trod lanes, no touching, no feeding, etc. It sounded easy, but as we experienced many times during the next week, these little creatures had no fear of humans. As we stood in wonder taking pictures of the boundless scenery and active wildlife a solo chinstrap or a group of gentoos would waddle next to you, around you, or over you if they could. They would also poop anywhere and everywhere they pleased, as evidenced by the soles of everyone's boots upon return to the Plancius after each excursion.

We were asked to stay 15 to 35 meters away from all seals, especially the larger fur seals and elephant seals. A few days later at Whaler's Bay I was barked at quite severely by a large, lazy fur seal who clearly did not wish to be disturbed, let alone pose for pictures.

Zodiacs 101 followed the IAATO talk. We learned how to get into, slide around on, exit from, and not fall out of a Zodiac, the 10 passenger motorized rubber boats that would ferry us to and from every shore landing. We would enjoy astonishing harbor cruises with live narration from one of the expert guides as we motored around massive icebergs, ice formations, ice floes, playful whales, and wary leopard seals. I tried each time to follow the instructions, "step carefully on or off the ship, sit your butt down quickly and slide over, when you step out you will get wet." It sounded easy but it was surprising how often someone forgot the process and ended up splashing and lurching their way into or out of the oversized raft.

Following the briefing we retreated to our cabins to gather up and bring back all outerwear, backpacks and any other equipment that would be worn, carried, or otherwise introduced to the Antarctic environment. We were handed mini-vacuums and proceeded to thoroughly clean each item, all under the helpful eyes of the expedition crew members. Preventing the introduction of exotic species into this pristine environment was taken seriously. As Sierra Club members we became big fans of the IAATO practices.

Task completed, we returned to our cabins to await the call to march to the 'boot room' just a few steps down the corridor to our right. When our turn came, we crowded into the cramped room lined with shelves of wetsuits, small life jackets, and a large selection calf-high rubber boots that we were required to wear anytime we left the ship. Every shore landing would be a 'wet' landing where we would be crossing snow, ice, mud, and penguin poop. The boots proved a welcome necessity. Mal stood by to help dig through the stacks—or to lend a hand to help a teetering guest stay upright—as we each tried to find the right size. He reminded us that the final critical step in the frequent boot-wearing process would be a thorough bio-cleaning on the outer deck whenever leaving or returning to the ship—another smart IAATO rule.

Margie had suggested in one of her six pre-trip letters that we bring insoles from home to improve the twice-daily boot wearing experience. It proved to be excellent advice and the insoles worked great.

Margie's e-mails began arriving nine months in advance of the trip with valuable suggestions for clothing, cameras, packing lists, and lots of useful tips. We had put every suggestion to use on our Ireland hikes, so we followed all her recommendations this time as well. Her clothing advice alone saved us from some wasteful purchases like renting expensive Michelin man-looking sub-zero jackets. I did follow her advice to order an inexpensive pair of water shoes, but I forgot to wear them at a crucial time—more on to follow.

That afternoon arrived as we crossed into the Antarctic convergence, a major boundary zone of the world's oceans that separates the waters surrounding Antarctica into Antarctic and sub-Antarctic regions. Within the Antarctic Convergence zone, the cold, dense surface waters of the circumpolar ocean sink and flow northward, thus creating a major circulation system south of the equator. More and more wildlife appeared, circling or swimming alongside us. I raced across decks from rail to rail snapping pictures of Fin-whales, Hourglass Dolphins and some long-finned Pilot whales racing past the ship.

I grabbed a quick shot of an Arctic tern as she soared over my head. At least that is what bird expert Celine called it as she circulated among the gaggle of amateur photographers crowding the open deck. I had no clue. Surprising I know, because I am also a bird expert, so long as you limit my choices to seagull, eagle, or hummingbird.

Lulled by the mild breeze and boundless waves, I lost track of time until Kathy appeared by my side. We held hands to follow the setting sun merge with the ocean; the fading yellow orb seeming to pause reluctantly before disappearing below the horizon amidst a flurry of phone clicks and camera shutters. A near perfect moment at sea. Yet the spectacle served as a mere warm up act. The real star of tonight's show rose above the waves ten miles off the starboard bow. The South Shetland Islands came into focus. Our first land sighting since leaving the south American shores. As daylight faded into night, we sailed through a large gap between two starkly beautiful islands—creating a majestic gateway to the white continent that lay ahead. I experienced a rare peacefulness of body and mind. The world of conflict and chaos faded as the distance grew and nature's relentless strength and beauty took hold.

We soon left the welcoming islands in our wake and entered the Bransford Straight, a stretch of sea that separates the South Shetlands from the Antarctic Peninsula ninety miles away. The passage was named for Edward Bransfield of the British Royal Navy who, along with William Smith, a sealer (sorry, no body of water named for the civilian), made one of the first recorded sightings of Antarctica when they sailed through the straight over two centuries ago on January 30, 1820.

I returned to the lounge in time to catch Dorette offering her expert advice on cold weather camera care and sharing her methods for taking great pictures of the wildlife and landscapes. I liked her Dutch-accented directness. It took Kathy longer to warm up to her, but Dorette would surprise both of us a few days later during a fascinating dinner conversation. On this night Dorette offered additional tips for proper framing and motion. She cautioned her attentive audience to watch out for how quickly the cold temperatures would drain camera batteries, and she demonstrated how to keep the cameras and lenses protected and dry. Not a surprise—keep them covered. (I soon discovered that this was easier said than done.)

She left out the advice about how to master all of this in an unstable Zodiac while 1800 total pounds of heavily clad Ansel Adams wannabes hang over one side to glimpse a humpback whale or a leopard seal swimming nearby during a freezing rain storm.

Celine Clement wrapped up the evening with her highly anticipated lecture about the most-commonly recognized inhabitants of Antarctica. Yes, the penguins. Celine's lilting French accent and engaging smile captivated me as much as—OK, maybe more than—her vast knowledge and expertise as a wildlife researcher, university lecturer and expedition guide. That night she described the difference between the two species we might run across on our excursions. Gentoos, the third-largest penguin species, weigh around 12 pounds and sport yellow feet and beaks. Chinstrap penguins have a little band of black feathers that run from the black markings on top of their head, through the white underside of their chin and back up—exactly like the chinstrap of a bike helmet.

Their breeding practices could be taken straight from a penguin soap opera. Male chinstraps race to find the absolute best nests, then wait for their mates to arrive. If a male cannot find a nest to his liking, he may try to force couples to vacate their own settled nests. Once he does lay claim to a nest of his own, he will give his mate five days to show up, before moving on. If his original mate catches him with another lady however, the female penguins will fight beak and nail for his affections.

To the disappointment of several penguin aficionados, Celine acknowledged that we were unlikely to spot the other two Antarctic inhabitants: Emperors and Adelies. The Emperors are the big ones—the movie stars made famous by Morgan Freeman—that head off around this time of year on their big march to their breeding grounds. The Adelies are the most widely distributed of the species, but again not often spotted along the peninsula. These two species are most often found to the northeast in or along the Weddell Sea.

One passenger asked, "How likely is it that we will see penguin colonies or possibly whales up close?" Celine smiled as one of the other guides in the back giggled.

"Don't worry," Celine replied reassuringly.

Kathy and I retired to our bunks that night for a little channel-surfing. Not much surf there. One channel posted the next day's agenda while another displayed a copy of the upcoming lunch and dinner menus. Channel three transmitted the feed from the bow camera—no use at night. The fourth channel played episode one of the great British series "Shackleton" starring Kenneth Branaugh over and over and over. A great series, but that was all we saw repeated on a loop for the entire cruise—episode one.

The remaining channels rotated an odd array of movies, including 2001: A Space Odyssey (even slower than I remembered), Death Wish (the original 1974 version), SALT with Angelina Jolie (not bad), RIPD with Ryan Reynolds and Jeff Bridges (so bad I had to watch it to the end just so I would never have to see it again), and American Gangster. That was a strange one.

Set in the 1970s with an impressive cast featuring Russell Crowe, Denzel Washington, Chewetel Ejiofor, Josh Brolin, Ruby Dee, and Carla Gugino. I watched sections of it five different times over six days, but never saw the entire movie in sequence. Each film repeated constantly on one of the channels for several days before disappearing. I wondered aloud if each crew member had selected their favorite before leaving the Netherlands and that is what we got.

RIPD seemed to be the favorite of our next-door neighbor Judy. How did I know this? Her infectious laugh resonated through the thin cabin walls every time it played. Thankfully, Kathy reminded me of that significant architectural feature a couple nights later during one of our more intense 'discussions.'

Before Kathy turned out her light she asked if I was excited about tomorrow. She knows that I prefer to wait until a thing happens before I get 'excited' about it. She loves it when I smile or display any type of happiness. I get that, but it does not always come easily or naturally.

"I will be tomorrow," I answered.

She also understood that I have always been cautious about allowing myself to relax and have fun. Here I am, racing toward semi-retirement—I cannot even just say the word 'retirement'—and I am still trying to figure that out. How to do it, and how not to feel guilty about doing it. Life was particularly good at that moment, though, I had to admit.

She observed that everyone sounded excited that night at dinner. And healthy. I repeated the critical numbers that encompassed our dinner discussion: 114 passengers, 48 crew members, 0 virus.

We speculated about events at home, but we had received no new information about the encroaching virus. Ignorance was bliss. We did not know that just one day earlier the White House had declared a travel ban prohibiting anyone leaving or entering the United States.

No one on board showed any signs of the Coronavirus. I wondered if our luck would hold.

———

SIX

ORNE HARBOR, DANCO ISLAND

"What big ice chunk? The one right in front of us?"

THURSDAY, MARCH 12: CRUISE DAY 4

POSITION:	64°37.9'S / 063° 32.3'W
WIND:	E3
WEATHER:	CLOUDY
AIR TEMPERATURE:	0C (32F)

6:00 am.

Amazing. Two humpback whales just swam by on my right.

I am standing in Antarctica. Well, I am standing on a ship in Antarctica.

To be exact, I am standing on a ship in Orne Harbour. Discovered by Adrien de Gerlache's 1898 Belgian Antarctic Expedition, Orne Harbour curves along the west coast of the area known as Graham

Land. Glistening, artfully shaped icebergs littered the small, one-mile wide bay surrounded by towering mountain peaks and stunning blue-white glaciers. Many bays in the region are considered harbors (excuse me, 'harbours'—the Europeans got there first) thanks to the dozens of snow-capped peaks that block the raging winds and offered calm, sheltered waters for the whaling ships of old. The mountains slope down to snow and rock covered shores marked by tiny ice caves. Creeping glaciers mark the slow passage of time.

I headed to the dining room. Breakfast is Kathy's favorite meal, so I have learned to like it. I do appreciate our Sunday mornings back home when we head out to a nearby restaurant to order an omelet, talk a little and relax with a real, honest-to-god newspaper. I must admit that breakfast on the Plancius impressed me, especially with the European slant. I never eat muesli at home—the American version is too thin and boring—but this stuff was thick, filled with raisins and meshed perfectly with the fresh and dried fruit selections. Along with a little smorgasbord of pumpernickel and cheeses (my Danish heritage arises) and occasional baked beans (my Irish side also beckons) I enjoyed a filling but not too heavy start to the day.

Kathy has often accused me of looking 'too intense' or not showing emotion. That morning was different. I could not hide my excitement. I know that the lack of visible emotion comes from growing up as the oldest of four children in an alcoholic home. Many years ago, a well-known author on the subject wrote that children of alcoholics "don't talk, don't trust, don't feel."

Almost accurate. Adult 'COAs' do experience strong emotions, but they learn not to show or express them as a form of self-preservation. Coupled with a different understanding of 'normal' communication or relationships, many ACOAs find it difficult to change that pattern, even when it proves counterproductive to growth.

That intensity and mental focus has served me well at times, whether building and running a twenty-year business or dealing with personal challenges. Jana claims to have inherited these same traits from me; I know that her mother would concur. And I believe that it saved her life. Baby Jana contracted pertussis—whooping cough—and two other respiratory illnesses at three weeks of age. She was placed in intensive care for five days. Kathy was recovering from an unrelated cold at that time, so she was unable to enter Jana's room for most of the week. So, I stayed by her side. On the third morning an attending physician with a god complex walked into the room trailed by four or five interns. After glancing at the patient record for a minute the silver-haired pontificator turned to the newly minted doctors and stated, "I have never seen a patient this ill who lived."

I stood up, stared at the man, and said, not loudly, but in a clear, low, sharp tone, the following:

"You need to understand something."

"This is my daughter. I know, and she knows, that she is going to live. She is going to beat this.

I know this, and she knows this, and if you don't absolutely know this, then you need to remove yourself from this case and get us a doctor who does."

He said nothing. A nurse in the room stepped back and hurried off in search of the head nurse. The doctor babbled something, trying to backtrack.

The head nurse appeared in the doorway and the doctor motioned to her, as though she could help fight off a potentially violent parent if necessary.

"Oh, hi Don!" She greeted me, then turned to the doctor. "This is the man who helped me get sober. You take care of him and his child!"

The doctor stayed on the case. Jana was discharged two days later problem-free and has not stopped moving since, not only running marathons but running circles around anyone who tells her 'no.'

As the clock creeped toward 9:00 am my head and my legs grew restless. Time for our first real Antarctic activity—Sea Kayaking. Kathy and I raced back to our cabin for our pre-kayaking challenge: putting on all the 'kit'. I pulled on my warm-but-not-too-hot base layers of clothing—my single layer consisting of a long sleeved t-shirt and long johns of thin fleece; Kathy added an additional three—or was it nine?—layers to keep her blood circulating and her footsies warm.

Next came the tight overalls-like wetsuit, then rubber half-booties instead of the big boots, followed by the kayak "skirt." The skirts are designed to fit the opening around your seat to protect your bottom half from the splashing water flung from your—or your partner's—paddle. Finally, we donned the special insulated dry jacket or "cam," and of course one must not forget a heavy woolen hat and thermal-lined gloves. We joined the single-file line in the corridor leading to a small covered deck on the starboard side. I stood parboiling in my overheated, overstuffed layers as I waited to swipe my keycard for "off ship," then gave a quick bio-brushing of boots and headed down to board a Zodiac.

The next challenge required proceeding down the slippery metal stairway to a small loading platform attached to the side of the rocking ship, reaching for the Zodiac pilot's extended arm and half stepping/half lurching into the bobbing black rubber boat. Each Zodiac fit ten passengers squeezed cheek-to-cheek on the top of each side of the craft. Most riders grasped a section of the thin rope running along the gunwales for balance. Others grabbed onto their spouse, partner, or a surprised new friend. Our Zodiac pulled away from the ship trailing seven kayaks tied end to end behind it. We motored into toward the ice strewn harbor. Once we had reached a safe distance away from the Plancius each kayaker carefully slid from the zodiac into one of the 2-person kayaks. Points for gracefulness were not awarded. Expedition leader Adam led the floating parade across Orne Harbor straight into an easterly ten knot wind. We ducked our heads and labored to a spot twenty yards offshore, just below the summit of Spigot Point, named for the towering black spire resembling a cask-like spigot rising 938 feet above our heads. We pulled up paddles and drifted while an awesome National Geographic scene came alive before our eyes. Gentoos and chinstraps waddled along the shore in front of us while fellow penguins dove past us, flying gracefully through the icy water.

Pippa had not exaggerated. Gentoos are the speedsters of the penguin world. Although they are not strong runners, they become guided missiles in water: When diving, they have been known to reach speeds up to 22 miles per hour. Quite useful for spending much of their day cruising for krill, squid, and fish.

We paddled on, our senses overloaded by stunning ice formations below and majestic glaciers above. Then came the morning's main event.

Fifty yards from our scattering of kayaks rose two large brown forms from the icy blue-gray water—a couple of humpback whales casually emerged to reclaim their territory. The bulging black minisubs appeared and disappeared without sound before reemerging a minute or two later in the middle of an ice floe. The residents quickly assessed the vibrations of our insignificant fiberglass-hulled intruders and deemed us harmless as they lazily cruised the bay.

I reached into my coat pocket for the waterproof camera I had purchased especially for this scenario. I had imagined bobbing two feet above the water in a wet, rocking kayak when I was reading several sad and desperate tales of iPhones slipping from cold hands and slowly sinking out of sight. I chose to leave my phone back in the cabin along with the expensive new Nikon DSLR I had purchased last August in preparation for the trip. I pulled out a little yellow digital number instead.

Well, not 'pulled out' exactly, more like fumbled through the special extra-heavy lifejacket, located the right pocket, realized I had to remove my glove to pull down the tough zipper on the right pocket, reached with swiftly cold-numbing hand for the camera, tried to find the right button to switch on the camera with my near-blue fingers, aim in the generally direction of the whales and take the shot. Too late. After my third or fourth shaking image of fuzzy blue waves and zero whales I started to get the hang of it.

I snapped shot after shot of the harbor penguins skimming gracefully across the water, while the two humpbacks rose and dove among the icebergs, even 'spy hopping' twice to check us out. Overhead I followed Antarctic shags staging their aerial show under intensely blue skies, quite unexpected for late summer in the

Antarctic. The birds, I later learned, are also known as Imperial Cormorants, King Cormorants, Imperial Shags, the *Blue-eyed Shag,* or the Antarctic Cormorant. They held their own among the incredible sights that morning. It was the first morning of the first day of our Antarctic excursion, and most of my expectations of the white continent had been met. Incredible. But the oddest sight that morning was none of the above.

While we sat in the small red kayak, dwarfed by this cold, alien environment, amazed by spectacle after spectacle, I watched the Plancius ship sail out of sight. That was weird. For the moment I felt adrift in a hostile world, sitting less than two feet above a vast cold sea. I knew that the mother ship had to keep moving to avoid being hit or hampered by icebergs or ice floes, yet it was quite unnerving to watch your only connection to the outside world disappear into a white void.

Adam had one more treat in store for us that morning. The expert kayaker encouraged us to follow him through the chunks and bits of ice floating in a large section of the harbor. His only advice was 'Don't stop paddling!'"

"Let's go!" I said. We sped up and slotted in right behind Adam. We were game to test our ability to power our tiny vessel fast enough through the icy slush to escape marooning on a low floating sheet of ice, but slow enough to maneuver around the larger chunks and avoid slamming into a mini-berg.

We took off through the partially frozen no-man's land.

Kathy (in the front): Watch out for that big ice chunk!" "Turn!"

Me (in the rear): "Where? I can't see it."

Kathy: "You can't see it? It's right in front of me!"

Me: "YOU are right in front of me."…CLUNK.

We soon got the hang of it and laughed our way back to the waiting zodiac. I loved it. Kathy loved surviving it. She admitted later that her laughter could be best characterized as the 'hey, I didn't drown!' version.

We reconnected with the waiting Zodiac and five minutes later bumped up against the rematerialized Plancius. I hoisted myself onto the tiny platform and clomped up the metal stairs. Grabbing one of the big brushes hanging on the side wall above two tubs of chemically treated water, I dipped one rubber clad foot at a time into the mixture and bio-scrubbed my boots before marching back to our cabin. Kathy and I performed a careful pas de deux in the tiny entry space between the door and closet while removing wet rubber boots, awkwardly heavy kayak jackets and the remaining ten pounds of 'kit.'

That afternoon we bid farewell to Orne Harbour and cruised south along the Errera channel. The nine-kilometer-long channel lies east of Anvers Island, in the shelter of the eastern side of the Gerlache Strait. In the middle of relatively calm channel sat Danco Island, our destination for Kathy's up-close-and-personal penguin encounter and the site for our overnight camping extravaganza.

Snow-covered peaks sparkled in the afternoon sun as we set foot on land for the first time in four days. We slid off the boat for our 'wet landing.' *Note: Everyone landing was a wet landing.* A welcoming committee of gentoo penguins perched on nearby rocks, some shuffling in and out of the water, some gazing down from rocky ledges along the shore while others ignored us altogether. We followed the natives as they made their way in ones and twos up the rock-strewn hillside. During Celine's shipboard lecture we learned that the gentoos were the most colorful of the species, sporting the familiar yellow-orange beaks and feet. By contrast the chinstrap penguins were all black-and-white, but easy to spot by the long thin black line running along each side of their head. Danco Island hosted one of the larger gentoo colonies in the region, containing over 1700 pairs of breeding penguins.

Our guides had not lied. If you did not keep one eye to the ground you could easily come knee-to-beak with a fast moving, perturbed bird. Twenty feet away a Discovery Channel episode played out before us. We spotted a mother penguin leaning down to allow her equal-sized adolescent to peck food from her beak. After a patient minute the mother decided that dinnertime had ended. She jerked her head up, turned, and scampered away. She had no more food to share, but the young bird was still hungry. He squawked and took off after her.

A third bird (jealous sibling?) noticed and took up the chase behind the two speedsters, but he soon fell off the pace. Mother and son scampered awkwardly across the rocky field, stumbling, falling, and dodging fellow penguins who took little notice as the mother maintained her steady one-meter lead. The miniature Olympic race-walk continued past a distant ledge until the family drama disappeared from sight.

We resumed our uphill hike. Navigating around a colony of gentoos was harder than it sounds. More than once I was forced to step quickly to one side as a seriously focused bird trudged down a well-worn path as though late for a meeting at the office.

Ten meters to my right two penguins perched side-by-side on a steep ledge, patiently enduring the late stages of molting, while nearby another dozen black-and-whites stood at attention while gazing motionless out to sea. I watched their heads swivel in unison to the sounds emanating from the clicking metal objects in the hands of the two-legged visitors squatting nearby.

I advanced gingerly up and over guano-slicked rocks to level ground. Dorette stood watch from a flat expanse to our left and offered to take some still shots of Kathy and me. She chose a picturesque mountain backdrop to frame the picture rather than the muddy, rocky slope on which we posed. This section of the island had much less snow than I expected. The shoreline and lower sections of hills were similarly barren. I wondered if this was normal for late summer or the result of increasing climate change. Still, a panoramic scan of the Errera channel revealed a stunning view of seemingly endless, untouched snow-covered mountain ranges. I thanked Dorette and paused once more to admire the views. Time to test my skill at employing Dorette's picture-taking tips. I raised my new Nikon and snapped multiple shots from each direction. Her advice worked. I captured one of my favorite shots from the entire trip; a great picture of the Plancius resting in center of the bay, surrounded by the stark beauty of the stunning bay and landscape.

"Hey hon!" Kathy called in a loud whisper. I glanced over.

"Don't move." I said.

I framed a close-up shot of a curious gentoo exploring Kathy's boot with its orange-tipped beak. Kathy stood frozen in place until her new friend, curiosity satisfied, waddled off.

The Plancius Trip Log offered this description of the afternoon's experience:

Along the hill we pass plenty of little gentoos rookeries. The little chicks are already left alone during the day by their parents. The parents go to sea and come back for feeding the chicks. What happens when you leave teenagers alone at home. They are just everywhere, they are bored, and they just checking out the bypassing tourists. The little teenage penguins have no clue about the 5m rule and approach us gentle, curious and in an unbelievable cute manner. We enjoy these new friendships and take a rest, sit down and inhale this fantastic landscape that the hill climb has to offer us.

The trip log continued: *The view is spectacular and we are impressed by this unique landscape. We get more than 3 hours time to enjoy and right when our free time on land finished the sun is settling behind some clouds. Maybe just to make leaving this island a bit easier.*

An apt description, though 3 hours never passed so quickly.

After three days of small ship confinement I really welcomed the hike up and down penguin alley. I am used to running at least three or four times a week. Doing next to nothing except stuffing my face had left me feeling restless and slightly 'off.' Kathy had the same reaction—albeit with less patience—though she denied that last part. I do get irritable after more than two days with no workouts, though, so we're even. (Nope, she does not buy that either.)

After a few hours of trekking up, down and around the steep hills and around the local resident waddlers, I had removed my jacket to cool off in the balmy 34-degree afternoon sun. There I was, standing in Antarctica clad only in a t-shirt and sweater. Bizarre. I was glad that I had lathered on the sunscreen before heading out that afternoon. Surviving skin cancer and living for forty years in Arizona had ingrained the habit.

Kathy announced that she was ready to head down to the Zodiacs, so I looked for an unoccupied penguin trail to guide our way down the slippery slopes. Our descent was interrupted more than once as for more picture taking and frequent stops to exclaim "look at that!" My camera was fully broken in by the time we departed Danco Island.

Snack time in the lounge. Kathy and I found two seats at a small table across from a young, friendly, dark-haired woman.

"Hi!" she said as she welcomed us to the table. "I'm Jennifer. We haven't met yet."

Jennifer was a slim 34-year old financial services professional from New York City. Kathy laughed and shared that she has a relative from Connecticut, also named Jennifer, also a financial services professional in her 30s' who works in New York City.

"That's where our daughter lives, too," Kathy added, smiling.

We spent a relaxing hour talking about New York City as she recounted her experiences in the global banking business. I related our tale of renting an apartment in the city during the previous November to greet our brand-new grandson Ryan, Jana's and Brendan's addition to the family. Jennifer knew most of the side streets and restaurants we had sampled on the trip. She sympathized when I described my first 'living in NYC' lesson: *Do not buy more groceries than you can carry in two hands for ten blocks.* I learned the hard way that it is only good for the biceps until the bag breaks.

Jennifer had grown tired of the banking industry and she had quit her job before leaving on the voyage. She had no idea what she wanted to do next. *Side note: After returning home we found out that Connecticut Jennifer had also quit the financial sector and had moved into a new field.* Future Jennifers take note.

Antarctic Jennifer was at peace with her decision after having toiled for over ten years in a high-pressure position. She admitted having done well financially, so she had embarked on the cruise as a welcome break between careers. I told her that I knew several individuals who made a similar move in their 30's, yours truly included. I did not know anyone who regretted the move. I added my opinion that the key for a successful shift is to move toward something meaningful, not just away from something. I shared how I had run a non-profit for eight years before leaving to start my own companies. I observed that even those endeavors had evolved over two decades from addiction treatment and EAP services to professional speaking and consulting work.

She asked what it felt like to start a new company from scratch. I said it felt like jumping off a cliff and making your parachute on the way down.

I asked if she had any ideas or avenues to pursue. Jennifer nodded and observed that she related to the "meaningful" part. She wanted to add more substance to her life, although she had not yet decided on her next course of action.

"Is there anything you are passionate about?" Kathy asked.

"I don't know. I have been too focused on my job for too long," Jennifer said.

"I will decide that when I get back to New York. I thought that this cruise would give me a chance to think about it more, but so far I am just looking at all the scenery!"

We continued the conversation throughout the cruise. A week later we offered our support as circumstances at home would push Jennifer in an unexpected new direction— away from quarantining in NYC to live with her brother in Dallas. Quite a change.

The Plancius passed through another spectacular gauntlet of blue-white icebergs as we sailed through the Errera Channel toward that evening's camping destination. I stepped through the metal passageway between the lounge and the outer deck. I peered over the railing, entranced by the large white irregular blocks drifting northward, shaped by the wind into giant swans and modern art sculptures. Iain's *"Good afternoon, everyone, good afternoon"* call interrupted my reverie and I headed inside.

Tonight's headliner: Pippa on the trials and tribulations of humpback whales.

Humpbacks are commonly described as roughly the size of a school bus, but I can now attest that the comparison hardly does the mammals justice. Up close they are immense. Humpback whales are not the biggest whales, though, that distinction belongs to the blue whale. Humpbacks grow to approximately 60 feet long and they can weigh up to 40 tons. Pippa pointed out that they do not actually have a hump on their backs; the name was derived from the way they arch their backs before a deep dive. Her colorful slides called attention to their two most distinctive features—their head and dorsal fin. The heads are rather rounded and covered with barnacle-like knobs called tubercles. Each tubercle was once thought to employ stiff hairs within it to function as motion detectors, though that remains just a theory. Most humpbacks are nearly all black on the upper (dorsal) side and mottled black and white on the under (ventral) side. The shape and color pattern on the dorsal fin and flukes are unique to each whale, like human fingerprints.

Pippa invited each passenger to take on the role of Antarctic whale researchers. She recommended checking out Happy Whale. International whale research organizations like *www.happywhale. com* invite members of the public to submit photos of fins and flukes of humpbacks to help the professional researchers identify, catalog and monitor humpback whale migration, population size, sexual maturity and behavior patterns across oceans. Pippa now appeared much more at ease than previously. Between the topic and the environment, she was clearly in her element.

Rustyn made his way to the front of the lounge to kick off the first night of camping. He reviewed the evening camping protocol, beginning by reminding us that camping was not guaranteed. He listed weather, safety, nearby wildlife, and penguin homesteaders as just a few of the independent variables that might negatively impact our adventure. Campers were advised to "Be prepared." He informed us that we would have a 30-minute notice if the night's excursion was a go. (Thus began the first of several hurry up and wait games, foreshadowing our final two days on board wondering if we would be allowed to ever disembark from the ship.) Rustyn handed the microphone back to Pippa as he proceeded to a Zodiac and headed out into the dusky gray light to examine that evening's campsite.

We gathered with our fellow campers for a light dinner. Our entire Sierra Club contingent has signed up for this night, so most of the group consisted of campers with the average age of 'retired.' Unsurprisingly, nearly everyone commented on Rustyn's caution that getting up to answer the call of nature in a cold, dark, snowy expanse would not be fun. Getting up just two or three times a night was considered a good night's sleep for most at the table, so our server Charlotte's workload lightened considerably that evening as fluid intake was minimal.

We all returned to our cabins for final preparations and to await the go or no-go announcement. Water bottles remained untouched and bathrooms were visited early and often as I sat and waited...and waited. I tried to read or watch the Shackleford episode for the fifth time. The evening light faded outside the port-hole. I knew that a second opportunity to enjoy a night under the stars was not guaranteed unless there were open spots for one of the three remaining nights. Yet as another hour passed, I thought to myself, "you know, another night would be OK."

A few minutes later I said it out loud. Kathy looked over at me and nodded.

"I am already tired. That would be fine with me," she agreed.

We continued to sit, stretch, and check the clock on the TV screen. I was rechecking my overnight pack for the third time when the intercom came to life. Iain gave us the official word—No Go. We headed back to the lounge. Rustyn, Pippa and Dave had just returned from surveying potential campsites. Thanks to the unusually high temperatures of the past week the preferred site was too wet and—this was my favorite part—the area had been taken over by a colony of gentoos. They checked out a second location but rejected it due to the danger of rockslide.

I was disappointed of course, but not alone. At least half of my fellow would-be campers admitted feeling some relief at the late decision to scrub the mission. Twenty minutes later we glanced out the windows. The exterior lights of the ship illuminated the driving snow slashing from port to starboard across the bow. The Oceanwide flag snapped furiously in the harsh, freezing wind. Yup, good decision guys. Nature 1, Campers 0. Kathy and I added our names to the waiting list for the Sunday, the final night available for camping. I hoped now that the weather would not interfere with tomorrow's excursions.

SEVEN

PORT LOCKROY, JOUGLA POINT & DAMOY POINT

"What's red and green and white all over?"

FRIDAY THE 13TH: CRUISE DAY 5

POSITION:	64°49.6'S / 063° 31.0'W
WIND:	NW4
WEATHER:	OVERCAST
AIR TEMPERATURE:	0

I needed one of those hotel elevator mats placed outside our cabin each morning that featured the day of the week printed on it. I had no clue. Time remained encapsulated by this small expedition ship traversing through limitless scenes of moving water, ice floes and jagged snow-covered mountain ranges.

The bracing Antarctic air smelled cleaner and crisper than I ever recall breathing, at least yesterday. The sun broke through a gray cloud blanket as the temperature reached a balmy 40 degrees Fahrenheit before dropping to 32F later in the day. Morning winds buffeted the ship before easing off as the skies brightened.

My hands froze after just a minute of standing out on the cramped Zodiac boarding deck. I hustled back to my cabin and slipped on an extra pair of socks and glove liners. The heavy-duty, super special REI gloves I bought for the trip were not quite up to the task. My hands and feet always pay the price, as I learned at age 11 after feeling—or rather not feeling—my feet go numb on a boy scout camping trip during one New England winter. Kathy earned her own frostbitten fingers while living in Vermont, but she had come provisioned with those little packets of chemical hand warmers. They worked incredibly well. Good things; small packages.

Properly attired, we embarked upon a frozen tour of the waters surrounding Jougla Point, a featureless outcropping on a nondescript island of rock and snow lazily guarded by a scattering of gentoos. Jougla Point sits at the entrance to Alice Creek in Port Lockroy. According to the large map posted onboard the Plancius, it lies on the west side of Wiencke Island in the Palmer Archipelago.

As we circled the bay my eyes drifted upward to the vast panorama of snow-covered mountain peaks, the scene accompanied by the sounds of calving glaciers to my right. The small booms of cascading ice produced smaller waves than expected. I wondered if the frequency of multiple breaks and avalanches occurring across the large expanse mitigated the effect. I continued to snap away on the DSLR as Iain steered us through choppy waters past glowing blue ice caves carved into odd shaped mini bergs, no two alike.

Seabirds appeared overhead. A large gray-white wandering albatross skimmed by low and fast. He darted back and forth over our boat, intent on his reconnaissance mission. He zeroed in on a spot twenty yards away to attack the floating remains of a former resident—likely a small seal. His find discovery attracted a flock of fellow sea birds who arrived amid much flapping of wings to grab a share of the mid-morning snack.

The most entertaining of arrivals was the lone Antarctic petrel who 'ran' past our bobbing zodiac on her way to the feast. The Antarctic petrel is the Earth's southernmost breeding bird, although they can be found as far north as New Zealand and Australia during winter months. This species appears to skip or run over the water before flight, which is how they got their name, with 'petrel' alluding to the water-walking Saint Peter. We spied a few of the low-flying, smaller Wilson's petrels darting by as well, but they chose not to perform for us.

The Zodiac bumped into the rocks buffeting the shoreline at Jougla Point. Iain hopped out to brace the boat as we hauled ourselves over the slick rubber gunwales into the icy, calf-deep water. I grabbed Kathy's hand as she stepped onto the uneven footing. We sloshed our way to solid ground under the impassive eye of a single chinstrap penguin inspecting us from a half-submerged boulder a few yards away. Kathy decided that the area was a bit too treacherous, so she stopped to engage in a penguin stare-off while I clambered over the rocks to inspect two large gatherings of whale bones. Previous divers had collected and reconstructed near complete whale skeletons using the aged, sun-bleached bones of different species that had been recovered from the surrounding bay. Two more chinstraps sauntered over to stand watch as cameras shutters clicked. After the gaggle of rubber-booted visitors finished posing inside this living museum piece, complete with directions like "move over and squat down by the penguin…no, too close!" Iain hailed us from the boat.

A brief dash across the water led us to our most treacherous landing to date: Goudier Island and the site of Port Lockroy, a former British Research Station. The island was discovered by the French Antarctic Expedition of 1903-05.

We edged our way along a narrow, wet, cliffside path overrun by arrogant gentoos, skuas and Snowy sheathbills. The sheathbills are small white birds so named because of the horny sheath that covers the upper part of the bill. They frequently scavenge penguin colonies for eggs, dead chicks, and other disgusting penguin detritus. Sheathbills are the only Antarctic birds that do not have webbed feet; thus, they are unable to fish for food like the other area inhabitants. Over 800 breeding pairs of Gentoo penguins make their home on Goudier Island, far outnumbering all other species and moving off their paths for no man or woman.

Two freshly painted structures came into view on a small hill above us. A small black storage shed sat closer to the water, its bright red doors formally guarded by a half-dozen tuxedoed birds. We skipped that one and trudged past a field of muck and penguin poop. We climbed the wooden steps to the front deck of the larger green building where Pippa stood waiting.

She directed us to a small side bench where we brushed off our boots before entering a small reception area just inside the open door. Two white framed windows brought light into rooms on each side of the open doorway. I entered the tiny entryway just large enough for leaving boots and hanging coats and took three additional steps forward along the narrow, dim main hallway. The British military set up WWII Operation Tabarin Base "A" here in 1944 and handed it over to civilian control after the war ended. The site lay abandoned from 1962 until rebuilding efforts began in 1996.

I turned right at the end of the hall and found myself in the middle of a 1940s style kitchen, complete with mid-twentieth century appliances. Three large wooden tables sat along the pale military green walls. On one the tables sat four large metal canisters labeled PREPARED AND DRIED VEGETABLES AND FRUIT. Above the tables attached to the walls were two ranks of narrow dark green shelves. I leaned in to read the faded labels on the dusty cans. The bottom shelf displayed age appropriate canned vegetables, soups, and undefinable meat products, while the upper shelf held coffee, a box of butter, six #10 cans of oatmeal and faded sauce bottles. I stepped back into the hallway and turned left into a small but bright and airy room centered by a long table covered with a familiar old style red & white checked tablecloth. Two chairs sat on each side of the table, with the end butting against the building's front wall between two windows. In the far corner sat a small round cast-iron stove. I moved over to the blue wall on my right. I looked above a padded bench seat to read from a display of four wood framed posters told the story of the station.

'From 1944 to 1962 the base at Port Lockroy was home for a small, very isolated community. Ships with mail, stores and relief personnel visited infrequently during the Antarctic summer (November to March). Once the ships had left for the UK, the bases were completely isolated. The only contact with the outside world was by radio, using Morse code, with the FIDS office in Stanley, Falkland Islands.

The normal term of duty in the Antarctic was two winters, which meant that men would be away from home for over 2 ½ years. They often moved to another base for the second winter. One advantage of this length of stay was that there would always be a nucleus of experienced men to provide continuity.

The conservation of Port Lockroy was started during the Antarctic summer of 1996 by the British Antarctic Survey with financial support from the UK authorities and is continued by the UK Antarctic Heritage Trust (UKAHT). The base is now a museum and Post Office operated by UKAHT.'

The weather-beaten structure had been described in our ship's literature as a "charming little museum." Fascinating, yes. Charming? Well, it was warm and did offer a respite from the constant, face-reddening breeze. The building also offered our first encounter with evidence of previous human presence in Antarctic. It was not hard to experience a sense of the weighty isolation of a (near) south pole winter.

Except for a brief glimpse of another small cruise ship as it passed beyond a distant iceberg, we had seen no one beyond our shipmates. I had read many stories of Antarctic explorers and adventurers. Standing there in my modern cold weather gear I could scarcely imagine the mental and physical stamina required to live and work in such ceaselessly challenging conditions.

I wandered across the hall to find Kathy winding her way through a room filled with tables of well-preserved communications and scientific equipment for all manner of wind, sea, and geological tracking. She stood entranced by the old charts and notebooks preserved under glass. Her excited eyes directed me to notations penned by hardy researchers and official visitors from decades past. She once remarked that in another world she could imagine life as a happy scientist.

At the left end of the T-hallway I entered a room brightened by two side windows on the far wall of a four-bunk sleeping area. Each bunk sat next to a small storage locker adorned with personal items—old watches, tiny leather-bound notebooks, and the like. Above one bunk proudly hung the torn half of a British flag. Nearby walls held two rows of shelving filled with shaving equipment and more books. When I entering the space, however, my eyes had focused immediately upon the walls opposite each bunk, each painted panel featuring an impressive hand-drawn, life-size mural of a 1940s 'pin-up' model, colorful, fading images of Jayne Mansfield and Doris Day among them.

Back in the kitchen Kathy noticed something that I had missed. She directed me to a bulletin board propped next to the stove. Preserved and posted on the wall hung my wife's favorite discovery of the day; a popular Port Lockroy recipe for "seal-brain stew."

She snapped a picture of the well-worn historical document to carry home. Future dinner guests are hereby forewarned. Tough to get all the ingredients at Safeway, I am guessing. Kathy does swear by Trader Joes, though, so I will remain on alert.

Here is the recipe:

- *1 Prepared Seal brain*
- *3 reconstituted eggs*
- *1 dessertspoon Tomato Sauce*
- *3 ozs Butter*
- *Grated cheese, hot toast*
- *Salt, pepper and a little grated nutmeg*

Chop the brains into very small pieces, mix together with eggs, tomato sauce, nutmeg. Cook slowly in a buttered saucepan until done. Add grated cheese and serve on hot toast.
Bon Appetit.

Port Lockroy's second claim to fame decorated the hallway just beyond the front entryway. A shiny red British postal box featuring the E II R symbol was affixed to the wall. Anglophiles would recognize the royal cypher representing HRH Queen Elizabeth II. The 'EIIR' cypher stands for 'Elizabeth II Regina'. The 'R' stands for either 'Rex' or 'Regina', which is Latin for King or Queen. The port remains one of the few active post offices on the Antarctic Peninsula, but the site is only occupied during the summer months of November through February. That year's museum staff had abandoned the site just prior to our cruise. We deposited three postcards each into the slot along with the exact amount of US dollars required for the necessary postage. The cards will sit in the box unattended until the following November. With luck they may be delivered in time for a new president's inauguration, but still too late for Ryan's first birthday.

The island delivered one more unexpected display. One of nature's harsh realities unfolded on the rocks a few feet from shore. I stepped out from the warm, protected walls into the brisk, chilly wind. Kathy had expressed zero interest in climbing up another hill just to peer in the windows of the small tool shed, so we stepped across the whitish muck to the water's edge. A cluster of gentoo penguins practiced jumping and diving off the low flat rocks just a few feet offshore. I did not see the leopard seal silently stalking the clueless birds as they hopped and shuffled around one of the ledges. The younger penguins continued displaying their newly developed skills to their friends, unaware of the predator lurking nearby. Sure enough, in full view of two dozen shocked witnesses the seal effortlessly glided up the ledge, snatched a young penguin in its teeth and slid back into the bay.

The serpent-headed star of the horror show swam a few yards out to open water, raised its head and thrashed the penguin back and forth to ensure its demise. Welcome back to Discovery Channel live. Later at a lecture on pinnipeds we learned that leopard seals are picky eaters, preferring only certain penguin delicacies like the liver, for instance, and leaving the rest for the circling birds to finish off.

"Poor penguin." "How sad." My initial reaction matched the chorus echoing around me. My second thought did not. This was the real world. Darwin was right. Slow learners get eaten, even if they are much cuter. It is the predator's world, too. Maybe if Morgan Freeman narrated a movie about cute seals...?

Back to the ship to warm up and fill up. No one's appetite seemed affected by the earlier native dining display. The lunch buffet offered perfect Plancius-sized (i.e. not huge but impressive) offering of salads, hot and cold pasta dishes, DIY sandwich options and Kathy's favorite—soups. As I sat down among our small group Charlotte materialized tableside with my soda, a nod, a smile, and a quick swipe of my all-purpose Oceanwide keycard. Water, coffee, and tea were free but on the ship Coke Light cost 3 euros—a small price to pay for a taste of home.

2:00 pm. Time for the afternoon excursion. Over the past few hours, the ship had traversed a short distance north through the Neumayer Channel to the shallow waters of Dorian Bay. Iain and Pippa created an arm chain to guide each passenger across the slick rock landing at Damoy Point.

Amazing sights became our daily backdrop. Exit the ship, stop, glance up at the array of stunning blue-white mountain landscapes. Glance over to a spectacular view of designer iceberg drifting in the bay. Walk, stop, repeat. We hiked a brief distance along a snow-packed path to a compact British Antarctic Survey (BAS) hut, erected in 1975 and now designated as a historic site. The BAS previously used this location as a staging-post for planes flying farther south. Pippa pointed out an area behind the hut where an ice runway had been cleared on the glacier.

Celine stood nearby to describe its use as a research station and waypoint for past scientific explorers. Now inactive and closed, but like most intact structures along the peninsula the hut is still used as an occasional refuge by intrepid scientific travelers. Rustyn called to us from higher up the hill. We waved an acknowledgement. After a hundred-yard slog we were greeted by the largest and highest gentoo penguin rockery on the island. It offered stunning views of the fjord below. I removed my bulky gloves to attempt a fancy panoramic shot on my super camera. Dark clouds approached our position as I heard Iain shout from the shoreline. "Let's go!!" Our pleasant uphill excursion, or as Kathy described it, "SLIPPERY, FREEZING and WINDY," was concluded.

I fumbled my gloves on, stashed the camera in my backpack and trotted down the hill. I asked Iain why we were cutting the afternoon short. He said he had gotten a call from the captain, who instructed that '*the swell at the gangway is getting deeper and deeper. Head back to base.*' One wet and wild dash later we pulled up alongside the ship.

The increasing waves made moving from the Zodiac to the small platform rather dicey. Kathy reached up to two friendly crewmen as they smoothly grabbed each arm and lifted her onto the platform. The male crew member turned to me with a slight challenging smile that said, "go for it, buddy." I had to time my steps in sync with the rising four-foot swell while Pippa worked to keep the bobbing boat close to the ship. One. Two…thr..JUMP! Made it. The crewman nodded. Respect for his elder.

Question of the Day: What the heck are Green Snow and Red Snow?

Any boy or pet owner knows where yellow snow comes from, but red snow? We had observed this strange phenomenon on several mountainsides since arriving in the region, but the various patches or streaks of multi-colored snow remained a mystery. At the afternoon program Tom Van Hoof, a burly Netherlands-born guide, supplied the answer and taught us a new term: snow algae.

Green algae 'communities' were protein-rich, had a high chlorophyll content and contained many metabolites associated with nitrogen and amino acid metabolism. The phenomenon's red color comes from carotenoids (the same pigments that make pumpkins and carrots orange) in the algae's chloroplasts. In addition to their crimson hue, these pigments also absorb heat and protect the algae from ultraviolet light, allowing the organisms to bask in the summer sun's nutrients without risk of genetic mutations.

Both communities contain bacteria and fungi and hide in snowfields and mountains worldwide. The algae thrive in freezing water and spend winters lying dormant in snow and ice; when summer comes and the snow melts, the algae bloom, spreading red, flower-like spores. *Note: This phenomenon was noticed by Aristotle way back in the third century B.C. I enjoy any reference to Aristotle.*

That is good for the algae but not great for the ice. According to Ukrainian Antarctic researchers (Ukraine is not cold enough for them?) it is easy for these blooms to kick off a feedback loop of warming and melting.

Since the red colored snow reflects less sunlight and melts faster, these snow blossoms contribute negatively to climate change. The more ice that melts, the faster the algae can spread. From that afternoon forward I was decidedly not happy to see red or green patches along the mountainsides. Sadly, we saw them at every stop.

So now you know...*and* there will be a quiz.

Tom himself was an entertaining character. A healthy, large-bodied Dutch native, he stood well over six feet with longish dark hair, a bushy beard, and a ready laugh. He ably fit Kathy's description of "a big bear of a man." I had read his bio posted along with those of other crew members in the ship's corridor. It mentioned a stint at the University of Arizona. When I told him that I lived in Tucson and attended graduate school there he responded with a mile-wide grin. I motioned Kathy over to enjoy his heavily accented recitation. Tom had conducted research studies around the world and had spent time at several educational sites, including a lab at the U of A. He laughed, recalling his amazement at living in one of the dorms attached to Arizona Stadium and working in the one of the labs set directly beneath the football field. He enjoyed hearing that they still existed. I got the impression that he enjoyed the Mexican food and beer just as much.

Our Sierra Club group had hoped to experience camping overnight together as a group, but after the first night's cancellation the second chance hopefuls were limited to signing up for any remaining openings. A few awaited the confirmation for that night's excursion. During our dinner conversations the official word arrived: Night Two was cancelled. Rain and high winds were expected in the target area. The forecast proved to be correct. The outer decks were marked off limits that evening as fierce winds blew the heavy rain across the decks. Two nights down, only two possibles to go.

I relaxed with a book in the lounge until 9pm before I headed down to our cabin for the night. Kathy was already buried in her bunk scanning one of her several hundred New Yorker magazines that must multiply in secret and follow us everywhere. I am sure that the ones she could not fit in her backpack were inviting friends over and partying on our coffee table back home.

Kathy's habit is to jump into bed well before 9:00, call or text a friend, turn on the TV (with the sound off) then read for relaxation until she is ready for sleep. I cannot do that. If I climb into bed before I am just ready to drift off, I will stay awake for hours. Even when I do lie down, I read for thirty minutes or so just to turn my mind off. Mysteries work best; non-fiction keeps me thinking too much.

That night I needed to talk.

"I think it's time for a change," I said.

"What?" Kathy dropped her magazine, propped herself up on one elbow and looked over to me. Her female radar jumped to high alert. She has told me before that her rational brain is listening, but those words set alarm bells clanging. Her emotional brain immediately jumps to worst case scenarios. "Is he bored with us? Is he unhappy? Is it me? What did I do? What did he do? What does this mean?"

Kathy's first reaction was worry. Kathy's first reaction is always to worry. I think Kathy would worry if she had nothing to worry about. I get it. Like many couples we went through a rough spot early in our marriage. For the past 39 years, though, I could not ask for a better partner nor could I imagine a life apart. Those words make her tense up, so I quickly add when appropriate..." with my dentist, ...with my brand of running shoes," etc. *Note: Those are just examples—Dr. M. and Asics are safe.*

Now I talked about cutting back, or semi-retirement, or whatever the hell I thought I needed to do. Kathy was heading toward the traditional form of retirement this summer (for the second time) but I was contemplating a different path. At age 63 I do not want to disengage completely, but I do not want to keep doing the same work I have been doing since I sold the business five years ago. I love speaking professionally, yet I have grown tired of giving the same series of talks in the same locations year after year. I felt honored to be invited back by organizations doing meaningful work, especially the native American tribes, but refreshing or recreating the same topics has reached its limit. I have continued the work out of respect for the friends and great people I have come to know well. One of my popular programs is "Managing Change," so I guess it is not surprising that I needed change and variety in my life again. I also admitted to something Kathy already suspected—someone new has affected my thinking. She knew who I meant.

Ryan, my new grandson. Now, I know all of you grandparents reading this just laughed because you have been there. You get it. But there is a twist. I have already been a grandfather for thirty years.

Chaz came first, followed by Caitie who was born shortly after their father Chip died. I have shared the story of my stepson's passing each Memorial Day because he remains close to our hearts. Here is the first part of that annual message:

You've seen more than one movie in which the military officer walks up the driveway to knock at the door—and inform a parent that their soldier-son or daughter had died.

On July 10, 1994 I answered that door.

A respectful staff sergeant reported that my stepson, Charles W. Rawls of the 101st Airborne, had died that day. It was left to me to inform his mother. It was the worst day of our lives.

My wife Kathy was widowed when "Chip" was two. She worked and raised him alone as a single parent until we married in 1981. No mother or son loved one another more.

A few years later Chaz's mom Tina asked if Kathy and I would step in as grandparents for her two daughters Brenna and Emma, now teenagers. So, over the years I have gained four wonderful grandchildren. None by blood but all by choice. I love them all. It is a joy to watch them grow up.

Last October 29th Jana and Brendan brought Ryan into the world. I admitted that seeing the three of them just a few times a year would not do. Kathy nodded; she would prefer to see them a few times a week. Cutting back on work would be physically easy but mentally tough. Choosing to cut back on non-stop work after 45 years is a foreign concept. I also feel some strange guilt about it, since I have friends who are working—or did work—full time into their seventies. Losing Chip at 25 and losing my parents in their 60s is a constant reminder that nothing is guaranteed, though.

My father died at 63—the age I am as I write this. That weighs heavily on my mind no matter how often I compare health histories. He had quit drinking in his forties and had quit smoking for over a decade. I learned after the fact that an ill-advised prescription medication may have contributed to his death, yet he appeared healthy and fit at the time of his surprise passing, likely from an instantly fatal stroke or heart attack. Losing my mother was no less sad. She died nine months after my father had passed away and only a few weeks shy of her 65th birthday, as much from grief as from a recurrence of the breast cancer that she had evaded for four plus years.

Until I pass Paul McCartney's invisible barrier—"when I'm 64"—I will not truly relax. That is why I get up early to run. That is why I work hard to stay in shape. This recent diagnosis of retinal melanoma hit me hard, though. I cannot deny it, especially when the specialist outlined potential treatments like 'sticking radiation pellets in the eye' for three days to kill the cancer cells—and possibly the eye. Who knows? Maybe I will live long and prosper; I will just lose a piece at a time.

But there is another reason I work at staying in shape. I made a promise that I must keep.

Kathy already lost one husband. She says that she cannot bear the thought of losing another one. She made me promise that I would outlive her. I promised her. Honesty and integrity are the values that matter most to me, so I always keep my promises. I must keep this one, no matter what.

Cutting back on work now and creating something new with Kathy feels very right and very weird. Neither of us are the inactive or non-participatory types. We both have a need to stay busy, to stay active in the community or helping others in some fashion. I may also suffer from IFOR—irrational fear of retirement. Part of me fears the "r" word as leading to a state of irrelevancy and a loss of connection to "the real world"—meaning my professional ties and associations. For 45 years I maintained a hyper-focus on achieving success and financial security for the family, and yes, I did benefit from some ego-gratifying recognition along the way. I don't need that anymore, but no one wants to be forgotten either.

I have advised others that creating a successful retirement requires more than just stopping one thing, but also moving toward another thing. Time to heed my own advice. Simply doing less of the same activities will not work for me. So what should I do? I intend to continue conducting behavioral health surveys and trainings for CARF as long as they want me, however, which allows me to contribute to a field that helps millions of people.

I plan to stick with local and global service efforts on behalf of ShelterBox— one of the world's top global disaster relief organizations—and Rotary, although I recognize the need to periodically review my purpose for engaging with each organization. Traveling is a must, although that does not excite Kathy quite as much. As we talked about seeing the kids more, visiting family and friends around the country, and checking out national parks I could tell that she was catching on to the benefits. I know that I cannot just skip from one activity to another to fill time, though. There is no satisfaction in that. I must figure this out.

But she relaxed as we talked about how soon we could head back to New York for a visit. I told her that I was ready to start making these changes as soon as we got home.

As we sailed along in our Antarctic bubble, I did not yet know that the world had other plans for us.

EIGHT

NEKO HARBOUR & ANDVORD BAY

"Why so blue?"

SATURDAY, MARCH 14: CRUISE DAY 6

POSITION:	64°50.9'S / 062° 32.5'W
WIND:	VAR 2
WEATHER:	RAIN
AIR TEMPERATURE:	+3C

How close do you have to get before you can claim that you have reached Antarctica?

Apparently, travelers and scientists maintain an ongoing debate about what constitutes visiting "the real Antarctica." The broadest definition gives credit for crossing the Drake at the Antarctic Convergence Zone. The "AAC" is a curved line that fully encircles

Antarctica, and which varies in latitude seasonally. It marks the point where the cold Antarctic waters meet, mingle, and sink beneath the warmer sub Antarctic waters. When the two regions meet, nutrients situated in the seafloor are carried to the surface, rendering the convergence zone suitable for the growth of micro-organisms such as phytoplankton and creatures like krill. These life-forms contribute to the food chain of the region's residents, including seals, penguins, whales, albatrosses, and fish. The zone is among the southern hemisphere's primary marine food sources.

The AAC curve changes in latitude seasonally and in differing longitudes across the Indian, Atlantic, and Pacific Oceans, between the 48th parallel and the 61st parallel of south latitude. The primary indicator of the change is a reduction in water temperature, which is recognized by a passing ship's instruments. The usual summertime water temperature north of the zone is 7.8⬚ (46F), which drops to 3.9⬚ (39F) upon reaching the Antarctic Convergence.

We crossed that line three days ago.

The South Shetland Islands, which we passed on the evening of Day 3, lie approximately 75 miles north of the Antarctic Peninsula and are included among the Antarctic Islands. Landing on one of the South Shetlands or any of the islands off the shore of the continent is recognized by most people as the first legitimate Antarctic arrival site. We would not set foot on any of the South Shetlands until making a final stop before heading back to Ushuaia. I believe that the proponents of this continental marker do have a point. If you first land on Nantucket Island off the coast of Massachusetts have you not arrived in North America? Since I grew up on Cape Cod, I am fully qualified to rule in the affirmative. But please do not ask me to explain "Nantucket red" shorts on men. I can describe them—they are PINK!—but I cannot explain them.

For all of you purists out there, today was the day. On Saturday, March 14, 2020 we landed on the mainland of Antarctica.

I could not stop smiling. A rare sight, I know. I was about to officially set foot on my seventh continent. As I said earlier, this was not a 'bucket list' thing. When I was growing up I always wanted to get away from home. As an adult I have always sought to visit new places, try new things, enjoy new experiences, understand other people's lives and other cultures. This cruise certainly fit all the criteria. I enjoyed every opportunity to learn about the lives and experiences of fellow passengers and—more interestingly—discussing working cruise life and expeditionary cultures with various crew members.

On my home office wall hangs a poster board-thick map of the world. Today's landing site in Neko Harbour is the place where I will stick a pin on the board. Each marker triggers rich and fascinating memories. Some of those memories—like our encounter in the Amazon with Montezuma's revenge—I describe as a "once in a lifetime experience, and once was enough."

It is estimated that only 70,000 people each year visit Antarctica. That seems like a lot. By comparison, though, that is the number of people that fill just a single large NFL stadium on a pre-pandemic Sunday.

Pippa maneuvered our black rubber taxi around the rocks and ice breaks as we approached the rugged, muddy shore of the continent. We sloshed our way onto the land. I stopped to look down at the blanket of white atop the rocky ledge. I retrieved my camera, pointed it at the snow and snapped a picture of that first boot print. My own personal Neil Armstrong moment.

We braved a short slog up a muddy hill through the light drizzle. Pippa said that the Scottish call it a *"driech"* morning. This bay was overfilled with glowing blue and white icebergs, two or three times as many as we had encountered at our previous stops.

The local gentoo colony ignored our arrival. The shoreline melee resembled the end of summer camp. Chattering penguins clustered in small groups squawking away while youngsters hopped and flopped along the shore before splashing into the water and transforming into sleek, darting sea missiles. Not a leopard seal in sight.

As we wandered up the slippery slope from one ledge to the next, I stopped every few feet to take in the amazing spectacle of sight and sound. The rumbling crashes of calving glaciers caught my attention on the right before I pivoted to the left to capture shots of sea ice sculptures fronted by an inexhaustible display of penguin antics. Farther up the muddy path we stopped to observe an older penguin constructing a nest.

With single-minded focus this hard-working bird waddled a few feet in one direction, grabbed a rock in her beak, raised the wall of her circular rookery another inch, then repeated the process. With fall just two weeks away I asked if it seemed late in the season for such efforts, but Celine described most penguin behavior as instinctive, regardless of need or calendar.

We tread carefully around the abundance of fast-growing chicks. The fluffy mini penguins hoped to lose the remainder of their down covering in time for winter. We watched one chubby chick after another chase the adult birds for food, some slowed by full bellies but most remaining undaunted in pursuit of constant nourishment.

"Whales!" Kathy called out as she motioned to a spot across Andvord Bay. She pinpointed three humpback whales easing by fifty yards beyond the shoreline. I moved to join her on a ledge to the side of the rocky path. My foot slipped on a damp rock and my thin blue backpack slid off my shoulder and hit the ground— with my fancy camera inside it. Clunk. "Crap." I pulled it out of the bag. No visible damage. I turned it on. It worked. I had left enough cushioning in the bag to avert catastrophe. Over lunch Kathy and I debated which would have been worse, breaking the camera or dropping my phone in the water. Fortunately, neither event occurred and a few days later the answer became a no-brainer. Without my cellphone we might still be looking for a way home.

We bid farewell to the local waddlers and headed back to base camp for a new layer of dry clothes and a meal. Next on the schedule: A two-and-a-half-hour Zodiac tour of Andvord Bay. The sun emerged from the heavy gray cloud cover just as we descended the platform and hopped into the boat. Darkened skies soon reappeared to deliver a mix of rain and snow, an occasional peek of sunshine, then wind, then more rain in rotation throughout the afternoon. We tugged our coats and face coverings tighter as we coasted around the iceberg-strewn harbor ringed by an endless succession of steep, glacier-covered mountains. As we glided around for close-up ice examinations, the striking blueness emanating from within the massive floating bodies seemed lit by a hidden high-end illumination system. Icebergs full of tiny cracks and crevasses glistened as we marveled at each unique combination of translucent pale aquamarine or turquoise layers above and below the crystal-clear water. Massive ice carvings, several of which equaled a two-story house, exposed colorful ice caves that receded deep into the massive iceberg.

Why so blue?

As Mal described in his imaginatively titled lecture "Ice", when glacial ice first freezes it is filled with air bubbles. As that ice gets buried and squashed beneath younger ice, the older ice begins to take on a blue tinge. As the ice grows denser, the bubbles become smaller and smaller. Without the scattering effect of air bubbles, light can penetrate ice more deeply. To the human eye this ancient glacial ice acts like a filter absorbing red and yellow light and reflecting blue light, creating the beautiful blue hues of a glacier.

In contrast, snow is white because it is full of air bubbles, which reflects the full spectrum of white light. The continent's great glaciers are like slow-moving rivers of ice.

When these flows hit a barrier, such as a mountain range, the deeper layers of ice are forced upward, like water flowing over a submerged rock in a riverbed. Blue ice also tends to surface on the lee side of mountains, where fierce winds strip away snow and ice. Over time, the older layers are revealed through evaporation. In Antarctica, the blue often emerges where glaciers tumble into the sea and form icebergs small and large...and larger. Summertime melting creates smooth patches of blue glacial ice on land and on the icebergs. During our tour around Andvord Bay we discovered one large, amazing iceberg so shiny and translucent that it looked artificial, like one of those plastic colored ice cubes, except this blue cube was the size of a cargo ship.

"Look over there!" exclaimed a younger passenger on the port side opposite Kathy. While we remained entranced by the floating art deco sculptures, the nearby Zodiac 'buddy boat' passengers had spotted a few sleepy humpbacks and cruising minke whales. We moved closer to enjoy the sight of curious minke whales, playful humpbacks, crabeater and Weddell seals freewheeling around the bay while checking us out in return.

Ten minutes later three highly active humpback whales arrived to further inspect our little convoy. Flukes flipped and pecs slapped within a few feet of our boats. Dorette and the other boat pilots shut down the engines as all aboard beheld the curious humpbacks diving near, around and under our oversized rubber rafts. Thankfully, no one toppled overboard as crazy whale watchers in each of the three rocking zodiacs shifted from port to starboard to record every move of the giant barnacle-crusted behemoths.

The performance was mesmerizing, but thoughts of hot chocolate and dry clothes beckoned once the huge creatures disappeared and the brisk winds grew harsher in the late afternoon light.

Dorette did not seem anxious to return to the ship. Kathy, on the other hand, was not thrilled with the meandering pace as we wandered among the ice floes, at least as far as I could understand through her chattering teeth.

Dorette: "I guess we should head back toward the ship. It is a bit chilly."

Kathy: "Great."

Dorette: "Wow, look at those great ice formations over there, shall we check them out?"

Three other passengers—all under 40: "OK, cool!"

Kathy (softly): "I am freezing."

We motored stately along, passing right by the Plancius, and moseying toward a remote section of the harbor. And by mosey-ing, I mean VERY SLOWLY.

Dorette: "What amazing iceberg shapes over there toward the sunset. Should we check those out, too?"

Kathy: "I can't feel my toes."

Eventually we made it back to the ship, thanks to the requests prompted by the highly motivated large prostates and small blad-ders of a few jittery septuagenarians on board.

Once I regained sensation in my toes, I joined Kathy and her 4pm wine club for the daily recap. (In fairness the time was now 6:30 and she still nursed her first glass.) Iain bounded to the front with his usual greeting and rated the chances of campers getting to spend the night on the continent. A 'wee bit unlikely' solidi-fied to a solid 'no" as the hour progressed. Bad weather made the score Antarctica 3, Campers 0. Mal's ice lecture proved much more fascinating than the name implied. As he concluded Iain popped back up to ask a question that revealed the evening's big surprise.

What better way to spend a balmy, slightly windy 30-degree evening than by enjoying an outdoor Antarctic Barbeque?

We paraded through the dining room and out the rear door-way to the stern. Under the protected cover of the upper deck a dozen picnic tables had been jammed against the outside railings. Opposite the stern against the steel wall of the ship the beaming kitchen crew (no doubt happy to escape the hot, cramped galley) lined up with tongs in hand behind three large grills covered with steaming sausages, steaks, and chicken. We worked both sides of an impressive buffet to fill plates with salads, corn-on-the-cob, beans, and breads before making our selections from the grill, "one of each, please" the most common request. Wine, beer, and lemonade flowed freely. Overhead speakers pounded out upbeat tunes as we laughed and shivered and pretended that enjoying a shipboard barbecue surrounded by Antarctic glaciers was a perfectly normal way to spend a mid-March evening. Passengers, staff, and kitchen crew sang and feasted while a few hardy guides grabbed a partner for a quick dance in the small center area. Our favorites servers appeared hefting huge platters of desserts just as we were headed inside to restore blood flow to our extremities. The heaping mounds of white chocolate and mango mousse proved irresistible, so Kathy, Meg, Margie, and I each filled a bowl as we moved into the dining room so our thawing fingers could work the spoons.

We claimed a long table in the nearly empty room and dug in. At one of the circular tables to my left sat a woman of similar age with short reddish-blond hair and a serious look. Her husband appeared to be a few years older, tall, and nearly bald, thin, and healthy-looking. I had wanted to meet the woman.

"You're the mystery writer?" I asked.

"Yes," she said. "I'm Rebecca Douglas."

We introduced ourselves all around and compared work and home histories. Rebecca and her husband lived in northern California. She had been a teacher previously but now made a living as a published author. He had been a professor and political junkie.

"Have you heard of the 'PTA mysteries'?" she asked.

I had seen them on shelves or on Amazon but had never read one. I did not tell her that part. I just said, "Yes, I have."

I lost track of time as we talked about writing. I admitted that I had written a few non-fiction books related to my profession, but never fiction. I love to read and solve mysteries, but I am not a natural storyteller. I took me many years to comfortably work stories in my presentations. I shared that I never have fictional stories with intricate plotlines pop into my head. Rebecca does. We compared different writing styles. I had listened to a podcast recently that featured John Grisham describing his highly organized writing method. He detailed his extensive preparation of story progression, chapter outlines and such. Rebecca said that she used a similar method. She told me about creating her website as a place to engage with her fans, too: www.ninjalibrarian.com. Great title. I liked her more.

Kathy seemed to enjoy our discussion, but I noticed that she had not said a word for the last fifteen minutes. I glance over to see her holding her head up with one hand, eyes fighting to remain at full mast. I said good night to our new acquaintances and farewell to a great evening.

Sleep is not my friend. A mildly distracting mystery helps me to relax and drift off, but it often does little good. If I get six hours of rest, I consider it a good night. I have always believed that working three years on graveyard shifts to pay for college screwed up my sleep pattern for life. I spent too many nights as a psychiatric aide in the 1970s at psychiatric hospitals in Oklahoma and California. Each night's shift offered an all-or-nothing proposition. On the 'nothing nights' I got a lot of studying done between rounds of checking vitals or calming restless patients. Other nights all hell would break loose. A new patient would arrive after hours via ambulance, often in the grip of attendants informing us that the reluctant visitor patient might be on PCP but was quiet "for the moment." One summer night in Santa Ana a patient was admitted just after midnight. He calmly asked an attendant to retrieve his guitar from the private car that brought him. He took the guitar, thanked the attendant, and then ran down the hall hollering while he smashed the instrument back and forth against each wall. I enjoyed the work during that time, and it proved to be great preparation for dealing with crazy politicians.

Back in the cabin I powered up my phone for the first time since leaving Ushuaia to learn what was happening in the world above the 55th parallel south. Oceanwide had provided each passenger with 100mg of free internet use on their satellite-based connection, so together Kathy and I could go wild with 200 mgs. I sent a quick text to Jana to let her know all was well. I sifted past the junk mail and useless messages. As I read news briefs and e-mails from friends a startling picture emerged.

I had gladly traded a few of my favorite annual events to enjoy this once-in-a-lifetime experience, but I was still curious to see how the Wildcats were faring in the Pac-12 tournament and the NCAAs. I was stunned. Not by the results; by the lack of results. The world we had left behind just five days earlier was shutting down—fast.

March Madness—cancelled.

All other sports—cancelled

All concert events—cancelled.

The Tucson Festival of Books—cancelled.

I should not have been surprised. Right before we left home #45 had assured all Americans that we had *"nothing to worry about."* Two days later on March 8 he announced: *"We have a perfected coordinated and fine-tuned plan at the White House for attack on coronavirus."* On March 11 he had proclaimed that: *"for the vast majority of Americans, the risk is very, very low."* In fact, on four occasions that week the president predicted that the coronavirus would "go away." Fool me once....

Like any half-aware American I had learned that his proclamations were as credible as his orange tan. Now, after seventy days of dithering an infected wave of reality had swept over the U.S. Worse still, credible reports later revealed that #45 and his administration had known of the threat since January and chose to respond with denials and blaming, rather than creating a national strategy for prevention and mitigation—Exhibit A for how NOT to manage a crisis.*

I ranted for a bit longer as I reviewed the electronic stack of horror stories. I replied that the response of the White House and their Senate cronies was nothing less than a failure of leadership, a policy failure, and a moral failure of historic proportions. There, I felt better. Well, no, not really, but I did eat up 100 megabytes in a flash. Kathy moaned once or twice in agreement, then rolled over and switched off the light above her bed.

I discovered that next morning that, after months of calling reports of the spreading pandemic a "hoax," #45 had finally declared the coronavirus a National Emergency. Our Antarctic bubble had burst. Soon more than just the ship's course would be altered.

---

* During our group dinner discussions I would sometimes refer to #45 as 'the current occupant.' Judy, our well educated and recently retired Iowa friend referred to him as 'doo-doo head.' You gotta love high school counselors.

NINE

PORTAL POINT & THE GRAHAM PASSAGE

"Is it a he or a she? It's a what?"

SUNDAY, MARCH 15: CRUISE DAY 7

POSITION:	64°29.7'S / 61° 43.8'W
WIND:	SE 2
WEATHER:	OVERCAST
AIR TEMPERATURE:	0

A squadron of blue-eyed shags offered a fly-by greeting as we stepped through the icy water onto the granite ledges of Portal Point. These intrepid residents are the only members of the cormorants to reside this far south. The seabirds sport a blue ring around their eyes that give them their name, along with an orange/yellow growth at the base of the beak that grows larger and brighter during the early summer breeding season. That blue ring is tough to spot when they soar overhead, but their white lower sections, black upper part and black tail confirmed their identity. Dorette stood next to me as we tracked their flight path. She added that blue-eyed shags do not travel far from their nests to feed, which always made them a welcome sight for sailors and explorers who would know that land was near.

I hopped from the rocky outcropping to the snow-covered path ahead.

"Wait, please!" Pippa called out.

Two six-foot long grayish white crabeater seals blocked our path. I froze in place to observe the unhurried shuffle across a narrow, uneven 30-meter spit of snow-covered land toward the opposite shore. These poorly named pinnipeds do not actually eat crabs at all. They use highly specialized teeth to filter water for the abundant tiny local crustaceans, but 'krill eaters' did not have the same ring to it.

Cameras sprung from bustling black, red, and gray parkas. Photographers circled the scene as the pair slip-n-slid down a short incline, inch-worming their way to a flat area midway to their goal. Exhausted or bored by the effort the seals stopped, rolled over and threw a bored glance at the motionless spectators on opposite sides of their rest stop. Under a blue sky the two animals could have passed for hefty summer sunbathers as they reclined on a white snow blanket with faces turned upward, indifferent to the gray skies and freezing wind.

The sound of four zodiacs drifted across the bay. Two groups of passengers motored off for an hour of whale watching and seal spotting among the coves carved by the Graham Passage.

The remaining boats carried the day's mountaineering group and kayakers to their wet and windy locales.

I employed the snow-shuffle two-step to navigate a narrow path past the two resting blobs and hiked up a nearby icy, white hill. Kathy and Meg trailed behind as we tip-toed to the top to join an extra-heavily clad group gathered staring out into the bay, seemingly at nothing.

A morning meditation group? Through a light curtain of falling snow I spied the Plancius drifting in the bay, but that was it. I pulled my collar up higher and my watch cap lower. In the past five minutes the temperature had dropped at least 5 degrees as the breeze stiffened. The light curtain of snow had morphed into a sideways-blowing sheet of thickening flakes.

I heard a now familiar yell from behind. Over there! I turned to follow the extended arms pointing beyond the edge of the low cliffs to our right. Three humpbacks emerged from the grayish-blue waters below. They disappeared just as suddenly below the calm surface, then a few seconds later, Whoosh.

A single whale shot up out of the water in a perfect breach position. Then a second whale outdid the first, executing a perfect slow-motion backwards flop and splash. Too late for the 'pull off gloves-grab camera-snap off shot' maneuver. I squinted through the thick falling flakes and waited for an encore. No such luck. The whales clearly believed in the tried-and-true adage: Always leave them wanting more.

Margie's smile widened as the snow fell thicker and quicker. She was gratified by our first glimpse of 'normal' Antarctic weather. I remarked that I was pleased to know that the region would be breaking no more high temperature records this season. She nodded. It was impossible not to think about the encroachment of climate change, especially after having spent the first two days walking on bare rock shorelines under relatively warm skies. The graffiti-like streaks of green algae defacing the pure white mountainsides had further served to remind us of what might soon be lost.

I side-stepped my way down the slick hill, one hand extended behind me to help steady Kathy as she followed in my fresh footprints. Trekking safely back to the slippery rock ledge we donned lifejackets and stepped gingerly into the calf deep water to a waiting zodiac.

By now we had the boarding process down pat; turn sideways, place butt on the black rubber gunwale, swing legs toward the stern and over to a sitting position, then slide sternward along the gunwale past the large black duffel bag filled with emergency equipment, leaving enough room for the pilot to stand and handle the outboard motor, all without inadvertently knocking a paying customer overboard.

We swung out and away from land for part two of the morning's excursion: another close-up whale watching tour. Separate pods of humpbacks wandered by in twos or threes. Pippa commented that they were likely cruising and feeding on krill.

After three straight days of seeing the large black humps and yellowish flukes appear and disappear one might think we had become accustomed to the site. Not a chance. Time passed without notice as we watched these majestic creatures suddenly appear, rising and diving around our tiny boats. With each languid pass they remained unconcerned by our presence, as though ignorant of their power to send our two thousand pounds of passengers and equipment flying with a single, dismissive flip of the tail.

As Pippa explained later that afternoon, krill constitutes the most abundant wild species of animal on earth and a key link in the Antarctic food chain. We had watched the whales glide through swarms of tiny krill, cavernous mouths agape, capturing the mini appetizers by filtering sea water through their baleens. The jealous krill oil advocates on board marveled at the sight of these heart healthy humpbacks consuming loads of $30 per bottle supplementals in a single gulp. For the rest of us, sitting three feet above the water as a wide-mouthed whale approached our tiny boat was not a sight soon forgotten. Lucky for us, our rubberized vessel and bulky Columbia sportswear were not considered delicacies in these parts.

What a privilege to encounter these gentle giants in their own habitat. I had experienced the same reaction during safari trips in Zimbabwe and South Africa. Each outing proved to be similarly unique and incomparable. Observing such large and amazing creatures in the native habitat has ruined me for visiting zoos or places like SeaWorld (a dying business, one hopes.) Even before I had the opportunity to travel to new lands, I never really felt any joy at seeing animals in captivity, but I can understand the attraction of viewing rare and unique living specimens from other parts of the world. I just dislike the sight of a regal elephant or performing seal confined to an area 10000 times smaller than home. The evolution of the role of zoos during the past few decades is encouraging, however, as they shift from entertainment venues to research, education and conservation centers for wild animals, assisting protection efforts and breeding programs designed to reintroduce extinct and endangered species back in their natural environments.

I recognize how fortunate I am that good health and a modicum of success have allowed me to fulfill my travel dreams. The great joy, however, is not received solely from the sight of amazing species in native habitats or stunning array of natural and man-made vistas. It is not even the incredible, sometimes eye-opening knowledge and understanding gained from engaging with other cultures who often face challenges unimaginable in middle-class America. The reward—what keeps me going—are the encounters with fascinating individuals who become lifelong friends.

Thanks to professional trips, vacations, or my current Rotary club's commitment to taking an active role in international service projects I have experienced the wonders of places like Peru, Brazil, Viet Nam, and South Korea. I still think Kathy kicks herself a little bit for not going with me to Sydney, but she would not have to twist my arm to go back. I have enjoyed speech-making visits to Ireland and Asia, but what I value most is discovering new friends on three continents. I am thankful that our global clan now extends to places like Waterford, Ireland and Victoria Falls, Zimbabwe, a troubled place that we have twice visited and the 'home home' of Bryson and Grace Tivatyi, whom we call brother and sister in our extended family.

We returned to the ship for a filling repast of not-krill. Iain's bouncy *"good afternoon everyone, good afternoon"* grabbed our attention midway through the meal. He announced that we were headed out to explore the Graham Passage, a narrow gap through which ships cannot normally pass due to large icebergs threatening any foolish captains.

Calm, ice-free waters had convinced the captain to declare 'Clear sailing, Full speed ahead.' An hour later Mother Nature changed her mind. Twenty-two knot winds raked across the bow as we traversed the passage. Gray clouds darkened the skies and dropped sheets of rain upon the ship. Iain and company had ventured out to survey possible landing sites for our afternoon activities. He returned to the ship's lounge soaked and dripping wet as he apologized for canceling the afternoon landing. He reported that the crew had checked three separate locations, but they determined that the risk of heavier rain and wind gusts was just too high for safety or fun. I glanced over at the windows, but the low clouds and heavy rain obscured any sight of land. Good call, Iain.

I felt a little guilty but not unhappy with an unexpected afternoon off. I was not alone. Unreserved Judy said, "Great. I need more time to warm up and dry out!" I entertained the thought of wasting a rare afternoon in the lounge with a warm drink and a book. My wife had other plans.

"Let's go down and air out all our socks, long sleeve t-shirts and mounds of fleece so they can fully dry," she said.

Uh, OK dear. She would do it anyway and I had no idea where my clothes might end up. I followed her down the stairs.

When we finished the exercise I surveyed the scene; clothing draped across both beds, long johns hanging from every bathroom railing, underwear covering the tiny wall lamps at the head of each bunk, shirts spread in, on, and over the closet unit, socks across the heater, and various other garments covering the small corner desk and the single chair jammed against it. Not a clear surface in sight—Kathy's favorite view. Drives me crazy. We have a standing agreement at home that when I get home from a three or four-day trip I will be able to see actual kitchen countertops and dining table surfaces. While I am away, though, all bets are off.

Pippa brightened our late afternoon by highlighting the various marine mammals who make the Southern Ocean their seasonal home. Her detailed knowledge and easy speaking style kept my attention, so I learned more than expected—or needed—about all the species of whales and seals that call the Antarctic home. She finished right on cue as Hotel Manager Alex announced the arrival of happy hour. Based on the crowd's reaction I half-expected horns to sound, streamers to fall, and penguins to dance on the waves. Thirsty loungers rushed to the bar to grab their adult beverages. Aromatic squares of oatmeal goodness arrived in two large baskets borne by a majestic dark-haired Philippine crewman who topped out at a generous five and a half feet tall. Baked goods, beer, wine, and plenty of Coke Light capped the late afternoon session on the high seas. Not bad.

I relaxed in one of the two swivel chairs bolted to the deck across from a padded bench seat surrounding two small tables near the front of the lounge. One of my fellow loungers asked if anyone had updates from the world back home. Kate had heard from her daughter and Margie shared updates from Sierra Club HQ. We pooled what little information we could piece together.

We recalled that in late January cruise lines begun stepping up health screenings and deny boarding to people who had recently been in China. We knew that when we filled out the Oceanwide Excursions forms before leaving home and then again prior to boarding. The Sierra Club was considering cancellation of future 2020 trips but had made no decision. Kate's daughter reported that no clear-cut directions yet existed for U.S. citizens.

Someone nearby had heard that a cruise ship, the Grand Princess, had left San Francisco on a cruise to Hawaii but quickly reversed course after passengers became sick en route. The ship sat dockside for several days before the American passengers were released to military bases for quarantine.

One of our party read from a news site that on March 8 White House infectious disease advisor Dr. Anthony Fauci had warned older people and those with underlying health issues to avoid cruise ships. That would not have stopped anyone present. One day earlier the CDC issued a 'no-sail order' for cruise ships. Not sure what that meant for us. Well, nothing, really.

Heads shook in unison when someone asked, "Can you believe what's happening back home?"

Margie shrugged. Meg smiled. Kathy asked me what I thought. I laughed once.

"Do you realize," I said, "that, right now, we are probably the healthiest people in the safest place on the planet."

No one thought "we're screwed." The real world was still back there somewhere. None of us had any idea that by the end of the day the United States would confirm 669 new cases of the coronavirus, bringing the total number to 3,485. The number of reported deaths had reached 65. We sailed blissfully through our secure world at the bottom of the globe.

A dry Iain reappeared looking considerably more relaxed. He favored us with his Scottishisms while warning us that our bunks would feel "a wee bit bouncy" this evening as we continued southward toward our next port of call. He handed the microphone to Steffi, who pushed a button on her laptop. A little red jellyfish-looking creature popped up on each screen.

Steffi asked, "What looks like a jellyfish but is quite closely related to humans?"

Her answer: a salp.

"A what?" Kathy asked me.

"I think she said a 'salt'," I whispered.

"I thought she said a 'sack,' Kathy replied.

Margie leaned over next to Kathy. "I think it is a 'salp—with a p," she said helpfully.

Judy: "A what?"

Margie: "Salp."

Judy: "How do you spell that?"

Salps, according to Steffi, are tiny transparent jet-propelled tubes whose life cycle alternates between an early period as tiny solitary swimmers before merging into aggregated colonies that can grow longer than a bus. As individuals, salps are innocuous. They do not sting. They do not hunt. They are gentle plankton eaters. But as Steffi described, once they create populous blooms salps wreak havoc. Salp blooms off the California coast a few years ago shut down one nuclear power plant and destroyed fishing nets

With her characteristic German directness Steffi revealed the peculiar life story of the sea salp. Each salp lives only a few days or a month in two stages: solitary, and in a colonial chain. And salps in linear chains are particularly skilled at this migration, traveling thousands of feet each night, at speeds around 10 body-lengths a second—like running a marathon every day.

During this process a solitary salp gives rise to a colony of genetically identical salps asexually. The chain of salps continues to grow over time until it eventually breaks. At the same time, each salp within the chain will reproduce sexually. Hand after hand shot up as audience members tried to keep the sequences straight. Steffi flipped slides across the screen that depicted how the male's sperm reaches a female's egg, forming a baby solitary salp that eventually swims out of its parent.

Steffi's demeanor softened as a sly smile escaped her face. "Here's the thing," she said before delivering the punchline. Each salp starts life as a female, then switches to male and never switches back. No one knows why. The women on the ship seemed to find this little nugget quite amusing. At dinner Kathy and Judy returned to the subject more than once, giggling through their dissection of Steffi's X-rated salpshow.

We passed the remainder of the evening in pleasant conversation before retiring to our cabins. That same day, unbeknownst to me, American Airlines had canceled our March 22nd flight from Buenos Aires to the United States.

TEN

CIERVA COVE & MIKKELSON HARBOUR

"Ice, ice baby."

MONDAY, MARCH 16: CRUISE DAY 8

POSITION:	64°08.2'S / 60° 57.0'W
WIND:	S 2
WEATHER:	RAIN
AIR TEMPERATURE:	+2

The sumptuous lunches and dinners were taking their toll. Alone in the half-lighted lounge at 6:30 am I stretched by the windows overlooking the bow. I had tried running/jogging around the outer decks, but unlike the larger cruise ships with their quarter-mile running tracks, the Plancius resembled a mini-obstacle course consisting of very short outside gangways that required stutter-stepping up and down metal stairs, ducking under machinery and maneuvering through steel doorways while trying not to get blown sideways into a cold, dark sea. Even my indoor workout was challenged by the rolling movement of the ship, though it did provide a great test of balance for a shortened karate workout. I stretched and kicked and shuffled through katas, all the while trying not to head bang a low-hanging monitor or kick-stumble into one of the small round tables when the ship dipped to starboard. Crunches and pushups proved to be safer options as the boat pounded northeast through the Gerlache Strait.

After breakfast Kathy and I descended the familiar metal stairway and with a now-routine hop, step, and sit I settled into for the morning ride. Five chilled minutes later Mal eased the Zodiac into the protected shelter of Cierva Cove. As we circled among brash ice and towering icebergs a curious Minke whale surfaced while suspiciously eying the two closest boats, giving the excited passengers a rare view of the smallest baleen whale in Antarctica. Minkes are known as a solitary, reserved species but curiosity seemed to get the better of this one. Mal eased our boat up behind one of the two lucky crafts but the Minke had seen enough of our group and sank below the waves, so I never got a good look at him.

Turning back toward land, Mal directed our sights toward rocky mountainside area where we spotted an impressive grouping of nine or ten faded red wooden structures, perched at various levels across the rugged slope. A large blue and white flag had been painted on the side of one of the larger buildings facing the bay.

Two words stenciled below the flag identified it as 'Base Primavera,' an Argentinian scientific base overlooking Cierva Cove. The cliffs below the site also served as home base for a mixed collection of gentoos and chinstraps. Gloves came off and cameras rose to record a raft of penguins soaring gracefully into the frigid waters to skim across the waves in search of breakfast. By the way, a group of penguins on water is a raft; On land they are identified as a waddle, rookery, colony, or huddle. I prefer "waddle."

Next up: The Amazing Seal and Ice Spectacular.

Jagged icebergs rose and fell in concert with the high swells. Each berg displayed a unique pattern of multi-shaped, multi-colored surfaces. I gazed up at a large sharp-edged rectangle the size of a strip mall while its smaller cousins featured surfaces heavily pockmarked by wind and erosion—smaller in this case meaning the size of a double 18-wheeler. One iceberg would flash a glistening white surface against the dark gray sky, perhaps the offspring of a floating ice shelf, while the next bobbing mass exposed the grayish brown remains of a land-based glacier. I was most captivated by the formations of mini caves boasting the clearest, bluest glowing ice that any interior designer would beg to re-create.

We drifted closer to the rocky shoreline where another family of twenty-foot-high glacial escapees violently rolled and groaned and split before us. Mal kept easing the boat back to avoid capsizing or smashing into a rogue piece of ice, but the hypnotic creaks and crashes mesmerized us, and soon our small vessel had drifted right up next to another one of these creaking ice monsters. I imagined a movie close-up of our ten passengers bobbing among the waves as the camera pulled back to reveal the vessel dwarfed by heaving, menacing icebergs, the lens widening further to include the amused penguins braced against the brisk wind eyeing the spectacle from shore. Finally, a wide shot pulls back to capture the glistening white mountains ringing the bay, looming over a lonely blue expedition ship drifting patiently across the bay. Buzz Aldrin coined the perfect term—"magnificent desolation"—as he placed the second set of footsteps on the moon. I thought of that description, but it did not quite fit the scene before me. I settled on this: I was awed by the endless beauty of Cierva Cove. I was breathing the cleanest air, viewing the whitest snow, and touching the bluest ice on the planet. I felt immersed in an alien world, as if mother nature had revealed her gifts and the earth was saying, "Look at what's here. Enjoy it. Don't blow it."

A single leopard seal glided just below the water's surface. I guess today was the day for curious locals to check out the tourists and this annoyed resident decided to make our boat and Pippa's nearby group the objects of his attention. For twenty minutes the seal dove around and under each boat, repeatedly emerging to eyeball us with a steady, malevolent gaze.

Mal announced that a similar-sized leopard seal had taken a bite out of a zodiac just two weeks earlier. Everyone yanked hands and feet back inside the craft and held cameras closer to the pontoons than the water. Pippa called over from the other zodiac. I watched her lean down over the stern and lower a long stick capped with a Go-Pro below the waves. I assumed that she knew what she was doing. These apex predators are known for their aggression, but this one maintained his composure though he still let us know who owned this territory. Later that evening we enjoyed her crystal-clear video of the leopard seal darting and diving through his frigid domain. Happily, all ten of Pippa's fingers remained present and accounted for.

The brisk wind returned with a vengeance as noon approached, so we headed back to the Plancius to enjoy a meal, giving thanks and swipe cards to the galley crew.

While we gorged on 'lite' courses of salads, do-it-yourself sandwiches, desserts and cheeses, the ship cruised several miles north to Mikkelsen Harbour, a two-mile-wide bay lined with ice cliffs indenting the south side of Trinity Island. Kathy could not shake off the morning chill, so she and Judy and a few like-minded women voted to take the afternoon off and hang out on the boat that afternoon.

No thanks. I did not want to miss a thing. I shrugged on the landing "kit"—jackets, heavy boots, fleece this-and-that, hats, gloves, and life jackets and headed out. As I looked around, I saw that Kathy and company were not alone. I joined half the normal contingent of happy wanderers for a swift ride to the northeast shore of the relatively small, flat D'Hainaut Island. A tiny scattered colony of Gentoo Penguins monitored our progress in a stinging rain that rendered three layers of cotton and fleece useless against the chill. Even the local colony seemed displeased with the worsening conditions, hopping cautiously along the chunky ice bank or slogging through muddy pools on their way to slightly higher ground.

Above the shoreline the late summer snow and ice had melted away. I eased through small rivers and dodged pink patches of penguin guano to head up a long incline. I stopped twice along the way to snap shots of scattered whale bones before arriving at a small, two room abandoned Argentinian refuge hut perched near the apex of the damp island. I took a quick glance at the bare interior though a misty window, then turned and headed back down the slope. On my right I watched two nearly full-grown fledglings waddle impatiently toward the sea. Ahead on a large rock a giant petrel feasted on a perished penguin. Whoever penned the Plancius log entry for that day nailed it: "The rather morbid scenes seemed to showcase the darker aspect of the nature...." I detoured across a shallow muddy pond and skipped over slick rocks to inspect the remains of a whaling boat marooned next to discarded whale bones. A squinty-eyed gentoo kept watch atop a nearby rock and scrutinized each visitor who approached the natural art exhibit.

To my right a line of six patient photographers fawned over the afternoon's star attraction: an immense fur seal posing lazily a few feet from the shore. The massive pinniped barely moved during the ninety-minute island visit. Periodically he (or she, tough to tell) lifted his nose and a lazy flipper to stretch or scratch himself, offhandedly casting a dismissive glance at his admirers like a retired movie idol. I recalled Steffi's explanation that fur seals, despite having the word "seal" in their name, are more closely related to sea lions. This one certainly fit the part. Like most of his species he featured longer flippers than sea lions, along with a rich luxuriant coat of fur that was so prized by hunters that it brought them to the brink of extinction in the 19th century.

Scientifically speaking, the word pinniped means fin or flipper-footed and refers to the marine mammals that have front and rear flippers. This group includes seals, sea lions, and walruses who live in the ocean but can remain on land for long periods. There are three families of pinnipeds: *phocids* (seals), *otariids* (sea lions) and *odobenids* (walruses). This fact appeared during one of our shipboard trivia nights.

I learned that phocids are sometimes referred to as earless

seals or true seals and are easily identified. They have ear holes but no external ear flaps. They also have small front flippers and move on land by flopping along on their bellies. The second type, *otariids, are* sometimes referred to as 'eared seals,' and includes sea lions and fur seals. Unlike true seals, they have external ear flaps. Their front flippers are large, and on land they can bring all four flippers underneath their bodies and walk on them. (We saw this up close during our excursion the very next morning.)

The third family of pinnipeds is the odobenids—the walrus. Both males and females have tusks and vacuum-like mouths for sucking up shellfish from the ocean floor, and air sacs in their neck that inflate like life preservers to allow them to float. Walruses live in the artic regions of the North Atlantic and Pacific Oceans, so they were not on our current itinerary.

Two more (weird) notes on pinnipeds. First, I cannot hear the word without instantly thinking of the H.M.S. Pinafore. I imagine a large brown seal flopping on the stage of a silly Gilbert & Sullivan set. Second, no one ever yells, "Hey, look at that funny pinniped!" In fact, no one uses the word "pinniped" unless one is delivering a scientific lecture—or wishes to sound pretentious. They are seals.

I lined up to wait for the last returning Zodiac. I stood encased in my fully soaked clothes; head down as icy rain dripped off the brim of the baseball cap I wore under the hood of my heavy 'water-resistant' jacket. It should have resisted harder. A hot shower and a hot tea beckoned.

Before long, the Plancius motors churned to life as we sailed north. I ventured out on deck for a last goodbye to the Antarctic peninsula. We were heading for the South Shetland Islands and

Whalers Bay. I anticipated one more unforgettable day before heading back across the Drake toward home. I had no idea how many other 'unforgettables' awaited unseen beyond the next day's horizon.

"La Fin De Monde"

The Drake Lake.

132

A colony, a rookery, or a waddle?

"What 5-meter rule?"

Life is tough down here.

Another berg, another beauty.

"They were all wet landings."

Port Lockroy station.

Seal brains for dinner?

"Welcome to my rock!"

Stealth penguin.

High-steppin' it.

A chinstrap penguin keeps watch.

Just a fluke shot.

Humpback tailgater.

No telephoto lens needed.

ELEVEN

DECEPTION ISLAND

*"Fog, sun, white snow and black beaches
made for a mystical morning."*

TUESDAY, MARCH 17: CRUISE DAY 9

POSITION:	62°59.1'S / 60° 33.6'W
WIND:	VAR 4
WEATHER:	SNOW
AIR TEMPERATURE:	+1

"Are you awake?"

I rolled to my right to tap my phone. The display lit up. 5:25 am.

"I am now," I replied.

"It's OK, I have been awake for a while." I admitted.

I had felt the rhythm of the boat shift during the past hour, the gentle rocking barely noticeable as the vibrations of the rumbling engine slowed our progress.

I got up, showed, shaved, and stuck my head out of the bathroom door.

"Happy St. Patrick's Day," I said.

I pulled my suitcase out from under the bunk, dug deep and pulled out my favorite Ireland t-shirt. I purchased it eighteen months ago in a little souvenir shop across from the Dublin bus stand by Trinity College. I threw on the comfortable soccer-style shirt, mostly black with gray vertical side panels trimmed in green and "Ireland" spelled out above the left breast over a shield of green clovers. That trip had marked my fifth time exploring my favorite destination. Hard to believe. The initial visit came seventeen years ago when I was asked to speak at a workplace alcohol and drug conference. Kathy joined me for a ten-day exploration of Dublin, the Ring of Kerry and Kinsale, but the real highlight was forming an enduring friendship with Waterford native Maurice Quinlan and his long-time partner Theresa.

Maurice had extended the invitation at the start of my year as president of our international EAP association, allowing me to fulfill a long time wish to see one of my family's ancestral homelands. Maurice is a proud, distinguished-looking descendant of Waterford mayors, and his slightly red face and lilting brogue mark him immediately as a son of Ireland. He is also fiercely loyal, strong-minded, and strong-willed. At a professional conference years ago my dear friend Dotty watched in shock as Maurice and a fellow Irishman argued boisterously for several minutes over a professional dispute in full view of passersby.

Dotty served as the group's president at the time and felt the need to intervene. I advised her to stay out of it. I knew that scene well from watching similar versions during childhood. "It's an Irish family squabble," I remember telling her. "If you jump in the middle of it you become the target." The next day we discovered the two men enjoying a laugh together over breakfast. Dotty just shook her head. Kathy once said that Maurice reminds her of older relatives on the Sullivan side—same ruddy looks, quick to anger and quick to laugh. Theresa is an equal delight: caring, warm, and quick to put Maurice in his place with a quip and a smile. I look forward to my next visit.

One more link connected that Irish trip to our current excursion. Our longtime Tucson friends John and Jenifer Misiaszek put together the group of eight friends for that very first Sierra Club expedition—a hiking tour of the Aran Islands and Irish west coast. As I noted earlier in this book our lead guide on that trip was the very same Margie Tomenko. During one of our van rides across Connemara I asked her about any future volunteer assignments.

"I am leading a trip to Antarctica in 2020," she said.

Sign me up now! I thought.

I had already become familiar with how Sierra Club trips worked, so I asked her my one deal-breaker question.

"Do you have to have a roommate?"

"Yes," she answered. There were no single cabins on the boat, she explained, and only eighteen spots reserved by the club. She said it was a popular destination and thought there might only be a few slots remaining open, even though the trip was still a year and a half away.

I looked at Kathy. Her expression spoke for her.

"Oh dear," she said, but that is when wife-of-the-year agreed to go.

I had plans to return to Ireland again in September 2020. Along with another longtime friend Alice, Kathy and I planned to visit Scotland for the first time before I delivered new presentations in Dublin and Limerick.

On March 18th, just two days later, my phone beeped with a text from Maurice. He notified me that all conferences in Ireland had been called off for the remainder of the year due to the pandemic, so he was forced to postpone the training events until 2021.

Could I come then?

Of course.[*]

St. Patrick's Day is a favorite day in our family, so before we headed to breakfast I sprung for the extra 5 cents to send a celebratory text to daughter Jana, son-in-law Brendan and our newest addition to the family: Ryan Killian Brophy. You cannot get more Irish than that name, especially on this twinkling blue-eyed, blond, happy little leprechaun. My phone beeped with a picture of him in a bright green shirt with "Little Hooligan" spelled out on the front. No, I did not tear up. It must be humid in this cabin.

Overnight the Plancius had coasted up the Gerlache Strait and across the Bransfield Strait to the entrance of Deception Island, a small horseshoe-shaped islet at the southwest edge of the South Shetlands.

I clambered out onto the fore deck feeling a bit down. Today was our last official day in the Antarctic region. The gray, windy skies reflected my mood. I shook off my emotional indulgence,

---

[*] After returning home I received an e-mail from him announcing that he was moving all future trainings online. I will still be speaking to Ireland, but not in Ireland. Maybe I will wear my t-shirt on camera.

though, as another stunning sight surrounded the ship. I fixed upon the harsh beauty of Neptune's Bellows, named for the strong gusts that blast through the 775-foot-wide entrance to Whalers Bay. An old shipwreck lay submerged next to a large rock below the surface in the center of the gap, so the narrowed opening challenged even the most experienced ship's captain. But wait, there is more. The whole of Deception Island is classified as an active volcano. The land was formed when the rim of the volcano collapsed and allowed water to flood in, creating a formation known as a caldera. The jagged tops of the cylindrical snow-streaked walls surrounded our ship as we sailed into the bay. Five fellow early risers took positions nearby and we quietly propped elbows on the railings, the only sounds coming from the steady wind and clicking cameras as the Plancius inched forward toward the anchoring point near Port Foster. The gray and white palette of ice and rock did little to erase the uneasy sense of venturing into a once active volcano. After all, the last eruptions had occurred during my lifetime, in 1967 and 1969, and both had surprised the scientists who monitor these things. One hopes that prediction models have improved in the last half-century.

Good morning, everyone, good morning!

Iain's jaunty greeting shattered the silence. "Breakfast in 30 minutes, then we will head out for our shore landing around 8:30am. We have a wee bit of wind and snow today, so dress accordingly!"

On my way to the dining room I glanced at the large map on the wall near the lounge entrance where the crew marked the ship's daily progress and location. After spending a week sailing among all the coves and bays and islands it now looked like a modern art piece, or a plate of spaghetti. Just over the past ten hours, for example, we had sailed through the Gerlache Strait, across the Bransfield Strait, 'into' Deception Island through Neptune's Bellows, and now rested at Port Forster in the dark, ice-free waters of Whalers Bay—or was it actually 'Telefon Bay'? Depends on which map you consulted or who you asked. Later I confirmed that we had indeed anchored in Whalers Bay. Telefon Bay sits at the northwest end of the island.

I suited up, plucked my life jacket from its wall hook, and grabbed a bag that I had prepared for one last special Antarctic event. We wet brushed our boots and joined the shoulder-to-shoulder swarm waiting for Dr. Helleke to give the 'all go' sign to head out. Our turn arrived and we eased down the metal stairway to board our rubber shuttle. In case I have not mentioned it enough already, the Zodiac rides are a blast. We darted across the bay and sloshed our way to shore.

I took a few steps up onto the sand before coming to an abrupt stop. I slowly scanned from left to right across a stark, near color-less world to discover a scene unlike any we had previously visited. As the ship's log accurately described, *"...the combination of fog, sun, white snow and black beaches made for no less than a mystical morning."* True.

Kathy bumped my shoulder and we continued side-by-side along a long, wide beach of black volcanic rock worn smooth by centuries of wind and water. To our right a few yards up from the beach scatterings of bright white snow drifted over the landscape, painting a perfect contrast against the black sand. We stopped to examine the gray, sand-blasted frame of wooden harpoon boat. The land behind the boat extended to the undulating foothills made of black ash and lava resting beneath severe gray-white peaks. To the right loomed the harsh beauty of the 425-foot- summit overlooking Neptune's Window.

A smattering of local seabirds circled the cliffs. We, and by 'we' I mean Kathy, pointed out skuas, petrels, and snowy sheathbills. Celine told us the island was designated an "Important Bird Area" by Bird Life International, and a hidden section of the island was home to a large colony of breeding pairs of chinstraps. Well, an important bird area. Quite an honor. I wonder if they knew? Did the other birds feel slighted? I had never met an important bird before, although come to think of it I did meet the San Diego Chicken once at a Padres spring training game in the 80's. Ah well. Fame is fleeting. We moved on. I spied three hulking fur seals tussle like adolescent boys in the shallow waters to our left. Farther along the beach seven older specimens jerked their heads, flapped their flippers, and shuffled toward each other while emitting random grunts and yelps. The scene looked vaguely familiar; I may have wandered into the morning meeting of the Whalers Bay Rotary Club.

Our shoreline trek resumed as we soon came upon the sad remains of a large whaling processing site. Two rust colored oil collection tanks leaned in faded glory about 200 feet from the shore. Behind them sat half-buried rusted brown sections of the former whale works, fighting a futile, slow-motion battle against time and the elements.

We continued past the sinking silos and hiked over a small rise toward another set of inwardly collapsing structures. A sign remained affixed to the faded gray wall next to an open window framed in once-bright red on the nearest building. The sign read "BISCOF HOUSE. The fading F had been an E once, marking the site as 'Biscoe House,' but no longer. The three interconnected wooden buildings originally comprised the housing, kitchen, meeting, and supply rooms areas necessary to sustain life and work in this frozen world.

By 1820 Port Foster had become a popular site for catching and processing seals and whales. On this day, the Plancius sat as the lone occupant of a bay once crowded with multi-masted whalers dropping off their spoils for processing prior to making the treacherous return trip to their homelands.

Stories are told of Whaler's Bay itself serving as a rich source of humpbacks and other whale species until human nature asserted itself and decimated the local population. Whales no doubt rejoiced when oil was discovered in Pennsylvania in the late 1800s and the process of oil drilling expanded. The high-risk whaling industry dwindled, and Port Foster was abandoned in 1931.

During World War II the British claimed it for a military base and added a critical landing strip for planes on a low rise a half-mile away from the base. After the war, the site was repurposed for use as a research station. Argentina and Chile made claims on the island and operated stations there, but all were abandoned when volcanic eruptions and earthquakes destroyed the research centers in the late 1960s. We were assured that today's chances were low. Had we seen the hot steam that rises from beneath the black sand beach at low tide we might have been a wee bit less assured.

I snapped a few shots of Kathy and Meg shivering before the faded buildings. Meg set off to examine the three structures more closely while Kathy and I headed toward a steep but narrow ravine extending from the gray foothills to the beach. We scrambled down one side of the frozen lava ravine and up the other. Atop a light dusting of snow lay three graves, two of which were marked by large piles of rock topped by solid wood crosses. Burned onto the horizontal section of the first cross was the name "Tommern. Hans Culliksen," and below it was carved the dates "7/4 '71–4/1 '28." The second cross was no longer readable, and the third grave was unmarked.

We noticed a crowd gathering down at the shoreline. The special event in which I had elected to participate was about to begin. Time to put up or shut up, but we encountered a brief delay on our way down to the beach. A determined fur seal lumbered across our path, clearly asserting his right of way. As I detoured around a corner of a ten-foot high section of half-submerged metal I was startled by a loud, deep bark; Fur seal-speak for "Get off my lawn!" Another grumpy local was using the wall as a wind screen. He reminded me that this was his domain as he grudgingly allowed us to pass.

I joined the crowd at the beach. Claiming a bare space on the dusty, black sand I quickly and ungracefully stripped down to a single pair of black long johns.

Kathy snickered. I knew what she was thinking.

"No dear, these are not tights." I said. I had neglected to pack swim trunks.

I reached back into my bag. Darn. The $10 pair of water shoes purchased just for this occasion remained safely hidden in my suitcase back aboard the Plancius. I jogged on tiptoes to the water's edge and stood alongside nine other brave idiots. The crew had marked off an area while two zodiacs patrolled the edges to discourage curious seals from joining the party. Two or three amused natives eyed us from shore, but none approached. "It's time," I thought. I high stepped it into the frigid shallows of Whalers Bay. Feeling more than cold I waded into hip deep water and dove in. I came up, jumped around a bit and completely submerged myself twice more to get the full effect. I rose from the deep with arms stretched wide as I bobbed and splashed back to shore.

Kathy tossed me the University of Arizona shirt and hat I had brought along and I wriggled them on before the adrenaline wore off. The U of A Athletic Director sends out a weekly e-mail featuring pictures of fans wearing the red and blue in all parts of the globe. Kathy took a couple of photos for later submission. My Antarctic Polar Plunge was officially in the books.

Did I mention that it was cold? Very cold. Mind-numbingly cold. The water temperature sat in the low-mid 30 degrees F. The frigid air, stiffening breeze, and light snow conspired to steal any residual warmth away from the skin. My jaw stiffened. My teeth were not chattering, but I could barely form words. My fingers failed to cooperate as I wrestled with each piece of clothing against the encroaching numbness, all while trying not to trip over or look like a total idiot. Kathy continue to record the show, no doubt in hopes of a 'funniest home video' moment. I achieved one out of those two goals. I probably did look like an idiot, but I did not fall. I credit two decades of martial arts training for the ability to balance on one frozen foot. I also knew that if I toppled over, I would get no help from Kathy; she would be bent over laughing too hard to lend a hand.

The wind grew bolder and colder as I raced to the nearest Zodiac for the four-minute dash back to the ship. I squeezed into the last seat as it readied to pull away from shore. Sorry, Kathy. (She waved me on.) Both of my hands were achingly cold. I stuck them under my armpits with little effect. I soon burst into my cabin, pulled my gloves off with my teeth and attacked each hand with the tiny hairdryer for ten minutes until they reattached themselves to my body and returned to duty. I was surprised to learn that we had spent less than two hours on shore. It seemed longer—pleasantly longer, unforgettably longer. The combination of stark landscapes coupled with the exhilaration of plunging into ridiculously cold waters for no apparent reason had frozen both time and limbs.

After lunch we exited Whalers Bay and escaped the shadow of Neptune's Bellows to travel a short distance to Yankee Harbour. Iain warned that our final excursion would be brief. He relayed the captain's desire to stay ahead of a following storm that could impact our run through the Drake Passage and jeopardize an on-time return to Ushuaia.

I spotted a large Weddell seal reclining on the rocks as we set foot upon the ice-packed shore of Yankee Harbor, our final Antarctic landing site. The seal casually rolled over on his side, exposing two areas of dried blood along one fin and below the jaw.

The red splashes looked less like battle scars than the remains of a messy lunch. We hiked atop the loose rocks toward a lone fur seal settled in the center of the narrow curving spit, contentedly rubbing and scratching himself while posing for a parade of amateur photographers grabbing a few last chance memories. Farther up the path a crabeater seal joined in the fun.

I turned to Kathy. "I think each species has sent a representative to see us off," I joked.

Kathy replied that she really needed this exercise before spending the next two days at sea. I concurred. We trooped farther down the spit to enjoy a goodbye visit with a small colony of gentoos.

This time I pulled out my iPhone to try out another of Dorette's video lessons. I remembered tip #3: Keep the shot steady and let the animals move in and out of the frame.

I squatted to record three of the little yellow-footed waddlers hurrying along in one determined direction—straight at me. They were not moving out of the frame; they were filling the frame. I steadied my phone as they ignored all social distancing guidelines and headed swiftly for their close-up. I moved six feet to the right. They never broke stride and delivered a perfect video send off.

Time to go. We nodded thank you to our gracious native hosts for the last time. I lingered on the rocks to take in just one more lungful of icy, pristine air, then slipped a lifejacket over my head and climbed into the last shuttle back to our temporary home.

The Drake awaits.

I washed up before changing into my shipboard attire of jeans, light long-sleeved pullover and running shoes. I was relaxed and ready for two full days at sea. Bring on the Drake.

Twenty minutes later Kathy and her hair were ready to make their way up for cookies and conversation. We entered a lounge full of smiling faces eager to enjoy a relaxing voyage home. We squeezed onto a padded bench on the starboard front section next to Judy, Kate, and assorted Sierra Clubbers. I contemplated the rain sluicing across the windows in the blustery late summer wind—an appropriate send-off from the last continent. The following storm had caught up. By the time Iain's "thirty-minutes-until-recap" announcement sounded all passengers were already present and accounted for. Anxiety tinged with excitement enveloped the room in anticipation of Iain's weather report. Were we about to experience a real storm-tossed Drake adventure?

Iain rushed his usual 'good afternoon' greeting as he strode to the front of the room. His taut features and slight frown communicated concern and a seriousness greater than expressed during the initial lifeboat drill. Once the room quieted, he read the following statement:

The Argentinian government has informed Oceanwide Expeditions that Plancius would not be allowed to dock back in Ushuaia until Saturday, March 21. We must stay at sea for one extra day in order to assure that all onboard will have been "virus-free" for a full fourteen days since entering the country.

Last night Alex and Dragan had asked each passenger to come by the hotel desk to document the first day of our arrival in Argentina. Now I understood why.

Several fellow travelers had already planned to spend an extra night or two in Ushuaia before flying out so the change in plans had minimal impact for them. Sierra Clubber Kate was one of them. She had stored her hiking gear at the hotel in Ushuaia where she had booked an overnight stay before heading to Patagonia for her next adventure. She was not the only one who had parked belongings in Ushuaia, a decision each traveler would come to regret.

I had booked a flight from Ushuaia to Buenos Aires soon after docking on the 20th on a flight that we would now miss. I had been excited about the prospect of spending two days exploring the Argentinian capital before flying home on the 22nd.

Kathy had been looking forward to two days of hot weather-walking on level ground. We needed now to change flights, inform the hotel in B.A. of our new arrival date, and cancel the guided walking tour that I had booked before leaving home. I was not too concerned or bothered at this point, though. We would still enjoy one night plus a half-day checking out the sights of the historic city.

Stuff like that happens on international trips. Three years earlier we were marooned in London for an unexpected three-day weekend while in transit to visit Bryson and Grace and join a service project in Zimbabwe. To avoid heavy jet lag, we had scheduled a twenty-four-hour layover before flying on to Johannesburg. Two minutes after I had checked out of our hotel, I received a call from British Airways—just four hours before departure—to report the cancellation of our overnight flight and a two-day delay.

Thirty minutes later we checked back into the same lovely establishment near Paddington Station. We capitalized on the unexpected break to savor a wonderful weekend exploring London on foot, traipsing through Hyde Park, visiting the British Museum, 221B Baker Street, the Globe Theater and plenty of historic neighborhood pubs and chip shops. As a result of the poor customer service and surprise seat fees I will never fly that airline again, but I do thank them for the unexpected holiday.

By contrast, Oceanwide stepped up to aid shipboard passengers who needed to re-book flights and hotels, notify family and friends, or otherwise change plans. Alex and Dragan handed each passenger another 250mb voucher for free internet use. I added it to the 100mbs that I had remaining and sent off a quick e-mail update to Linda, our travel agent. Well, I tried to send it. To no one's surprise the ship's satellite-based internet immediately crashed when 114 new users attempted to access the system simultaneously. Thus begun the first of many days of connection frustration. I held off until late in the evening to shoot off another e-mail. This time it went through. I waited for a response. None came.

TWELVE

RETURN TO...USHUAIA?

"The Drake Shake"

WEDNESDAY, MARCH 18: CRUISE DAY 10

POSITION:	60°18,4'S / 61° 25.0'W
WIND:	NW8
WEATHER:	RAIN
AIR TEMPERATURE:	+4

Captain's Wisdom dictates that if you have a smooth passage across the Drake, the day will come for you to pay the price.

All the movies and YouTube videos we had scanned depicting a raging Drake Passage came to life. We slid and tossed around our bunks as swells rocked the ship though the night. The morning light brought 50 knot headwinds as wave after wave crashed over the bow and slammed at the windows at the front of the lounge.

Iain's weather forecast had accurately predicted a race against hurricane force winds bearing down on us from the west. Still, such a storm remained powerless compared to hearty and hungry shipboard diners. We grabbed neighbors and table corners to brace ourselves at breakfast. Tablecloths had been replaced by webbed rubber mats to hold plates and cups in place. I glanced at the starboard windows to capture waves up to 18 feet rising over the top of the windows. By 9am the sea had backed down to five-foot swells as the sun peeked out. Kathy and I headed to one of my favorite places on the ship.

"Permission to enter the bridge."

I called up from the bottom of the inner stairway leading to ship's nerve center. (Not its 'head'—that is a quite different place on a ship.) My call out was probably unnecessary but as a former Coast Guard brat I respected the tradition. I appreciated the open access to the bridge during most hours—a great feature on Oceanwide ships.

First Officer Miia and Second Officer Jan offered hearty welcomes as Kathy and I emerged from the steep entryway into the center of the action. Miia smartly answered question after question, her enthusiasm matched only by her endless patience. Jan proudly demonstrated the workings of the various consoles, explaining how he monitored positioning, weather, icebergs, and other ships at sea. Earlier in the cruise Margie, Rebecca and I had made an evening trek to the bridge. That night Jan showed us how to track the height and distance of a large iceberg a few miles dead ahead. My eyes flip-flopped between windows and consoles as the iceberg loomed closer. I looked over at Jan just as the Captain rang the bridge and suggested that perhaps his second officer might consider altering course a bit. Jan had laughed, turned a few dials, and the band played on.

Outside the port and starboard sides of the bridge sat small platforms called the "wings." Kathy and I kept a tight grip from handrail to handrail as we ventured out on the starboard wing to fully grasp the image of this small expedition vessel sailing alone across vast Southern Ocean.

I have always loved boats. Since I was a kid growing up in East Falmouth, I loved spending time in, on or near the ocean. Most summer days were spent swimming or rowing around the Atlantic. In my teens I taught rowing and canoeing and small boat sailing at three different scout camps. I learned how to row the hard way. The summer before fifth grade we lived for a year in a two-story Cape Cod style home a half mile from the beach and just a block away from a boat harbor. I became quick friends with the son of the harbormaster who lived next door. We spent hours checking out every fishing boat, fancy sailboat, and mini yacht along the docks. My friend had a rowboat that we often hauled over to the small beach just beyond the last set of docks. I would push the boat into the harbor and jump in while my friend maneuvered us around to inspect the newly arrived vessels or annoy the amateur fishermen leaning over the small bridge bisecting the narrow bay. One morning as we returned to shore, I confessed that I did not know how to row. My friend had the solution.

He stepped out of the boat so we could switch places. I reached for the oars. He grabbed the bow and shoved the boat back into the water, laughing as the current pushed me to the center of the harbor.

"You'll figure out!" I heard him shout. Eventually I did.

A year earlier the Coast Guard held a version of "take your kid to work" day. My father woke me up before dawn for the 45-minute ride to his New Bedford base. I stepped aboard the USCG cutter Vigilant. *Note: A few years ago, I visited the Coast Guard Academy in New London, Connecticut and discovered a model of that same ship displayed in a lobby.* My father served as the ship's corpsman, often spending three to six months at sea patrolling the North Atlantic. I remember climbing up and down stairways and through hatches exploring every nook and cranny. I recall sitting in the galley at lunch asking question after question of my father's smiling—and extremely tolerant—fellow crew members. It remains one of my favorite childhood memories.

The skies darkened and the angry Drake reasserted itself. Winds gusts buffeted the ship and the sea grew wild as we ducked back inside the Plancius bridge. A huge wave slammed against the bow. Coffee cups spilled and cookies flew off a high counter to smear across every clean shirt in the vicinity. I grabbed for the nearest railing; Kathy grabbed for my arm as I held on. We thanked Miia and the crew for the visit before weaving down two flights of stairs and careening into the lounge in time for the morning lectures.

Pippa captured my attention by opening with the rich history of Antarctic Whaling. Most folks immediately conjure up visions of Moby Dick. I did too, but I fondly recalled Nathaniel Philbrick's book "In the Heart of the Sea," an engrossing tale of the tragedy of the whaleship Essex, the actual event which inspired Melville to conjure up his classic featuring Ishmael, Starbuck, Ahab, and the white whale.

Pippa expertly transported us to Herman Melville's nineteenth century, when whale hunters employed only handheld weapons thrown from a small boat and hoped to survive a wild ride until the whale exhausted itself and they could tow it back to the larger vessel. By the time Antarctic whaling flourished around the turn of the last century, the industrial age had brought forth explosive harpoons and small, steam-powered 'fast catcher' boats.

Ships would be sent south to harvest the whales with no notions of sustainability. The plunder of Antarctic whales was more akin to mining than fishing. The south seas frenzy decimated virtually all the world's whale species. Today, nearly a half-century after large commercial whaling has ceased, total whale counts still represent a fraction of the pre-whaling numbers.

According to Pippa, Antarctic whaling increased when the first whale processing site was completed around 1904 at Grytviken, a site located in the South Georgia Islands. The number of stations like Port Foster in Whalers Bay soon flourished until 1925, when so-called 'factory ships' appeared on the scene and provided an efficient means of processing whales at sea. Ships rarely operated within the territory of any one nation, so there were no regulations or limitations on catch size, species, age, or sex of the catch.

Humpback whales were considered the favored catch since they swam slowly and stayed closer to land. The arrival of faster boats allowed the whalers focus to shift to the larger and more profitable Blue Whale, previously safe due to their incredible size and speed. A single 90-foot blue whale could yield up to 120 barrels of oil, and the slaughter of blue whales peaked in 1931 when over 29,000 were killed in one season. Belatedly, the International Whaling Commission (IWC) banned all hunting of blue whales in 1966, but by this time their numbers had fallen from over 200,000 in pre-whaling days to less than 2000.

The desire for certain types of whale products changed over time. In the late 1800s sperm whales were sought for their spermaceti, an oily, waxy substance produced in great quantity for which the whale got its name. Spermaceti was harvested from the whale's head for use in fine wax candles, ointments, cosmetic creams, and textile finishing; later it was used for industrial lubricants. According to the Encyclopaedia Britannica, the substance was named in the mistaken belief that it was the coagulated semen of the whale.

Near the end of the century extraction of oil and gas from underground deposits delivered cheaper alternatives for lighting, so the harvesting of sperm whales declined. There remained a demand for whale oil from the blubber, now sought mostly for the making of the finest soaps, varnish, cosmetics and less 'finest' margarine.

Sperm whales also produced a substance in their digestive tracts called ambergris. From the French for "grey amber," it had been valued since ancient times for use in cosmetics but also love potions, wine, and headache remedies. In more recent times it was used to enhance the potency of expensive perfumes.

In 1946, the world's whaling nations signed the International Convention for the Regulation of Whaling (ICRW) in an attempt to preserve the whale population, though primarily for the benefit of the whaling industry. Today, due to increased anti-whaling sentiment and dramatic decreases in demand for whale products, only a few countries still hunt whales.

Estimates from the past decade suggest that Japan, Norway, Iceland, and a few smaller nations combine to kill approximately 2000 whales each year, despite the current IWC moratorium on whaling. Pippa's recitation prompted more questions about whale preservation and happywhale.com.

Rustyn took over the microphone for the second show, and his energetic enthusiasm turned a dull-sounding exposition on the "Evolution of Gear" into a fascinating historical review of the people and science involved in the evolution of clothing, tools and techniques for cold weather camping and mountaineering. Pippa, Rustyn, and their fellow presenters impressed me every time with their ability to expertly mix science, history, and biography into entertaining and educational 15-30-minute briefs.

Each presenter kept our attention, if not their balance, against the re-energized Drake. They kept a firm grip on the center console railing as the side-to-side rolling motion increased. The wall mounted TV monitors swung dangerously on their hinges. The tables were secure, but I dared not put my glass down. My seat was firmly bolted to the floor, but two women sitting nearby were not. I grabbed one of them as she came flying off her chair, so no harm done. Fortunately, I had heeded Kathy's suggestion the night before and downed a promethazine, so my only discomfort that morning came from maintaining a too tight grip on the swiveling chair seat.

Iain asked for our attention from the rear of the room. He announced that, for safety reasons, the captain and Alex decided that lunch would be served to us in our cabins. Dining room visions of flying silverware and mass casualties danced in my head; this was a good call. I kept my eye on a few human-size wobblers, some looking decidedly green around the edges as they stumbled down the hallway toward the safety of their bunks.

At 12:30 we heard a knock at our cabin door. Lunch was served.

I held tight to the hallway railing as Pippa and Tom held out a cardboard box filled with 4-inch subs and apples. I made my selections from the two well-balanced crew members before stumbling back into our room. I had forgotten to bring water or soda down with me, but my travel bottle and the bathroom faucet sufficed.

To no one's surprise, the afternoon lectures were canceled. I watched the relentless waves grow larger in the porthole; the whistling wind punctuated by loud bangs whenever a rogue wave crashed against the bow. I heard another crash as the ship rolled violently to starboard. This crash, more of a thump, was accompanied by expletives rarely heard from my wife unless she accidently views Fox news for more than a minute. She emerged from the bathroom rubbing a bright red mark on her posterior, courtesy of falling backward against the inside door handle. I sympathized, having had a similar accident in the shower that morning. My slight bruise paled against her black and blue monstrosity, however, as she reminded me for the next seven days until the soreness disappeared.

I credit my parents for introducing me to great books at an early age. I have loved reading since I could put words together, and the Hardy Boys were a surefire gift for every birthday and Christmas. I had devoured them all by age twelve. Mysteries are still my favorite distraction, but I read both non-fiction and fiction, and I usually have at least one of each going at the same time. Kathy says I inhale them. Long trips used to require extra bag space or a duffel just for reading material. My e-book is a prized possession, but I still carry a paperback or two for emergency backup. Harry Bosch and Rachel Maddow helped make short work of the afternoon.

The Drake's rain-soaked rollercoaster ride persisted. Iain's afternoon update via intercom concluded with an expected addendum—dinner would be delivered to our cabins.

A small appetizer? A mini course of fish and chips? No such luck. This time Felicity joined Pippa at the door. I picked over the same selection of sandwiches offered at lunch. I considered my choices; Ham and cheese, or cheese." I smiled. The scene reminded me of an old Eddie Izzard sketch about English Inquisitors questioning the accused:

Tea and cake or Death?

Uh, cake?

Sorry, out of cake.

So, my only choice is "or Death?"

Our intrepid crew did offer a welcome treat along with the sumptuous dinner—Ritter Sport chocolate bars, including my favorite chocolate-coconut combination. (Thank you, Pippa, for the extra one.) Earlier I had run up to the lounge and filled our water bottles with ice so we could dine in style that evening. I was quite proud now of my strong stomach and sea legs. The thin walls revealed that same could not be said for a few of our neighboring Sierra Club friends.

During our dinner of 'sea-rations' Kathy asked me again if I had thought more about the future.

Constantly, I replied.

She wondered how any abrupt changes would affect both of our lives. I understood that.

Between bites of a tasteless cheese sandwich I reflected on how tough and weird turning age 63 felt. My father had passed away at that age, just two months before his next birthday. He had seemed perfectly healthy, too, when he woke up and died one night of a suspected stroke/heart attack. I only learned recently that he had been taking medications for several years that may have contributed to his early passing. As I had mentioned earlier, my mother died nine months later due to a recurrence of breast cancer and, no doubt, grief for the loss of her husband of 43 years.

I thought of friends who have lived long past the age of their fathers, and how I always try to shift my thoughts to my grandfather George, who worked into his 70s and lived into his mid-90s. He was once fired from his job at the age of 50 for being 'too old.' Yes, he was actually told that—it was the 1960s. He responded by starting a rival company (still family owned and operated today) and outliving the two younger guys who tried to put him out to pasture. Success is indeed the best revenge.

Still I felt somewhat adrift. How does one proceed when all your previous identities no longer fit, when, in my head, they still exist?

The 15-year-old new-kid-at-yet-another-school still exists, eternally feeling like an outsider not privy to the shared secrets of the group.

The 30-year-old competitive athlete still exists, thinking that I could jump on the court for 5-on-5 at any time, possible torn Achilles be damned. I believe this even as my daily runs take a little longer to complete each year. I still try to run a couple of half-marathons annually, but soon I will have to pack a lunch.

The 50-year-old driven business owner, community volunteer, and political junkie still exist.

The challenge to succeed never dims but it has been surpassed by the need to remain of value; to my family, to my community, to wherever it matters. I sometimes envy my retired friends and acquaintances who enjoy just reading, or tinkering, or traveling or playing golf with friends. I cannot do that. That's not me—well, except for the travel part. I don't ever want to stop exploring the U.S. and the world. I certainly comprehend the well-earned desire for relaxation and socialization, but I cannot disengage from a swirling world that affects our families, friends, and futures. I certainly get the desire for family contact, too. That is part of my equation. I want to enjoy watching our new grandson grow up, to play an active role in his life, and not simply appear as an occasional face on a phone or laptop screen.

But am I wasting an opportunity to share years of skills developed and successful experience? Or is that just ego talk?

Kathy pointed out that I would still employ my skills when surveying behavioral health organizations or speaking on behalf of ShelterBox USA. That was true, I agreed, but would I be satisfied simply doing less of the same?

Her standard response (and it's not wrong) is to seek out a new goal or a new passion. Years ago, I had written a couple of professional books and penned another one specifically for my daughter. I had toyed recently with the idea of developing one based on my more recent endeavors focused on advising small business leaders and creating effective workplace teams. Leadership books are a dime a dozen, though, and I just could not get excited by that idea.

Kathy interest—and patience—seemed limitless that evening but I had done enough ruminating for one night.

"So, if I had my mid-life crisis in my late 30s, I asked, what do you call this?"

She smiled, then rolled over and reached for her book. I plugged in my laptop for the first time since leaving Ushuaia. My timing was good. I broke through the internet logjam and spent an hour catching up with the outside world. I did receive some good news: Linda had read my e-mail from the previous night and by noon had confirmed the necessary changes to our itinerary. She had also been notified of our Buenos Aires to Los Angeles flight cancellation and had rebooked that flight as well. We were good to go.

Then the other news. Whoa, I said. Kathy looked up.

Every headline screamed 'global disaster ahead.' I had no idea how quickly the coronavirus had spread. I checked the U.S. numbers—over 8700 cases with 115 deaths. Incredibly sad, but the numbers did not seem that alarming, only because I really had no context for it. I kept reading.

The IRS had postponed Tax Day for 90 days. OK, that is a bit of a surprise, but I had filed ours before the trip.

The US government recommended against gathering of 10 people or more. OK, that is a big deal. This must be serious.

Then came the kicker: The CDC has declared the spread of the Covid-19 virus a worldwide pandemic.

Excuse me? What?

I kept searching for any indication of how the CDC's pronouncement might affect our return trip beyond spending one additional day at sea. I read that twelve countries had closed their borders to outsiders in the past week and others had begun shutting down business and all personal activities. I scanned the list of nations: Italy was the first, Ireland—I knew about that, and others in Europe and Central America were now listed as well. Peru and Ecuador were the only two South American countries on the list.

Argentina was not. The little shadow of concern hatched by the Ushuaia delay grew larger and darker. I had the uneasy feeling that we were now racing against an invisible clock.

THIRTEEN

COURSE CORRECTION

"The ship is taking us directly to Buenos Aires."

THURSDAY, MARCH 19: CRUISE DAY 11

POSITION:	56°58,1'S / 27,9° 27,9'W
WIND:	W 8
WEATHER:	RAIN
AIR TEMPERATURE:	+8

Rumors spread from breakfast table to table reporting that all flights in and out of Ushuaia had been delayed until March 25th and that hotels were no longer open to new guests. Questions flooded in: Did that mean we could not extend our hotel stay further if the flights were indeed delayed? Would flights be canceled altogether? Are just Ushuaia flights affected or all Argentinian flights? Would Oceanwide dump passengers on the dock with nowhere to go?

It was 8:00 am on the ocean, but way too early for me to contact Linda—we were four time zones ahead. I checked my phone. I had not received any e-mail updates overnight, but with spotty internet access I could not be certain.

"Good afternoon, everyone, good afternoon. Please assemble in the lounge for a special briefing."

Iain confirmed the early morning rumors as fact. No one expected to hear the words that came next as he read the following update from Oceanwide headquarters:

The coronavirus was spreading faster than predicted. The global pandemic had reached Argentina and the Argentine government had responded. Due to the government's demand for self-quarantines and the shutdown of all Argentine domestic flights, docking in Ushuaia was no longer an option. So...

The Plancius was bypassing Ushuaia and sailing directly for Buenos Aires.

How many additional days we would spend at sea? Not yet known, came the reply. With no definite arrival date not only was our ability to book new flights 'up in the air,' so to speak, but we could not even be certain if planes would actually BE up in the air by the time we reached Buenos Aires or whether flight cancellations would continue.

The new world had collided with the m/v Plancius, or vice versa, but it was a world in flux. A fellow American asked whether Oceanwide or anyone in the room had received any updates or reports from the U.S. government. Iain replied that he had no further information from the cruise company. A quick scan of fellow U.S. passengers elicited only the same regurgitated statements found on the previous two days. I shared the sense of frustration communicated by a nearby countryman who whispered the words 'typical' and 'dysfunctional' as he reacted to the lack of news from Washington.

As Iain concluded the tense, challenging session his brow furrowed and he took a half-step back, shocked and clearly puzzled by a spontaneous round of applause. A short time later I ran into him out on the forward deck. As I complimented him on his handling of the crowd, he admitted that he was puzzled by the supportive response from the passengers. I told him that I had some experience with workplace crisis response, and I had learned that people facing an unknown challenge always desire one thing above all: Honesty from the leaders, and in a way I described as transparent communication. In this case these world travelers needed a second thing, too, of course—a way to get home. Heading to Buenos Aires actually eliminated one step in the process for many on board, since all flights from Ushuaia had been destined for the Argentinian capital anyway, albeit several days later than planned. Iain's practice of reading verbatim the letters sent from Oceanwide Excursions headquarters, coupled with his openness to all questions and willingness to say "I don't know" or "I will find out" had engendered a sense of trust and fostered an atmosphere of shared experience. The staff's follow-through supported the understanding and acceptance that we were all, literally and figuratively, in the same boat.

During the prior briefing I had tapped out another quick text to Linda.

"Hello again! Due to shutdowns in Ushuaia the ship is taking us directly to Buenos Aires. No definite arrival date as yet other than approximately "a week" at sea, so possible arrival on the 26th. Also told no hotels open to guests in B.A. so will have to go directly to airport AND must have a reservation. So, if we have one on the 26th we should hold on to it, but it could be 1-2 days later even. I will stay in touch as I can."

"Next item: A Tucsonan friend and fellow passenger Meg Weesner asked if you could work with her and make her arrangements too. If so, I will get her information to you."

Thanks,
Don

Like many passengers onboard Meg had been stymied by limited internet connections and limited flight options. For two days she had tried without success to link to the internet and, like many passengers who had made their own reservations through Expedia and similar sites, she now faced repeated delays, drop-offs and frustration attempting to navigate the third party travel sites.

Both Bill and Jim from our group spent long hours attempting to rebook flights directly on the LATAM Airlines website. Their tired faces reflected the agonizing delays that more than not culminated with a loss of signal or a frozen website, forcing them to repeat the process late into the evening.

We might now be headed to Buenos Aires, but the Drake Passage had not finished with us. The day had begun with only two-thirds of the usual contingent staggering toward the dining room, but this iron stomach crowd (myself included) desired a full meal after a day of cabin rations. We would not be denied, even as navigating the shifting hallways proved to be an adventure all its own. Take one step forward, stumble to the right, grab a rail, take another step and lurch to the left, then fall forward into the person ahead of you...A third of the tables remained empty as the heaving ocean exacted its revenge.

Tablecloths might have been replaced by rubberized mats, but the chairs had no anchors. Every rogue wave brought forth a scream or grunt as a diner tumbled onto the deck or tipped left or right into their neighbor's lap. Kathy went for the two-fer. When the ship suddenly pitched forward, she slid off her chair toward the floor, clamping onto my arm to avoid tumbling under the table. Naturally, her actions stopped her momentum as she transferred the energy to me. I fell (or was I pushed?) to the floor while my dear wife floated most gracefully down upon my back. A few random expletives were quickly drowned out by the kitchen cacophony of crashing plates and glasses. The spotless crew smiled through it all, not missing a beat. I assumed that Oceanwide must factor breakage costs into every trip.

The morning show featured our huge, heavily accented teddy bear guide Tom (Kathy's description.) He kept us entertained that morning with a plain-English lecture about Antarctic geology, the opening of the Drake Passage, its implications and impact on the development of icecaps on Antarctica.

A few of our greenish-tinged friends appeared at lunchtime. LaRae managed a bowl of soup while her fellow survivors nibbled on tea and toast. Terry from Minnesota asked if the sounds from their cabin bothered us during the night. We lied and said no.

Actually, that was not a lie. I could hear the discomforting noises, but I was not bothered.

One sympathizes, especially one quite familiar with the experience. I told them about our miracle medication and offered to share. Over the next three days I took on the role of unofficial prescriber for three or four grateful users—hey, international waters—as I distributed a few wonder pills to my self-proclaimed new best friends.

The afternoon lecture featured a video presentation from Celine that demonstrated how to track sea birds and marine mammals, and how they can track us. All I recall is that they are much better at it than we are. The program was followed by another surprise call from Iain. We assembled for the unusual early afternoon briefing. He gave a quick update on the latest news regarding final approval for docking and disembarking at Buenos Aires. The capsule version from his comments: 'Nothing new to report.'

After the unenlightening update and subsequent Q&A session concluded Margie headed off to attempt contact with Sierra Club officials. I checked for word from Linda. Nothing. Jim and I remained in the lounge while attempting to break through the satellite squeeze. Someone suggested searching again for any updates from the U.S. State Department. The only new travel advisories suggested that we reconsider travel to Micronesia or Tajikistan. Uh, OK.

I did locate a story that reflected our own growing frustration. The report quoted several anxious State Department employees having received little or no guidance for conducting business during the pandemic, even as one employee tested positive at the U.S. embassy in Jamaica. Nothing about Argentina.

I found this statement posted in the center of a State Department webpage:

On March 14, the Department of State authorized the departure of U.S. personnel and family members from any diplomatic or consular post in the world who have determined they are at higher risk of a poor outcome if exposed to COVID-19 or who have requested departure based on a commensurate justification. *These departures may limit the ability of U.S. Embassies and consulates to provide services to U.S. citizens.*

Hoping to keep up the spirits of the passengers, Iain and his team sought ideas from passengers and fellow team members to help fill the remaining days at sea. To the good-natured cheers of his crewmates and travelers, Rustyn was immediately promoted from camping guide to cruise director and entertainment manager for the duration. He invited interested passengers to suggest or help create new activities, new entertainment, or friendly competitions. A small group of thirty-somethings gathered to make their pitches. Several women volunteered to lead fitness activities, including yoga classes and ship aerobics, once we left the Drake for stable waters.

Pippa stepped up and invited willing passengers to deliver any presentations of interest to the group. I volunteered to give a brief talk. I offered a few topics that I thought might entertain and engage the crowd. She selected one of my programs titled "He Said, She Said: Gender Differences in Communication." I had waffled on whether to bring my laptop on the trip, but I was glad now to have access to my video/slide presentations. I could easily trim it to 20 minutes.

After dinner, the complete expedition team gathered to host the first Plancius Pub Quiz, testing our knowledge of Antarctica, the Plancius, and crew member trivia. Rustyn prefaced the competition by admitting that the 'end of cruise' quiz was normally held on the last evening before returning to Ushuaia. It made no difference that night to the ten enthusiastic teams eager to relive the week's experiences. Our team of bright, distinguished, competitive veteran voyagers finished a middle-of-the-road fifth after struggling with challenges like 'how many bottles of wine are consumed during a single cruise?' Two teams of fanatical millennials fought it out to the bitter end. The winning team was awarded with…yes, a massive bottle of wine.

FOURTEEN

CRUISING THE SOUTH ATLANTIC

"Why penguins don't need socks."

FRIDAY, MARCH 20: CRUISE DAY 12

POSITION:	53°29,1'S / 64° 39,7'W
WIND:	NW9
WEATHER:	PARTLY CLOUDY
AIR TEMPERATURE:	+9

I watched the sun rise over the crystal blue expanse. We had escaped the perilous Drake and crossed an imaginary line into south Atlantic waters, heading north toward Buenos Aires. Waves continued to pound the ship ahead of the persistent gale force winds, but the change in direction toward warmer waters should knock down the winds considerably by afternoon. I could sense the rampant physical discomfort of the past two days transforming into a shared ship-wide anxiety. I felt it, too. What happens when we arrive in Buenos Aires? What can we expect there? Can we get home? I wondered. I had expected to be packed and ready to disembark this morning. Instead I watched through my binoculars as the islands of Tierra Fuego—the entrance to the Beagle Channel and Ushuaia—faded into the distance.

Iain called us to the lounge after breakfast for the first of several briefings that day. He wasted no time delivering the latest shocker:

"Buenos Aires is now locked down until the 31st of March 2020."

Questions flooded the room. What does that mean—is the whole city locked down? Does that include the airports and docks? Are we approved for docking at all? Do we have an arrival date? Can we stay on board? Will we be required to quarantine in Argentina? When should we book flights? Are planes still flying? I watched the number of anxious faces multiply.

I sweat easily, and I could feel a trickle starting down my back, as though the room temperature rose along with voice levels.

Iain relayed the word from the Plancius bridge that they expected to reach Buenos Aires in approximately 5 to 6 sailing days. Without a definite date of arrival, though he advised everyone not to begin booking flights quite yet. I stayed silent, but that made no sense to me. If every traveler waited as long as possible to book a flight, I could foresee two outcomes—neither good. First, good luck to everyone trying to acquire an internet signal without jamming the satellite's limited bandwidth. If someone did get through, then they faced the challenge of connecting with a functioning airline or agent. If I wanted to induce groans or gritted teeth, I need but ask someone "How it's coming with Expedia?"

Second, I assumed that, based on all the recent flight cancellations, there would be a limited number of flights available. If everyone engaged in a last-minute rush to book a seat, how many seats would still be available? I decided that it made more sense to keep Linda apprised of each update and re-book flights as soon as possible. I would rather cancel or change travel dates daily if necessary, rather than start a new search. I counted ahead and decided to shoot for flights on the 26th of March. That would give us an extra day's leeway if docking were delayed. I typed out a quick e-mail to her and hit send.

Iain grimaced as more hands shot up but kept his cool until the rush of unanswerable questions petered out. He exhaled a noticeable sigh of relief and promised to hold more briefings as updates arrived. His honesty and patience eased tensions a bit, though dozens of eyeballs remained glued to their cellphones. Our group of American English-speakers agreed that Iain's bright, lilting Scottish accent helped make each pronouncement sound a wee bit less dire.

A chorus of passengers had asked, "Can we get more internet access?" Oceanwide responded within hours. Iain announced that all aboard now had free and open access to the ship's Wi-Fi system. To no one's surprise a mad tech scramble ensued. Fingers flew as stranded cruisers tried to get in touch with family members, travel agents, or airline websites to update plans, check available options and simply connect with the outside world. Predictably, the ship's limited satellite bandwidth produced a range of muttered expletives and the whooshing sounds of deep yoga breathing as the digital herd stampeded through the narrow canyon of internet access.

"We get to watch human nature under stress now," I whispered to Kathy.

She nodded. We watched millennials reattached themselves to their cellphones, instantly oblivious to all movement and murmurs around them. We smiled as older passengers matched them grimace for grimace. Frustrated hisses of 'damn' and 'come on' escaped from every corner.

"I made so many mistakes on this trip." A young Australian admitted this to me over sodas a few days earlier. He had recounted his DIY travel planning and we had talked about the best electronics for world travel. I found him now sitting by a window, oblivious to the sparkling ocean outside.

"I am still frustrated," he said, fingers attacking his iPad.

"Well, you will figure it out. The experience helps. That how I learned." I replied, trying to sound more reassuring than amused. But I could relate.

"What experience?" he asked.

"I made mistakes," I answered. "That's the other name for 'experience.'"

I did pass along one critical bit of knowledge that I had gained the hard way: I suggested that he get the best international calling plan he could find. I mentioned getting stuck in Bangkok once with a sick wife and "no signal" popping up on my phone screen. He asked for details, so I told him the story.

I was attending a Rotary International Conference forty minutes outside of Bangkok. Kathy had stayed in town enjoying a relaxing boat tour with a friend until she began experiencing severe chills and fever. She headed back to the hotel but could not reach me by phone. I returned that afternoon to find her in bed, quite unwell.

After twenty-four hours she added aches and pains to her temperature swings. I headed to the front desk to ask them to call a doctor. I also asked the woman at the desk if we could extend our stay, since my wife would be in no condition to leave the next morning (Thursday) when we were scheduled to fly to Vietnam with our friends Deb and Randy. The woman barely glanced at me,

"Sorry sir, we are all booked up."

"My wife is quite ill," I repeated.

"I am sorry sir; I cannot help you."

I asked again if a doctor was available and then requested firmly (and politely, I must add, though it took effort) to speak to the hotel manager. I was not moving from that spot.

The energetic young hotel manager appeared and listened to my two requests.

"Of course, we will extend your stay," he responded with no hesitation. "No worries. No let me call a taxi to take you and your wife to the ex-pat hospital. It's only twenty minutes away and that is your best option."

Thanks to three visits in three days to an excellent hospital whose service and low costs put all U.S. systems to shame, extremely expensive phone calls to the indefatigable Linda to reroute our travel, a brilliant hotel manager and a fully recovered Kathy, we caught up to our friends in Vietnam and completed another memorable trip.

Kathy reminds me to this day of the isolation and panic she felt when she could not contact me.

I told my young friend that for just $10 per day of use I saved time, money, and a happy marriage by adding global calling and data plans. The service automatically activates upon arrival in any country and (I did not know this) on ships at sea that have the right communication systems. Texting became my unexpected lifesaver on this voyage.

Even a random phone call would sneak through. I picked up the buzzing phone one morning to hear "We are calling to confirm your eye appointment for March 25." Another voice message confirmed that "Your taxes are filed and ready for pick up." Weird to hear your phone ring in the middle of the Atlantic. Fortunately, that was a rare occurrence and the sporadic signal discouraged any outgoing calls.

The previous night I had texted my daughter to update her on our shifting itinerary. My phone buzzed with her return message. It was our first contact since Ushuaia and, thanks to Jana, our first glimpse of life outside our bubble. Kathy and I peered at the screen together.

5/20—Hi! Well I'm so sorry—I'm sure it's stressful and concerning not knowing when you'll come back, but honestly a ship in the Southern Hemisphere is a pretty good place to be. It's a very weird world right now and while I'm still working—it feels as if everything else has stopped. NY is almost on the verge of a police state—all bars, restaurants, retail shops, nail salons, barber shops, public parks, schools are closed. There's talk of limiting what you can buy at the grocery stores and some delivery places are throwing in a free roll of toilet paper with purchase.

Work is nuts. Too much to go into but just send good vibes that our (plan) on Tuesday go well.

Ryan is great. His sleeping is not but he is definitely getting bigger and more fun! Brendan is doing well. Yvonne is in the hospital—she has fluid in her lungs and suffered a mild heart attack. Mike can't visit because they won't allow it so that's been a bit stressful.*

Chaz is good. He's off work but getting paid so he's excited except he is freaking out about "all his money and stocks and needs Grandpa back ASAP"

I will continue to play secretary and be in touch with all your friends :) I will reach out to Carla and Ellen.

Good luck staying sane and with any presentations!!!

Ryan's smiling face appeared below the text. Kathy teared up instantly, accompanied by a prolonged "oohhhhh." I smiled, pressed my lips together and squinted hard. I looked away for a moment. No tears escaped. That's my story and I am sticking to it.

The crew instituted their newly expanded daily programming. Steffi kicked off the session with a lecture about how plants and animals adapt to the polar regions. Today's homework kids: Look up 'counter-current heat exchange.'

Here is a capsule version:

---

* Yvonne and Mike are Brendan's parents and Jana's in-laws. Sadly, Yvonne—a bright and bubbly wife, mother, and friend—passed away a few weeks later.

The major source of heat for 'endotherms' (humans, birds and animals) is the metabolism of their internal organs. There are several measures that an endotherm can take if it begins to lose heat to its surroundings faster than it can generate heat. In simple terms—when one gets cold. Most common is to increase physical activity. At rest, muscles make only a small contribution (about 16%) to body heat. This increases during vigorous exercise. Without exercise the same effect results from shivering.

The loss of heat occurs first in the extremities, due to a sharp reduction in their blood supply. In extreme cold the blood supply to the fingers can drop to 1% or so of its normal value.

Many animals, however—including humans—have another way to conserve heat. The arteries in the arms and legs run parallel to a set of deep veins. As warm blood passes down the arteries, the blood gives up some heat to the colder blood returning from the extremities in these veins. For example, fish use it in their gills to transfer oxygen from the surrounding water into their blood, and birds use a countercurrent heat exchanger between blood vessels in their legs to keep heat concentrated within their bodies. Thanks to this process a sea gull can maintain a normal temperature in its torso while standing with its unprotected feet in freezing water.

The key takeaway? After decades of wonder, Steffi announced, we now understand why it is penguins do not need socks. And yes, that too will be on the final.

That afternoon Iain delivered a fascinating tale, complete with pictures, of three winters spent working on an Antarctic base. His anecdotes depicted life with a small, isolated group of scientists surviving in an environment unknown to most outsiders.

He shared fond recollections of a socked-in 'Christmas in July,' exposed the lack of privacy in a cramped, communal atmosphere with too many open windows and doors, and highlighted a last-minute race to rebuild an ice-bound runway before the seasonal supply plane made its return. The impact on his life was apparent, as was the slight desire to do it again.

The South Atlantic seas took pity on us and stopped flinging us from one wall to the next. While Kathy wined and whined (unwhined?) with friends I attempted a cramped workout inside our compact cabin. I am sure that I looked ridiculous running in place while mixing in burpees, pushups, and sit-ups between the narrow-spaced bunks. I did benefit from the built-in treadmill, heading 'uphill' as the ship rolled to port and then worked my core to avoid crashing into the desk during the reverse tilt. The workout was more useful for my mental health than physical condition, but both were needed. After a quick shower I used the free time before the next briefing to head out on deck. The southern breeze smelled different than the pure Antarctica version. I felt the air temperature rise against my skin.

New seas, new voyage, new world? I thought.

At the late afternoon daily recap Iain read directly from the letter received a few hours earlier from Oceanwide Expeditions Headquarters:

The following message has been sent to our passengers, staff and crew on board and to the agents that have these passengers booked:

Vlissingen*, 20th March 2020, 11.25am

Dear Passengers, Captain, Crew and Staff, Agents,

This is to keep you informed on the current situation.

All our vessels have now either departed Ushuaia or have deviated towards Buenos Aires. The Oceanwide fleet of Hondius, Plancius and Ortelius are moving together northbound.

Plancius has onboard 114 passengers and 48 crewmembers
Ortelius has onboard 98 passengers and 50 crewmembers
Hondius has onboard 59 crewmembers

We are still working very hard to get approval to enter Buenos Aires. But as stated earlier Argentina will be in a total lock-down until 31 March.

We have daily contact with embassies and they are pushing hard to allow a port entry in Buenos Aires. We are aware that embassies are working very hard to arrange extra flights for repatriation, these discussions are ongoing between embassies and the Argentine Government including major airlines.

At the same time we are working on Montevideo and Brazil. The Falkland Islands/Malvinas are closed so those are no option.

---

*

We have opened up the Wifi-access onboard so you should be able to keep your relatives or others updated of your whereabouts. We will also regularly update our social media channels with up-to-date information.

While we understand the concern of your relatives please ask them not to contact our offices with questions, because many at this stage we cannot answer.

We will keep you updated and our social media channels with latest information, please refer homefront to that.

As stated we are aiming at Buenos Aires for the 26th, but this is not confirmed yet. We hope the weather conditions will make that possible and off course the authorities.

Please rest assured that our goal is not getting you off the ship, we want to get you home! While there are many uncertainties and changing situations we hope for your good spirit and cooperation. We are dealing with a situation new to all of us.

We have to make the best out of it as long as we are together in this!

Stay safe!
Michel van Gessel—CEO
Mark van der Hulst—COO
Oceanwide Expeditions

Alex posted each missive on a wall near the main desk for passengers to review. I found the exhortations like "We have to make the best out of it…" quite amusing coming from land-based folks thousands of miles away. Still, I appreciated this confirmation that efforts were under way to get us home.

Off to dinner. After two weeks at sea we gravitated automatically to our preferred tables closest to the large oval starboard windows and bench seats. Despite the rolling decks our expert serving staff maneuvered smoothly through the room regardless of the condition of the waves or the guests. The occasional interlude of breaking glassware receded as normal dining resumed.

I smiled at a familiar couple as they squeezed past our seats. During our second morning at sea Kathy and I had shared a center oval table with a friendly but uncommunicative emergency medical technician from Connecticut. Traveling with his mother, an accomplished nurse herself, the fortyish, the light-haired, slightly round gentleman barely nodded when I introduced myself and asked his name. His mother answered for both, then glanced at her pale-faced son and asked, "Are you OK?" He shook his head slightly as he kept his unfocused gaze down at his tea and toast. The sparse meal should have been a clue. Without warning he projectile vomited onto his plate and across half the tablecloth.

I reached over with my napkin but before I could offer assistance two servers swooped in with towels and napkins. Within the space of one minute the table was completely cleaned and reset. Clearly not the staff's first rodeo. The gentleman quickly mumbled his apologies and headed for his cabin. By the end of the week he appeared to have recovered his health and his appetite and we enjoyed a delightfully uneventful follow-up lunch conversation a few days later with the two east coasters.

I won tonight's dining room shuffle and sat near of the large windows. Near, but not next to the window; that was Kathy's domain. Chivalry lives. We faced Bill and Dottie, a striking couple from Tampa sat across from us. Bill and I had swapped histories during introductions back in Ushuaia. He had identified himself as a retired Tampa police detective.

With short cropped gray hair, bristle mustache, deep Gulf Coast tan and low-key manner Bill looked tailor-made for the role, although he did admit to some past undercover work while fighting the Florida drug trade. He recounted an early training stint at Quantico and his experience coordinating with the FBI, which finally allowed me to share my pride in our daughter's exploits with someone who understood her work from the inside. Bill and I also connected as fellow Eagle Scouts.

He and Dottie kept us laughing with tales of chaperoning young scouts on trips to various jamborees, including a memorable excursion to Iceland with a handful of extremely active teenagers. He recounted the challenge of monitoring adolescent boys wandering the land in search of food orgies and Icelandic blondes. He chuckled and claimed to have achieved his one goal, which I understood to be "just bring them all back in one piece."

We also talked about the recent stock market crash and frequent fluctuations that seemed to follow each bizarre White House tweet. Bill shrugged and said, "Well, as long as you don't take money out right now then you haven't lost anything."

Sort of true, and it may have been the right attitude for the time. Bill's low-key demeanor no doubt kept his blood pressure low when two nights later he spent five hours trying to book flights as prices skyrocketed on a balky LATAM Airlines website.

Dorette greeted us in the lounge that evening with an impressive video she had compiled and edited of the Antarctica portion of our extended journey. She added that all her videos and pictures were available for downloading from the two computers in the small library. Dorette had also created a shareable folder in which passengers and crew post and exchange pictures. Very gracious. It proved a popular draw for all aboard. The library—later the scene of some very suspicious behavior—remained open to passengers 24/7.

The evening's highlight: Another Pub Quiz titled "Do you know your guide?" Pippa, Steffi, Dave, Rustyn, and Tom took turns reciting a story from their lives. In each of the five rounds only one story was true. Our mixed team of Kathy, me, Judy, Margie, Colorado honeymooners Ian and Maggie struggled to finish in the middle of the pack. Ian and I found it easy to pinpoint the lying males, but the female storytellers proved far too devious. Pippa recounted her path to making the Scottish national rugby team; Steffi described her parachuting exploits and claimed a romantic encounter with a Saudi price; Rustyn talked of setting a swimming record as a youth. He laughed and fake-pouted when no one voted for his true story—but in fairness he was the smoothest liar.

Dave's entertaining story about getting arrested by Australian authorities for speeding on a sailboard was the only true bad boy tale. With only three correct picks we learned a valuable lesson: our guides were excellent liars. We made one additional observation that I filed away for future reference. Except for Dave's story, the true tale turned out to be an accomplishment for which they felt the most pride. A great character study and a good night's fun.

I waited until after 11:00 pm that evening to try to access the internet. Yes! Success. No, crap. My morning e-mail to Linda failed to send. She was not yet aware of our possible arrival date in Buenos Aires. After four failed attempts I gave up and turned off the light. I did not see the latest advisory that appeared on the websites of all U.S. Embassies.

We call your attention to the State Department's Global Travel Advisory issued March 19, 2020:

The State Department has issued a global travel advisory advising all U.S. citizens to avoid all international travel due to the global impact of COVID-19. In countries where commercial departure options remain available, U.S. citizens who live in the United States should arrange for immediate return to the United States, unless they are prepared to remain abroad for an indefinite period. U.S. citizens who live abroad should avoid all international travel. Many countries are experiencing COVID-19 outbreaks and implementing travel restrictions and mandatory quarantines, closing borders, and prohibiting non-citizens from entry with little advance notice. Airlines have cancelled many international flights and several cruise operators have suspended operations or cancelled trips.

If you choose to travel internationally, your travel plans may be severely disrupted, and you may be forced to remain outside of the United States for an indefinite timeframe.

FIFTEEN

AT SEA TOWARD...?

"Where's my wife?"

SATURDAY, MARCH 21: CRUISE DAY 12 +1

POSITION:	49°28,4'S / 62° 04,7'W
WIND:	S2
WEATHER:	CLOUDY
AIR TEMPERATURE:	+11

Day thirteen of our twelve-day cruise started off a wee bit less bouncy and a lot less cool. With temperatures rising I searched through the bottom of my suitcase for lighter clothes. Hidden below all the now useless thermals I dug out two t-shirts—my Ireland favorite and a thin orange souvenir shirt from the Civil and Human Rights Museum in Atlanta, a fascinating place to visit by the way. I highly recommend it. Over the next few days each my fellow voyagers could be identified by their limited selection of lightweight base-layers, shorts, or sundresses packed away in anticipation of temperate post-cruise destinations.

Big news arrived overnight. Shortly after breakfast we heard the call: "Briefing in fifteen minutes."

The Oceanwide Expeditions home office had fired off an update earlier that morning. Iain delivered the latest shocker:

Buenos Aires has officially closed its port to all cruise ships. We were no longer welcome there.

The following message has been sent to our passengers, staff and crew on board and to the agents that have these passengers booked:

Vlissingen, 20th March 2020, 10.15pm

Dear Passengers, Captain, Crew and Staff, Agents,

We have just been informed by our contacts at various embassies that Buenos Aires is not an option for us anymore.

The latest decision from Argentine Government is to deny all disembarkation of passenger vessels in Buenos Aires.

Although expected, it's a change of plans again, same as the old explorers in Antarctica had to change their plans continuously and so will we.

Next stop Montevideo!

AT SEA TOWARD...?

We have just been informed that passengers will be allowed disembarkation if passengers are in possession of a valid air ticket and we are preparing the exact details of arrival times in Montevideo which would be needed for flight bookings.

We are also in contact with embassies to see in what way governments can assist with flights as we are aware that that commercial flights are very limited available, if any.

But we can take at least the required bunkers there and some provisions which are needed for Plancius.*

We are also working on making sure we have the necessary additional (passenger's personal) medication for our passengers for a longer stay onboard, should this be needed.

To be clear; our vessels have been at sea since: Plancius 9 March Ortelius 16 February Hondius 24 February

All people on board are in good health and we have no signs of COVID-19 infections.

Michel van Gessel—CEO
Mark van der Hulst—COO
Oceanwide Expeditions

---

* For oceangoing vessels, the term bunker refers to the storage of petroleum products in tanks, and the practice and business of refueling ships. Bunkering operations are located at seaports and include the storage of "bunker" fuels and the provision of the fuel to vessels.

Kathy looked at me with raised eyebrows as others exchanged similar bewildered looks.

The first hand shot up. "Where is Montevideo exactly?"

Iain brought up a map on the video monitors. He pointed to a dot to the right of Buenos Aires.

"Right there," he answered.

"Oh," exclaimed several relieved voices.

This may be good news, he explained. Not only does Montevideo lie in relative proximity to our former destination, it is located near the head of the large opening to the same river route that leads to Buenos Aires. In other words, our new destination lay several hours closer to our current location.

More hands rose.

Question: "So, our docking and disembarkation in Montevideo is definitely confirmed?"

Answer: "Well, not quite."

Question: For what day should we make our flight reservations?

Answer: "We think it's premature at this time. We are being advised that it's best holding off on booking flights until we have a definite docking date and know how long we will be allowed to stay in port."

Our new hoped-for destination came with a Catch-22 scenario. According to the letter and reports from officials in Montevideo, only passengers with flights all the way back to their home countries that were booked and confirmed in writing would be allowed to disembark. However, at this point we did not yet have a confirmed arrival date or time, and no final confirmation that we would be allowed to disembark at all. For travel agents and especially for most passengers who had booked their own flights this created several dilemmas and generated additional questions. Should they book multiple flights on different days? Will the airlines allow this? What airlines are flying out of Montevideo? If payment is required at time of booking, can they pay for multiple flights and will they have any chance of reimbursement for the unused flights?*

I decided not to wait. Immediate after the morning's briefing I texted Linda (no more e-mail attempts) and asked her to find flights for us out of Montevideo on the 26th. I sent the text at 6am Tucson time, so I knew it would a while before I heard from her. This time it worked. Linda responded a few hours later. She agreed that the timing made sense and went to work. That proved to be the smartest move of the week.

I headed up to the bridge and enjoyed a relaxing conversation with the captain and second officer, relishing their tales of past voyages and minor mishaps at sea. I asked for their thoughts on the potential outcomes we currently faced. Based on their projections they said it was most likely that we would reach Montevideo by the 25th. That was the good news, the captain admitted.

And the bad news, I wondered? He turned his gaze back to the sea and continued to speak. If we were refused debarkation in Uruguay then his only choice would be to sail on to their home port in the Netherlands, complete with a full contingent of 114 passengers. I asked how long that Atlantic crossing would take. He shrugged. "Another three and a half weeks at sea."

---

* Linda is still chasing a reimbursement for us from Aerolineas Argentinas for our canceled Ushuaia to Buenos Aires flights. I told her that I view it like a loan to a family member: I consider any return of funds a surprise.

I headed back down to the lounge to a chorus of heavy sighs and mumbled curses. The rush of desperate digital detoxers back to the internet had slowed the satellite connection to a bottlenecked crawl. Impatient males paced the room; a small group of single women huddled in a corner, heads together as though planning a coup.

Dozens more scattered in the halls and stairways braving carpal tunnel syndrome as their fingers flew across cellphones and iPads seeking passage to Sao Paulo, Brazil or Santiago, Chile—the only two destinations available from Montevideo for repatriation flights and connections home. The crush of data became so great that it created a brand-new problem.

Mal strode to the front of the room and reached for the microphone. The room quieted. He calmly informed us that the high internet usage was interfering with the bridge officer's ability to transmit or receive weather updates and urgent messages from Oceanwide HQ. In fact, during the previous evening several passengers began spreading the rumor of the closure of Buenos Aires ports before the Plancius officers had received the official word. He asked those passengers without an urgent need to get online to cut back their usage. A sea of heads nodded around me. No one wanted to interfere with official communications; kind of important when you are looking for a place that will allow you to dock, disgorge passengers and resupply, we agreed.

Mal offered an instant IT Support workshop. He expertly shared the ability to impart, in plain English—well, in plain accented New Zealanderish English—an understanding of cellphone operations, internet connections and related mysteries of the digital world known only to the under-35 group and those with live-in grandchildren. He walked us through how to turn off automatic notifications and updates, limit downloads, and employ other simple tricks to limit bandwidth use and free up the satellite for critical ship communications. He concluded with another please to limit internet use to flight searches and critical contacts. Status updates and Instagram feeds could wait.

Time for some fresh air. Celine invited interested folks to meet on the narrow stern section of deck five for a bird watching workshop. The distraction tempted me more than did the subject, so I followed the crowd. Celine delivered a fascinating, eyes-on lesson covering the various types of petrels and albatross soaring around the ship. As she spoke a dozen dolphins dove into view from the port side and cavorted their way past the appreciative crowd. Once our live-action nature show concluded I headed to the bow to find the answer to a new and puzzling question: Were we headed in the wrong direction?

One of my favorite cell phone features was the built-in compass. I noticed that the ship had swung to the west, then south and now east. We were sailing in a circle. The ship had reduced speed overnight and now we were drifting along a counterclockwise path. As noon approached, we ceased moving altogether. Was something wrong?

The intercom crackled with a message from the bridge. Iain announced that we were awaiting the arrival of the Ortelius, the sister ship to the Plancius which had increased speed overnight to catch up to us. The Ortelius had been at sea for thirty days on a voyage from New Zealand to the Antarctic. They too had been refused disembarkation at the port of Ushuaia but had been allowed to dock and resupply there before continuing northward.

Oceanwide Expeditions operated three "ice-strengthened cruise ships" to carry passengers on expeditions in both the Antarctic and the Arctic. The third ship, the newer and larger Hondius, had managed to dock and disembark all passengers in Ushuaia just ahead of the travel ban, so it continued on course back to the home port at Vlissingen.

The Ortelius grew from a dot on the horizon into a fully formed vessel as it approached from the south. The ship carried additional provisions, including surplus medical supplies and a few extra crates of fresh fruit and veggies for the Plancius. I leaned over the portside rail to watch as Pippa, Steffi and Alex set off in a zodiac for the half-mile dash. Once they matched the Ortelius's speed, pallets of goodies were skillful transferred from the bobbing beast to the tiny boat a few meters off its starboard side. Mission accomplished; the zodiac sped away. The intrepid crew were welcomed home with cheers from all decks. We returned the waves and yells from our mirror image on the sister ship as the Plancius re-oriented to the north. Just like that, the Ortelius and the Plancius were on the move again. The ships sailed in tandem toward Montevideo at an average speed of 10 knots. Each day I searched for an occasional glimpse across the waves as the Ortelius remained about one mile away to port.

My Pavlovian stomach rumbled as the 12:30 lunch call neared. The extra days at sea had taken a toll on the ship's stores, however, and the delightful salad bar buffet was a thing of the past. Lunch was now served at the tables and, like the dinner menu, offered three selections, one of which was a vegetarian option—quite often the best choice. The chef and staff had not missed a beat. My futile attempt to cut back on calories was soon abandoned in the face of fresh fish dishes and chocolate mousse.

"May I join you?" Dorette asked.

"Of course!" I replied and motioned to the empty seat across from me.

"I decided that with the extra days at sea I should get to know people a little better," she said, a bit shyly.

I asked her if photography was her full-time profession. She smiled.

"Not really." She loosened up and continued.

"Are you familiar with a TV program that originated in England called "Antiques Road Show?"

"Yes! We have it in the U.S. too."

She leaned forward and her voice lightened as she described life as the executive producer for the same show in the Netherlands. She smiled as she described how she spent several months each year traveling around the country with a small crew filming odd people with odd heirlooms. Her eyes sparkled with each story. I had judged her to be bright but a bit standoffish; the person before me now revealed an introvert reaching out to connect. It figured. We rarely recognize ourselves in others unless someone points it out. Kathy pegs me—correctly, I think—as an introvert as well, which she described (based on a New Yorker magazine, I am guessing) as someone who is inward focused, who gains energy from time alone, and such. I mentioned that I do get accused of not smiling enough in social situations. OK, guilty, but I plead for mercy under the rule that "I can't always control how my face reacts." Judge Kathy usually rejects that argument. So, it came as no surprise that I enjoyed the conversation and I enjoyed getting to know Dorette, who taught me once again that first impressions mean little. It reminded me once again that the greatest joys of travel are usually found in the people you meet.

Felicity, the quietest and least visible of the expedition guides, took center stage for the first time to educate us about common modern-day threats faced by all marine life—notably ship strikes, entanglements, and overfishing. Several audience members attempted to introduce the impact of climate change into the discussion, but she tiptoed past the issue and left the topic for a future program. I gathered the distinct impression that Oceanwide did not want to rock the boat (so to speak) with politically tinged discussions on a pleasure cruise. After a week's immersion in a near pristine wilderness of water, ice, and land, it was impossible not to consider the issue based on the first-hand evidence we had observed.

The next day Mal took up the mantle and squeezed in a highly interactive talk on the subject. Several guides contributed slides taken during visits to the same locales over the past three years. The severe encroachment of snow algae and the loss of snow and ice on the mountains offered sobering evidence of the accelerated damage to the natural earth cycles.

Doesn't all ice float?

Mal enhanced the previous ice discussion by highlighting, in words and video, the plight of floating ice shelves. He described how floating ice shelves have accounted for 30 percent of the ice loss in the western region.

Floating ice is lost in two ways: by calving of icebergs and through melting from underneath by a deep current of warmer water that circulates around the continent.

I was surprised to learn that the loss of ice across the Antarctic continent was an uneven process. The continent gained more ice in parts of East Antarctica but was losing it more rapidly on the western side and up the Antarctic Peninsula. The difference is attributed to increased precipitation in the east, where a greater accumulation of falling snow is compressed into ice and thickens the ice sheet.

Because floating ice is, by definition, already present in the water, it does not add to sea level rise when it calves or melts. But the ice shelves act as buttresses against the grounded ice behind them; when they thin out they allow the advancing ice to flow faster. As the previously grounded ice reaches the water, it adds to rising seas. Researchers recently reported that, from 2003 to 2019 the continent had lost enough ice to raise sea levels by about one-quarter of an inch (six millimeters) during that period.

The highly verbal crowd kept the discussion going for some time. Unfortunately, as is typical for any such gathering a handful of puffed-up passengers preferred to waste time flaunting their own subject knowledge—or ignorance—rather than ask a meaningful question. Mal's patience and New Zealander wit prevailed once again, however, and the session ended with an abundance of applause for his willingness to address the issue squarely.

"Abandon Ship!"

As Chief Officer Miia saw it, having access to a ship full of restless bodies provided a wonderful opportunity to test her crew's readiness to conduct a simulated fire/abandon ship drill. At 4pm sharp alarm bells clanged throughout the ship and the intercom blared: "All passengers report to their muster stations!"

Not 'stations,' since only one muster station existed for all passengers: The Observation Lounge. I grabbed my bulky orange jacket and headed through the corridors and up the stairs. Crew members took up their positions and began scanning cruise cards. But the Chief Officer had added a twist. A day earlier Miia asked for a few volunteers to play various roles as "difficult passengers" in various states of distress to further test the crew's skills in the crisis.

I could not resist the chance to have some fun. Kathy readily agreed to join in. While I headed for the lounge an anxious and frightened Kathy stayed in the cabin wondering where her husband was. I dutifully presented my card at the doorway and entered the lounge. I looked for my wife, whom I assumed had preceded me. No Kathy in sight. I fought my way back to the doorway against the tide of the incoming crowd. Senior staff member Dragan stopped me as I tried to exit. I raised my voice and informed him that "I must go to our cabin and find my wife."

He told me that I could not leave. I shook my head and tried to push past his sturdy six-foot, three-inch frame. He stayed cool and repeated his instructions. I repeated myself more forcefully. He said that a crew member would be sent to find her.

"Who is going? Send them right now!" I demanded.

"You want to know who is going?" he asked, surprised.

"Yes. Right now!"

Dragan stayed cool. He continued to check in the rush of life-jacketed passengers while blocking my attempts to slip past him. At that moment Kathy bounded up the stairs into view.

"There you are!" she cried out.

She informed Dragan and I that a crew member had knocked

and entered each cabin. She initially refused to leave, telling the determined crewman that "my husband would come for me." Kathy reported that the crew member handled her well and she relented.

Our role-playing efforts complete, we sat down to enjoy the remaining performances, including the drunk guy, the oblivious partyers, the weeping and wailing wife searching for her husband, and the shrieking 'We are all gonna die!' woman who collapsed in the center of the lounge. Once all cards were swiped accordingly, we lined up and marched single file through the corridor out to the stern deck behind the lifeboats for a final count. After standing for ten minutes while baking in the bright Atlantic sun Miia declared the drill complete. We applauded the staff and crew. I ran into Dragan at dinner and complimented his professionalism. He chuckled and said I was quite convincing. My wife responded with "He was just playing himself." Thank you dear.

The daily recap brought us no new information. The Plancius was not yet approved for docking in Montevideo. I leaned over to Kathy and whispered that another visit to the Netherlands was not a bad alternative. She was not amused.

Tom followed the briefing with a short slideshow that answered the other big question that had been on everyone's mind for two weeks: Who the heck was Plancius and why is there a ship named for him?

Tom wove a rather interesting tale. Petrus Plancius (1552—1622) was a Dutch-Flemish astronomer, cartographer and clergyman. Born in Heuvelland, West Flanders on the western edge of Belgium, Plancius studied theology in Germany and England. At the age of 24 he became a minister in the Dutch Reformed Church.

Plancius fled from Brussels to Amsterdam in 1585 to avoid

religious prosecution by the Inquisition after the city fell to the Spanish. In Amsterdam he became interested in navigation and cartography and, having access to nautical charts recently brought from Portugal, he was soon recognized as an expert on safe maritime routes to India and the nearby "spice islands". This enabled colonies and port trade in both, including what would become the Dutch East Indies, named after the Dutch East India Company that set up shop there in 1602. He was fascinated by the little-mapped Arctic Sea and strongly believed in the idea of a Northeast Passage until the failure of Barentsz's third voyage in 1597 seemed to preclude its viability. Had he only known about global warming...

For his pioneering contributions in the history of celestial cartography, Plancius is considered to be one of the notable figures in the Golden Age of Netherlandish cartography (c. 1570s–1670s). Who knew there was a Golden Age of Netherlandish cartography? Oceanwide Expeditions seemed to have an affinity for naming their ships after such gentlemen. The profession was shared by fellow mapmakers of that era named Abraham Ortelius and Jodocus Hondius.

Tom amused us further with a bonus history lesson covering the Dutch war for independence with Spain. He compared our current status to the plight of another 'ship without a port,' a Dutch ship refused entry to Spanish harbors during wartime. Well, our ship's cabin did have its own head (bathroom), night lights, fresh water, and entertainment, but otherwise, yeah, exactly the same.

That evening Margie delivered an official Sierra Club update for the gang of eighteen. She reported that senior staff at S.C. headquarters were monitoring our trip and attempting to contact the Uruguayan embassy. Other Sierra Club tour groups in Israel, Central and South America were being evacuated back to the U.S. and all international trips scheduled for April and May had been canceled. Margie added that her home state of California had just ordered all 39 million residents to stay home.

She updated us on the current news from home. Over 300,000 people worldwide had contracted the coronavirus. The term 'global pandemic' had officially emerged from the shadows and would henceforth insert itself into nearly every conversation within our little onboard community.

I took a moment to review a text that had pinged in from Linda. She was now receiving all updates from American Airlines and from Oceanwide Expeditions. She reported that she could now track our ship's location on the Oceanwide website. I read her message twice, but the gist of it remained the same: No change.

I stayed awake for a long time that night wondering how Jana and Brendan were coping. I wondered what kind of world we would encounter when we finally made it home. I thought our voyage into the unknown had ended. Perhaps so, but a new one had begun.

SIXTEEN

AT SEA TOWARD…MONTEVIDEO?

"Murder on the Plancius."

SUNDAY, MARCH 22: CRUISE DAY 14

POSITION:	45°35,6'S / 60° 13,9'W
WIND:	WNW 5
WEATHER:	PARTLY CLOUDY
AIR TEMPERATURE:	+15

My phone dinged. A flood of text messages had arrived overnight.

From Jana:
"Everyone is OK, but New York City has become an odd and scary place."

I smiled, thinking of the fortunate decision made by Brendan and Jana to move out of Manhattan in favor of a small town north of the city just one month earlier.

From Randy in Tucson, my former business partner and good friend of thirty years:

"It has become pretty weird here with the corona. All bars and restaurants are closed, except for delivery. Gun sales are up. California Governor has locked down the whole state. We are very concerned about you two."

From friends John, Paul, Bill, and David:

"It's getting really bad at home. Toilet paper shortages, 24-hour scary news updates."

"Maybe just keep sailing for a few months. Chaos and overreaction here. Stay safe and dry."

"You and Kathy are better off staying on the ship."

"You will be coming back to a different world."

From brother-in-law Steve:

"Grab some toilet paper on you way out, 'cause there is none in Tucson! I have never seen anything like it. Totally bonkers—no canned goods, paper goods, meat, bread, dairy, bacon, bottled water. Just stripped bare."

He continued:

"There are 23 cruise ships in a holding pattern on the Atlantic side of South America. There are 12 within 200 miles of your ship (just north of the Falklands). None of the South American countries are allowing anyone to dock, nor are any of the Caribbean islands. I hear West Africa is nice this time of year!"

Steve shares my dry sense of humor. I let out a laugh. Kathy asked what was funny. She just shook her head when I read the text.

Then she frowned. Worry took over her face. I could not blame her. We have had major challenges on international trips before, but nothing like this. Home was sounding more and more like a foreign country, and we still had no certainty about how and when we would return there—or what to expect when we arrived.

The morning briefing lived up to its name—it was brief. Iain continued the wise practice of reading verbatim from each letter sent from Oceanwide headquarters. Always a smart move, as we had agreed earlier. In times of crisis a leader rarely goes wrong by overcommunicating; his or her mistake is typically the reverse. Experience has taught me that when information is scarce the affected group, whether it is employees, family members or cruise passengers, will always, ALWAYS assume the worst.

The overnight letter from Oceanwide read:

The following message has been sent to our passengers, staff and crew on board and to the agents that have these passengers booked:

Vlissingen, 21th March 2020, 7.23 pm

Dear Passengers, Captain, Crew and Staff,

Since we heard late last night that our next destination will be

Montevideo instead of Buenos Aires we confirmed to our local agent our intentions and are now working out the details and possibilities.

All embassies in Uruguay/Montevideo have been updated about our change and that our course is now towards Montevideo.

We are exchanging details with them and we are making the planning with the ships-agent.

Our ETA there will be on the 25th. But we do not know at what time we will be allowed inside. Perhaps we will need to stay there 25th and 26th but those details we are discussing now with agent and embassies.

The same applies in Montevideo as it now does in many other places. You will need a valid flight ticket to be able to disembark. Flights are however very limited. But, I hope more get available as there are more vessels than ours heading towards Montevideo carrying a lot of people wanting to go home as well.

Because of Plancius not being able to take bunkers and provisions in Ushuaia we need to stop there anyway to be able to take bunkers for the vessels and to get provisions for Plancius. Without those the vessel cannot proceed.

We have received the list with the medication that is needed for our passengers and will order that as well.

I hope that we soon get more detailed information from Montevideo that we can share with you.

Trust to have informed you for the moment

Michel van Gessel—CEO
Mark van der Hulst—COO
Oceanwide Expeditions

I paid careful attention to what was not said in that letter. I was not the only one. Iain pointed to one of the agitated hands fluttering in the back of the room.

"So, we are approved to dock, but that doesn't mean that we have approved for disembarkation yet. Is that correct?"

"That is correct." Iain answered.

"What if we are denied?"

Iain reconfirmed that Oceanwide assumed responsibility for every passenger until they left the ship. He reconfirmed that the Plancius would load sufficient provisions to serve passengers all the way to Vlissingen if necessary.

Half the room groaned. Kathy's eye widened as she grabbed my arm.

I decided that it was not a good time for a joke.

The humanness that Iain displayed at each briefing eased some of the tension in the room. "No more questions?" He repeated the offer as often as necessary before exhaling a relieved "cool" once the barrage of jittery outstretched hands ceased.

Alex requested that all passengers and crew members to bring their passports to the main desk so he and Dragan could scan them for the Uruguayan authorities. While I waited by the desk, I overheard Alex on the phone in discussion with an Oceanwide representative. I discovered that a significant debate was underway between embassies and local authorities who were struggling to create an acceptable method of transporting passengers directly from the ship to the airport and onto a plane. I took it as a sign of progress. Pippa was standing nearby and grinned. "Uruguay was not really planned on our agenda anyway," she remarked.

The seas calmed and the air grew warmer as we swept northward toward the equator. My Ireland t-shirt made its second appearance. As I climbed to the uppermost deck, I moved to one side to make room for a parade of smiling, squinting individuals shuffling back to their cabins, arms full of blankets and binoculars. The Antarctic campouts may have been cancelled but these intrepid folks would not be denied. The first of two on-deck camping nights had just concluded. Thirty-five bleary-eyed steel deck adventurers swore they had a wonderful time gazing for hours at the Milky Way and the multitude of southern constellations in the clear, black night. They claimed to have no aching backs after sleeping on the cold hard deck. Except for the stiff gaits and groans I almost believed them. The stars at sea were undeniably stunning, though. I spent a few minutes just gazing out at the watery expanse and felt an odd mix of anxiety and relief, like a simultaneous sense of stress/no stress. I explored the source of this dichotomy.

I recognized it as another unforeseen consequence of the pandemic. It looked something like this: All work and travel commitments had been cancelled, thus 'No Stress.' That also meant 'No Plans,' never a comfortable state of mind for yours truly. No plans also meant 'No Direction,' which equals Stress. I would have to work on a plan, which could be even tougher amid all the current uncertainty.

A View to a Kill.

In addition to aerobics, chess tournaments and a popular multiplayer board game called Catan that I had not seen before, Rustyn and friends had created 'The Murder Game' for restless voyagers. Over eighty passengers jumped in, eager for the diversion. The rules were deviously simple.

1. You draw a piece of paper from the bowl, which had printed on it:
   - Name of your victim, example: "Don J,"
   - Their cabin number,
   - Location for murder to occur in a public area, e.g. 'library,'
   - Weapon, such as a barf bag (plentiful throughout the ship), glove, key card
2. After a successful 'kill' you take their paper identifying the next victim and go after them.
3. Continue until only one survivor remains.
4. No running.

We drew names and planned strategy. Thirty minutes later a menagerie of serial killers began their rampage. Anxiety and paranoia gripped the ship as one hundred homicidal maniacs roamed the decks. Screams echoed from the hallways. Within three hours over half of the participants transformed into the walking dead. One young woman kept poking her head inside the dining room, afraid to enter in case her attacker lay in wait. Hunger got the best of her, as did her so-called 'friends' who lured her back in. She survived two minutes before being slapped from behind by an unforgiving sock.

It's Always the Quiet Ones.

By late afternoon the handful of players still alive were mostly women. Steely-eyed millennials and unassuming grandmotherly types were knocking off the male players with cold-blooded glee. I had been dispatched after just one murder to my name. While descending a stairway on the way to lunch I said hello to James, a young expert videographer I had gotten to know and like who stood at the corner of the hallway. "You look like a stalker," I said to him. "I am," he replied as he tapped me with his keycard and emitted a dastardly laugh. James the Merciless.

Kathy racked up three kills before her number came up. Her second victim: fellow Sierra Clubber Jim from Evanston. He had just bounded into the lounge and was gleefully recounting his latest kill to Judy and me when Kathy called out from the library. "Come see this!" Jim hesitated for a moment—the small library was the most difficult site to lure people. Kathy convinced him to enter to see "incredible whale pictures" with Dorette sitting innocently at the computer.

As we looked over Dorette's shoulder Kathy patted Jim on the back with her glove. "Sorry, Jim, you're dead!" "Nooo!" he groaned, "You're heartless!"

At lunch I watched Kathy glide to the other side of the room, pick out her target and all but leap across the table as her victim tipped back her chair and screamed. Just as Kathy reached over to apply the final blow, she felt a tap on her own back. Another one bites the dust. The real assassin in our midst was quiet, unassuming LaRae. She racked up kill after kill with her deadly stealth. What happened to Minnesota nice? She was still alive at the end of the day. At the afternoon recap the rules were adjusted slightly for the surviving six. I had wondered what would happen when all killers were known.

The next morning at breakfast I sat across from a young man named Jason, a professional game designer from L.A. Jason had helped Rustyn create the murder game, and he explained to me why a rules reshuffle was necessary to avoid a no-win scenario. Simply put, the final few players would know their stalkers and simply avoid them for the remainder of the cruise. Jason was a bright young guy and I enjoyed debating game theory vs. real life and learning about the multi-billion-dollar gaming and e-sports industry. I found it fascinating, but I still argued that anything you can do in pajamas from your bedroom cannot be called a sport. (No, not that either.) Later that day the prize for 'deadliest among us' was claimed by a slightly evil-looking grinning, skinny, thirty-something woman. "Too skinny," murmured my victory-deprived homicidal cabin mate.

Pirates of the South Atlantic

The kitchen crew prepared another delicious outside BBQ—this time with a theme: *Pirates on the Plancius*. Eager partiers were encouraged to create a costume using only items found in their suitcases and cabins. Closet bars became swords, hairdryers transformed into parrots, Sleep masks and photo hardware were fashioned into eye patches and other accessories, and bound arms and legs were 'lost at sea.' Rustyn emceed the walk of fame for the wannabe pirates, who snarled across the open deck to the shouts and cheers of their admirers. The top 10 costume winners earned a free shot of cheap rum along with lifelong respect…or regret, depending on the source of the rum.

Between laughs Margie, Meg and I considered the juxtaposition between our current situation—enjoying a safe afternoon at sea—and the reports of fear and disruption at home. We sat on the sun splashed deck for quite a while contemplating the uncertainty of the new world ahead. We still did not know if we would be allowed to disembark at Montevideo or forced to sail on to Europe. We did not know whether planes were flying, or if we would need to quarantine wherever we first landed in the U.S.

We did learn something new about Adam Harner that afternoon. He agreed to show an award-winning documentary "As the Crow Flies" about a record-setting sea kayaking adventure he and a team in Great Britain completed in 2014. One online source described it this way:

On 17 May 2014 a team of four set off to complete Beeline Britain—a journey from Land's End, the extreme southern point of mainland England to John o' Groats in a straight line.

This never before attempted route was completed in 28 days and required the two biggest sea kayak crossings ever completed in UK waters.

- *The first crossing went direct from Land's End to Pembrokeshire—a distance of over 200 km which took 34.5 hours to complete.*
- *The second crossing went direct from Pembrokeshire to Anglesey—around 170 km and taking 24.5 hours to complete.*

The team then kayaked, biked and hiked the remainder of the route via the Isle of Man and required traversing Ben Macdui, the second highest mountain in the UK and across the Moray Firth before reaching John o' Groats, considered the northernmost point in Great Britain.

The project was devised and managed by Ian O'Grady. He recruited the Team GB Paralympian Nick Beighton, Adam Harmer, a professional kayak coach and University Lecturer, and Tori James, the first Welsh woman to stand on the summit of Mount Everest. Beeline Britain's aim was to raise funds and awareness for Blesma, the limbless veterans charity. The project gained full royal endorsement from the Royal Foundation of the Duke and Duchess of Cambridge and Prince Harry, and raised over £20,000 for Blesma.

A very impressive feat.

Afterward I stood at the starboard rail marveling at two dolphins passing by the ship, framed by a beautiful ocean sunset. I had been kidding with Kathy, but I really would not mind spending another three weeks at sea. Compared to the dire warnings of store closures, stay-at-home demands, and toilet paper shortages, quarantining on board the Plancius sounded pretty good right now.

As I sat down to dinner that night Pippa tapped me on the shoulder. She asked if I would kick off the guest presentations with my 'He Said, She Said' talk the next morning at 11am. I agreed.

I always preferred speaking before lunch when folks are awake and engaged—as long as you do not drag Q&A time into the lunch hour. I spent some time in the cabin that night tweaking my talk for this unusually mixed, semi-captive audience.

"Are you nervous?" Kathy asked.

"No. I enjoy it," I said as I put the finishing touches on my slides. "I would be a nervous wreck" she said.

She knows my routine. I believe that preparation is always the key to a good presentation, even if I have given the same talk a hundred times. She asked me what I thought about the unique circumstances for my debut as a cruise ship speaker. I reviewed with her how I always consider the demographics of the audience, their knowledge of the subject, and which segments of the talk I think will resonate best with each subgroup. I considered the best tone for the audience. How much of an academic tone to employ vs. a lighter and more humorous style?

Humor was a definite yes for this crowd. I had already checked out the room setup, the audio and video equipment and the anticipated crowd size, all of which affect crowd engagement and response.

I saved my file and tried until midnight to get the latest updates from the outside world. Midnight found me staring in vain at a stagnant screen, waiting for the 'connected" icon. Nothing. I closed my laptop and called it an evening.

SEVENTEEN

STILL AT SEA

"The Importance of Whale Poop"

MONDAY, MARCH 23: CRUISE DAY 15

POSITION:	40°55,0'S / 57° 29,5'W
WIND:	NW 5
WEATHER:	CLEAR SKY
AIR TEMPERATURE:	+17C

I hardly slept last night. I rose more than once to stare at the slice of ocean visible through the porthole. A long line of bright lights shimmered a mile or so off our starboard side. At daybreak I hiked up to the bridge and asked the lone senior officer what I had seen. He pointed to one of the radar screens and pushed a button. Markers for over 30 fishing boats appeared by each dot, identifying each vessel by name and number. The dots bunched together in a line running from south to north.

"All of these names look Chinese." I said. The short, olive-skinned officer nodded. His weathered face hinted of years at sea.

"That's what you saw last night," he said. "Most of those boats are from the same China company." He traced the line created by the dots on the screen, demonstrating how the Chinese fleet would crowd right up against Argentina's presumed international fishing border.

We were cruising through a prime fishing area for squid, he explained, which is a highly desirable catch for the Asian fleets. The Chinese boats would shine huge spotlights toward the water at night to attract them.

Iain delivered the latest update after breakfast. Another message had arrived overnight from Oceanwide headquarters. He read aloud:

The following message has been sent to our passengers, staff and crew on board and to the agents that have these passengers booked:

Vlissingen, 22nd March 2020, 7.11pm

Dear Passengers, Captain, Crew and Staff,

Our efforts for a call to Montevideo continue.

We have some very active embassies that are working hard with the Uruguay government. They are updating us twice a day about their progress.

The Government has been discussing about the preliminary ideas for their "corridor sanitaire". And they have issued what looks as their draft requirements.

One of those, is that we need a scanned copy of all passports. The Hotel staff will start working on this.

So on one hand there is something happening, on the other hand we need to be careful and temper your expectations.

The requirements remain, that passengers may disembark only when in possession of a valid flight ticket departing Uruguay, homebound, with flight departure on the day of your disembarkation. However, until the exact details and requirements from the Government are known, we do not know exactly what the disembarkation date / flight departure date will be to book and/or when we will be allowed into the port.

And then the question, will flights be available?

As we are not the only one…several vessels are anchored off of Montevideo with the same wish; getting their passengers disembarked and travelling home.

Collectively, we are pushing for Governments taking a lead in this and try if they are willing to arrange extra flights, we as vessel operators have no influence on the availability of flights off course. We have 27 nationalities onboard our vessels, so we assume you all need to travel to different places.

One of the aspects that we are really looking into is keeping our vessels healthy. We have absolutely no signs of COVID-19 onboard and we want to keep it like that. We are asking questions and want to have clarity from the government of Uruguay, if and why there is the need for people or authorities to board the vessel upon arrival in Montevideo. Especially because ultimately our vessels will be at sea for more than three weeks until Vlissingen. Hopefully with only crew but of course we do not know that at this stage.

Your safety and those of our crew is our greatest concern! We trust to have informed you for the moment.

Michel van Gessel—CEO
Mark van der Hulst—COO
Oceanwide Expeditions

Well, now we knew why the hotel staff had scanned our passports again yesterday.

After Iain patiently restated each nugget of available information to the roomful of tense questioners, the level of shipboard stress skyrocketed. I could sense the anxiety rising even among our own little group of experienced travelers. I huddled with Margie, Meg, Kathy, Jim and the others as we laid out three unanswered questions:

NUMBER ONE: Will be allowed to disembark, and if so, when?
Rumors spread about another ship that had successfully off-loaded guests and crew members in Montevideo. A "corridor sanitaire" had reportedly been created to get potentially infected passengers

and baggage from the docks to the airport, but we could not get confirmation of this, nor could anyone find a description of the so-called Uruguayan health corridor.

NUMBER TWO: Will flights still be available? I had already begun another text-and-wait exchange with Linda. Because she had booked our original itinerary through American Airlines and their partner airline LATAM, she was able to update, change and monitor flight options directly through AA. As a frequent traveler on American I held Executive Platinum status, so we hoped that this might prove to be an advantage for keeping our seats. It had not done me any good in Buenos Aires on Day One, and I did not know if that would make any difference this time. (I do not know to this day.) I was frustratingly aware of my complete lack of control over flight cancellations, multi-national flight restrictions or airport shutdowns. The battle between 'control freak' and 'go-with-the-flow' global traveler continued inside my head. As far as I knew, our flights on March 26th from Montevideo to Santiago, Chile and Miami remained confirmed.

NUMBER THREE: If the answer to either question one or two is no, what happens? Does that really mean we will have to stay on board and sail for another 25 days to the Netherlands? And what then?

Even those of us with confirmed flights remained anxious and on edge, thanks in part to the series of callous, confusing, or misleading statements emanating from the US State Department offices in Washington and the U.S. embassy in Uruguay.

I reread the March 8 US State Department Release on my iPhone screen:

Passengers on Cruise Ships:

U.S. citizens, particularly travelers with underlying health conditions, should not travel by cruise ship. CDC notes increased risk of infection of COVID-19 in a cruise ship environment. In order to curb the spread of COVID-19, many countries have implemented strict screening procedures that have denied port entry rights to ships and prevented passengers from disembarking. In some cases, local authorities have permitted disembarkation but subjected passengers to local quarantine procedures. While the U.S. government has evacuated some cruise ship passengers in recent weeks, repatriation flights should not be relied upon as an option for U.S. citizens under the potential risk of quarantine by local authorities.

Someone on our group recalled that on the same day, the Sunday before our departure from Ushuaia, #45 had boasted, "We have a perfectly coordinated and fined tuned plan at the White House for our attack on the coronavirus."

We sat there for the hour before the morning lectures and scanned our devices for every news reports, interview, or update that we could find. The message from the White House and Secretary Pompeo reverberated loud and clear with the unmistakable warning: 'You are on your own, pal.'

A few hours later Jim found this update that he pulled from the homepage of the US Embassy in Uruguay:

Travel Alert for U.S. Citizens:

The government of Uruguay has implemented measures to limit the spread of COVID-19. All international passenger flights are suspended as of March 23, 2020. We are considering all options to assist U.S. citizens in Uruguay. Continue to monitor the U.S. Embassy's website.... The Department of State has issued a Global Level 4 Health Advisory for COVID-19. Many travelers world-wide have reported unexpected flight cancellations and limited flight availability. If your travel has been disrupted, please contact your airline.

Alex and Dragan instructed all passengers to bring evidence of their confirmed flight information to the front desk at lunch time. Oceanwide had tasked them with the job of collecting and transmitting the information to the Uruguayan officials and each of the 27 embassies as requested.

Back to regular programming. Pippa kicked off the morning programs with an unusual audio session: 'Ocean Sound—Acoustics in the Southern Ocean'. She played recorded snippets of all the Antarctic marine mammals as we imagined swimming alongside them twenty feet below the ocean's surface. I tried closing my eyes, but I kept imagining hungry sharks drifting into view, so I followed the jumping lines of audio tracings on the TV monitors instead. Pippa differentiated each chirp, squeak, and whale song by species. Some of the calls were slightly adjusted for our limited hearing range. The frequency of communication and the volume of undersea chatter astonished us all. Thus endeth the official series of staff lectures.

We took a fifteen-minute break before the next speaker—yours truly. I would be kicking off the first of four passenger lectures over the next two days. No pressure.

I sat down on one of the bar stools at the rear of the room next to Pippa during the break. One minute before the start Pippa leaned over from the next stool. In a quiet voice she asked, "Will this make people uncomfortable at all or be political?"

"It's a little late to ask that now," I thought.

I assured her that most folks would relate to the content and promised that no one would be offended. I added that I had delivered this presentation to many different audiences in north America with good result. I had also shortened it for this group to keep it on the lighter side. Her face relaxed, slightly. She stood and introduced me to the curious audience of 75 folks:

"We now have Don Jorgensen with the first of our passenger lectures, 'He Said, She Said: Gender Differences in Communication.'"

She handed the mic over to me and I made my way forward, doing my usual deep breathing exercise along the way. Maggie, our delightful new friend from Colorado, touched my arm. I paused to listen to her remind me that she worked as a couple's therapist and really looked forward to hearing my take on the issue.

Dorette stepped over to me as I reached the front and turned to face the crowd.

"I am very interested to hear your talk."

"Thank you." I reached for the microphone.

"I used to teach gender studies at a university in Amsterdam."

"No kidding!" I answered, taking one more deep breath.

OK, then.

Dorette, Amy, and the other members of the jury took their seats. I began speaking.

"Two items I want to address right up front," I began.

"First, I apologize for having a boring American accent, and not a beautifully lilting tone like Iain, Pippa or Celine." A few smiles appeared as heads nodded.

"Second, I do hereby vow that in all future presentations I will work in the phrase "It's a wee bit bouncy." A few more smiles. Off we went.

I kicked it off with a brief, amusing video depicting a typical male-female exchange ('You just want to fix everything...!") I confirmed that our understanding of gender roles and identity continues to grow and evolve, noting that Facebook now offers over 70 gender options for personal profiles, including an option to create your own—or leave it blank. I heard a few "wow's" as more heads nodded. The women sitting before me nodded in agreement when I warned the group that I would expose as fraudulent the traditional belief that the typical male communication style is normative and that common female communication styles are deviations from the norm. Different, yes. Better or worse, no.

A sample scenario from my talk:

"What did you talk about at the game?" That is the question my wife asks me when I get home after attending an Arizona basketball game with my good friend John. John and I have been going to the games for over three decades. He and his wife Jenifer are two of our closest friends.

I asked the men in the audience to answer the question for me.

"Guys, when my wife asks me what we talked about at the game, the answer is?"

They responded immediately. *"The game."*

Correct. I added that I also knew it was quite likely that my wife and Jenifer had, in fact, already completed a conversation over the telephone or over wine, or both WHILE John and I were at the game.

So, her response might likely be, *"Did John tell you that Julie was pregnant, or that Michael is coming to visit?"*

Me: *"No, we talked about the team schedule, and how this team compares to last year's team, and THE GAME."*

I offered common examples of how men commonly use communication with others to seek information, while women view communication foremost as a means to seek connection. The information vs. connection theme was highlighted by another scene:

As we were driving toward home...

"Do you want to go out for dinner tonight?" asks she.

"No, not really," I respond.

"Oh," comes the reply with a hint of disappointment.

Oh, Oh, I think to myself.

I asked the audience to shout out the correct answer to the dinner query.

"Yes?" guessed some of the younger men, tentatively.

"No?" ventured another brave young man.

Most of the women and older couples chuckled as several turned to smile upon the naïve young-uns.

"The best answer is...?" I asked the group.

"What would you like to do, dear?" called out a voice of experience.

The corollary to the Information vs Connection difference was the Goal focus vs. Process focus. I used to think that every question required a direct answer. Experience in marriage and politics set me straight on that one. Nope. Experience, otherwise known as "my wife," taught me that the question *"Do you want to go out for dinner"* is just the starting whistle for a discussion of whether to go or not to go, where to go, what to eat, when to leave, who else should we invite, where John and Jenifer went last week, and how this exchange compares to the discussion we had four years ago on the same topic.

And as I explained to my nephew on his wedding day: "Remember, every question is a test."

My bright, active audience of ocean trekkers kept it lively, especially when I threw out questions like: *"What are the 3 hardest words for a man to say?"*

I asked the women to wait a beat.

A few of the men ventured a guess, most look puzzled. Their response is barely audible.

The women shouted out the answer instantly: "I am sorry!"[*]

I wrapped up with two tips for partners of any gender:

1. Ask for what you need or let the other person know what you need, whether it is information, advice, or just support.
2. Actively engage verbally with the other person. Give them your honest attention. (Yes, put down the cellphone or the remote.)

---

[*] Rather than give you the answer in this book, I was tempted just to write "if you do not know, ask a woman. Then I thought that if you did not already know the answer, it is likely that you do not have a woman around to ask!

The younger members of the crowd usually congregated on the port side of the room and the more senior travelers to starboard. I appreciated the lively comments and applause at the end of the half-hour from all sides of the room.

Dorette nodded. "Very good," she said in her clipped Dutch accent.

Maggie smiled and nodded.

As I walked to the rear I was stopped by Jaroslav, a short, dark haired physician from Slovakia, who introduced himself. He was traveling with his wife and adult son and daughter.

"My son said that he now understands why his girlfriend broke up with him," he shared with a wide grin.

More than twenty folks who had listened to my talk stopped me over the next three days to share something they had enjoyed or learned from the presentation. That meant a lot. I have delivered speeches and presentations in venues around the world, but I had to admit that I felt rather good about my first 'cruise talk.'

Later at lunch Kathy admitted that she had rushed over from a mid-ship hallway yoga class to catch my lecture from the back of the lounge. She had snagged a seat by the bar next to the other Kate, a delightful silver-haired single traveler from Bristol, England. According to Kathy, when I concluded my talk Kate from Bristol leaned over to her and remarked,

"You must have a perfect marriage."

Kathy broke up laughing.

She chuckled again while reciting the story. So did I.

As Kathy and I exited the dining room Debra (not her real name), a friendly, attractive 40ish woman from the U.S. asked if she could speak with me. I had seen Debra and her male companion around the ship once or twice—with only 114 passengers you see everyone—but we had never spoken. I listened as she poured out her frustrations with her fiancé, whose reluctance to verbally engage with her had worsened as the stress of booking flights while facing an unknown world increased.

She acknowledged that the tension had led to second thoughts about their own future, which was complicated by a recent joint home purchase. Kathy and I tag-teamed some reality testing with her, and Kathy related her own experiences with yours truly. Note: I know when to stay quiet. She shared that as our relationship advanced and time becomes more precious, we always try limiting the time spent arguing or 'staying mad.' After 39 years together we have managed to cut it to about 20 minutes, at which point one or both of us realizes that a) maybe, just maybe, that person might have been a little bit wrong, or b) this is just a stupid argument and not worth the time, or both. It is usually both.

Debra gave a rueful smile and admitted that she and her fiancé had spoken little for the past two days. We suggested a few personal coping strategies and gave her a couple tips for opening their next conversation. Over the next three days she approached Kathy or me several times for follow-up conversations and updates. We kept an eye out for the two of them, hoping for signs of improvement. We spotted a few, but we were greatly relieved to learn that the couple had agreed to see a therapist back home.

Nick (the drunk guy from the fire drill) kicked off the afternoon with the second passenger lecture by declaring himself and expert on 'Snowology.' He entertained us with his deeply researched, slide-assisted explanation of very technical terms such as biggies (big snowflakes) and smallies (small snowflakes). He presented his ranking of the best snow movies (I believe 'Frozen' topped the list) and his assessment of the really, really serious global threats to snow, like snow cones and snowball fights. Hysterical. It was the perfect time for humor.

Real-life meteorologist Dave had a tough act to follow, but he succeeded with his serious climate talk addressing the weather systems that affect the Antarctic Peninsula. He discussed the causes of the recent record high temperatures in the region and explained how the change in the polar weather systems is related to global warming.

The most memorable lesson of the day came that evening; a surprise addition to the program from the quietest member of the expedition team, Felicity. Her captivating talk covered a brand-new subject with the unforgettable title: "Poo-nami. The Importance of Whale Poop in Carbon Capture."

Felicity transformed a silly-sounding topic into a wondrous bit of science fact. Employing just a few slides and easy-to-understand graphs, she highlighted the surprisingly important and effective carbon capture potential of whales. As she explained to an enraptured audience, whales accumulate carbon in their bodies during their long lives, some of which stretch to 200 years. The Felicity-named "Poonami" effect occurs when the whales die and their body full of carbon sinks to the bottom of the ocean. This mass amounts to an average of 33 tons of carbon dioxide. In contrast, a tree during the same life span contributes an amount equal to just 3 per cent of the carbon absorption of the whale.

Why does that matter? Wherever whales are found, so are phytoplankton. These tiny creatures produce every second breath we take, by contributing to at least 50 per cent of all the oxygen in our atmosphere. They also capture about 37 billion tons of carbon dioxide—the equivalent of four Amazon forests' worth. Whale poop has a multiplier effect on phytoplankton as it contains iron and nitrogen, the elements phytoplankton need to grow; so, the more whales, the more oxygen.

Sadly, whale populations today have shrunk considerably, representing just a fraction of what they once were. Biologists estimate that there are slightly more than 1.3 million whales in the ocean, a quarter of their pre-whaling number of 4 to 5 million. Yet the economic value of these creatures is immense. A report by the International Monetary Fund (who knew they studied whales?) put the value of the average great whale, according to conservative estimates, at more than US$2 million, and the current total value of all great whales at present over US$1 trillion.

So, whale poop matters. How did we not know this?

EIGHTEEN

HEADING FOR URUGUAY... OR EUROPE

"How far to the Netherlands?"

TUESDAY, MARCH 24: CRUISE DAY 16

POSITION:	36°41,5'S / 55° 10,8'W
WIND:	NNE 5
WEATHER:	CLEAR SKY
AIR TEMPERATURE:	+23C

The sun glinted off the sparkling Atlantic. I inhaled the invigorating salt breeze. Albatross and petrels glided by in search of breakfast on the waves. Thanks to Celine's on-deck tutorials I now had a clue about the identities of the circling wildlife. I had sworn off the hot chocolate now that temperatures nudged the 70F mark. Definitely no longer the cruise we signed up for, I thought.

237

I closed my eyes and let the breeze chill through my thin t-shirt. After three uses the shirt needed the air more than I did.

My cellphone buzzed. I opened a text from my brother-in-law Steve, who had been tracking our progress online:

"This is from the US Embassy in Uruguay:

The government of Uruguay has implemented measures to limit the spread of COVID-19. All international passenger flights are suspended as of March 23, 2020. We are considering all options to assist U.S. citizens in Uruguay. Continue to monitor the US Embassy's website for updates. Please e-mail MontevideoACS@ state.gov if you have an urgent need to depart."

I typed out a quick response:

"We are getting two stories—have found that the US Embassy has not been the most reliable source to date. As of this morning flights were still a go. Subject to change without notice of course. A charter flight is trying to get arranged, but only for folks with the second flight from Santiago or Sao Paulo. A possible back- up option. We have the Sierra Club in touch with Oceanwide and getting our info to the Embassy as well. Hope for another update in PM. Right now docking is set for tomorrow."

Moments later Steve texted this gem.

"There is a ship that was refused entry to all ports in South America and now is going from Chile to Florida—if they let it go through the

Panama Canal. The Zaandam, and it has 42 sick people aboard. I'm telling you, Uruguay is better than here...."

I answered:

"I would stay. Kathy would kill. Reportedly LATAM is still providing repatriation flights."

Steve:

"Good luck. It is going to be dicey, I think. There are 40 cruise ships out there that cannot dock. South America seems to be the worst right now."

"By the way, you are almost directly over the wreck of the German pocket battleship Graf Spee."

Steve is a former Navy submariner and an expert internet navigator, so I trusted his information and appreciated his knowledge of the world at sea. I ran into Mal a few minutes later and showed him the note about the wreck. He also thought that bit of trivia was fascinating. A tall, severe-looking German standing by the window overheard our conversation about the sunken boat. He leaned in, eyes twinkling and posed a question.

"Do you know what lies twitching at the bottom of the ocean?"
I offered the expected response. "No. What?"
A nervous wreck."

I chuckled. Not bad, I thought. It was the first time I had seen that guy smile in two weeks. I guess dad jokes are universal.

Rumors of the Zaandam crisis had filtered through the ship for the past 24 hours, but no one on board knew how badly the passengers had fared. According to a story in the Washington Post, the coronavirus infected passengers and crew on at least 55 ships that sailed in the waters off nearly every continent, about a fifth of the total global fleet. The virus killed at least 65 people who traveled or worked on the ships, although the full scope of deaths is unknown.

Two ships, the Celebrity Eclipse and the Coral Princess, had reported 150 coronavirus cases and six deaths among their passengers. On the Coral Princess, passengers had received a letter on March 20 from the senior physician assuring them that the risk of the ship's exposure was "near negligible." Two people died on the Coral Princess before passengers were allowed to disembark in Miami.

I did not know about those two tragic cruises, but as the Plancius sailed into the waters outside Montevideo we did hear about the Zaandam—a cruise liner carrying 2047 passengers and crew. Before that cruise ended April 2, the virus would claim four lives and sicken hundreds as port after port turned the Zaandam away.

Our greatest concern had been realized on board the much larger Holland America ship; the Zaandam had indeed been left to fend for herself.

Holland America's president penned an op-ed a few weeks later, stating that "It's tempting to speculate about the illnesses that may have been avoided or lives saved if we'd gotten the assistance we sought weeks ago."

As the Zaandam coursed north, more people got sick. On March 24, 77 people were ill, including 47 crew members. Three days later the cruise line announced that four passengers had died and 138 people on board were sick. The Zaandam tried to medically evacuate two critically ill patients with COVID-19 to Mexico, but the Mexican authorities turned them down.

The Zaandam struggled to return to Florida, having been denied docking at ports along the South American west coast and initially blocked from transiting the Panama Canal and returning to Miami. The callous, short-sighted governor of Florida refused to offer any humanitarian assistance, stating that it was the cruise line's responsibility to care for its sick and that dropping off a load of ill people in the community "didn't sound good." He ignored the fact that the Zaandam's passenger list included two dozen Floridians.

"Good morning, everyone, good morning." Iain brought everyone to attention by announcing that he had a 'wee bit' more news this morning. The latest Oceanwide update had arrived. The lounge grew silent.

Vlissingen, 23th March 2020

Dear Passengers, Captain, Crew and Staff,

We have just heard from one of the embassies that this evening that, one of the other vessels in the same situation as ours, that was waiting for disembarking their passengers, have successfully done so through the "corridor sanitaire" as instated by the authorities in Montevideo.

The embassy states that they have no reason to believe that the same would not work for those still having to disembark passengers in the coming days, and thus we hope we will get the confirmation of our port days soon. We have now asked for 25 and 26 March but as said, we are awaiting confirmation.

The letter continued:

One of the embassies have informed as follows:

Flight schedules and availability remains subject to change and / or cancellation at very short notice. The embassies understanding is that flights to Sao Paolo and Santiago are still available. LATAM confirmed that there are 20+ seats available for general sale via GDS* from MVD to SCL on Thursday 26th March with an onward connection to London with British airways on Friday 27th March.

We also know that embassies are still working hard to make other (commercial) flights available. That is not an easy process and we do not know if this will be in time. They are keeping us updated.

About the information sent earlier today about a possible charter flight we once again need to state that this is an initiative from a travel-agent and we are not further involved in this, nor with any onward travel.

The number of flights that might be available during our port dates we do not know unfortunately, as you understand this is changing

---

* The Global Distribution System (GDS) is a network that enables travel agencies and their clients to access travel data and book travel.

continuously, we also do not know if there will be enough flights for everybody.

We want to state, and this is important to realize, that there will be a time that we need to proceed with our vessels. If there is no outlook to either commercial flights and/or Government operated flights at short notice, our vessels will have to continue onwards. Even though, how much we would like you to travel homebound, if restrictions prohibit us to disembark you, we need to accept that and deal with that situation.

Between Montevideo and the vessels final destination Vlissingen, The Netherlands, there are not really viable ports anymore; either due to the current restrictions of mandatory quarantine period of 14 days when disembarking the vessel (even given the time already spent onboard), or not accepting the vessels at all.

We only want to disembark people when there is a reasonable expectation to reach their homeport and not being stranded at an airport, or being quarantined in a foreign country, and we hope as well that you understand we cannot call every port underway in order to try disembarkation.

This might have an unfortunate result that some of you will have to remain on the ship until we reach Vlissingen, The Netherlands. That is a rather long journey of approx. 3.5 weeks.

We understand that each and every one of you has a clear wish to go home as soon as possible. Unfortunately the current situation in the world does not provide us the opportunity to do so in a quick way. We have no influence on the restrictions Governments put in place and have to deal with the limitations that these bring.

Should it turn out that as mentioned above, we can only provide you the continued safe environment of our vessels which, we will off course do so.

After our call in Montevideo, our vessels will have enough provisions for all onboard and enough bunkers to reach Vlissingen.

But such a journey requires a lot!

From you, our passengers, but also from our Crew and staff.

As once we set sail from Montevideo, it's important to realize that this is for a period of 3,5 weeks.

On the other hand, in many places in the world, people are required to remain inside their houses for the same period of time in order to avoid further spreading of the COVID-19 Virus.

By being in contact with your relatives and from reading news online, we assume that you have a better picture of what the situation in the world is today.

The situation you are in, is very unfortunate and we hope for your continued understanding and support.

Then lastly, a practical matter:

We have opened up the internet for your convenience but have learnt that because of extreme usage (which we do understand), your and our email did not transfer during a large part of the day. We see heavy downloads of computer and program updates in traffic logs and we would really urge you to refrain from large downloads. We need our communication means to be available at all times.

Therefore we might on certain moments need to temporarily shut down access, this is for making essential communication or receiving essential navigation information possible. We will open it back up again, as soon as possible. We hope for your understanding.

We trust to have informed you for the moment.

Michel van Gessel—CEO
Mark van der Hulst—COO
Oceanwide Expeditions

Hands flew up. Iain calmly fielded each question. He responded time and again with the same response, "I have no additional information." I scanned the lounge. Half of the heads tilted forward; eyes and ears intent on capturing every nuance and utterance.

The rest of the crowd leaned over cellphones and pads, frantically seeking a connection to the outside world. Humid air tinged with a slight aroma of panic filled the room. Stress pacers roamed the narrow spaces as thirty- and forty-somethings fretted about missing work. Nervous laughter and jokes about being marooned on a ship to nowhere trickled out from various corners. Crew members whose contracts had already ended maintained their professional façade. A handful of them admitted to me during a few private asides that they were experiencing the same frustrations. I could not traverse a single hallway or deck that day without stepping around a frantic typist fighting for a connection as airplane seats or entire flights disappeared.

After Iain finished his update our gang of eighteen gathered to check each person's travel status as we cycled through the latest good news and bad news.

Good News: Another ship has docked at Montevideo and passengers successfully transited the corridor sanitaire to the airport. Flights were still taking off.

Bad News: The Plancius had not received approval for docking at Montevideo, and we were likely to come in range of the port later that evening.

Good News: There were still seats available on a shrinking number of flights out from Montevideo to either Santiago, Chile or Sao Paulo, Brazil.

Bad News: Fewer flights and fewer seats remained on limited flights over the next two days.

More Bad News: All flights—even those that were already booked—remained subject to change and/or cancellation with very short notice.

Good News: There was still talk of a charter flight being arranged by another travel agent supposedly in contact with the US embassy.

Bad News: We had no confirmation of a charter flight, nor any details regarding when, where to or from, how many passengers, or how much it would cost per passenger.

Good News: Oceanwide was taking full responsibility for all passengers on its vessels, and no one would be kicked off the ship and left high and dry.

Bad News: If Montevideo was closed to us, or if we were unable to arrange for travel home, a 3.5-week transatlantic cruise awaits.

Good News: The internet connection was open free of charge to everyone on board.

Bad News: An ongoing crush of internet usage led to frequent shutdowns to allow for official traffic.

We were sailing through limbo. Nervous compatriots compared their queasy stomachs to the discomfort of crossing the Drake Passage once again. The triple crown of fear, anxiety and stress had reached its peak. Frustrations erupted and passive-aggressive behavior played out before our eyes. As I relaxed out in the lounge with a few travel companions a young woman stomped past us and flopped down at the next table. We listened in—it was impossible not to—as she exhaled theatrically and whined to her compadres, "I guess we are not allowed to have fun anymore!" Apparently, her little band of revelers had been asked to leave the bar last night after complaints arose from disturbed sleepers in nearby cabins. Elsewhere in the room an occasional 'I don't know!' hissed from nearby couches where couples traded exasperated shrugs or stares while stabbing at their phones.

I went wild racking up nickel-per-text charges as I reached out to Linda several times that day. I tried to keep watch for any American Airlines or LATAM notices or investigate the latest travel rumor floating through the ship. Kathy joined me and we briefly contemplated a return trip to the Netherlands. We had enjoyed a wonderful three days exploring the streets and museums of Amsterdam nine months earlier, but we were not quite packed and ready for a return visit. On the serious side, we anticipated that trying to get home from Europe while the pandemic continued its global devastation was not a likely prospect for mid-April and beyond.

Irregular morning programming commenced with a mix of guest lectures, an indoor passenger-led aerobics class, a group workout outside on the upper deck, and another bird-watching session with Celine. The first talk featured Maria, a medical specialist with a program on TMJ disorders. Maria's program was followed by a presentation given by our couples' counselor-friend Maggie. Pippa made me laugh when she whispered that Maggie's tips would come in handy for cruise staff who had yet to inform their partners back home that they had to remain at sea another three and a half weeks.

A few passengers viewed a potential transatlantic voyage as an acceptable option, and at least one person preferred it when compared to what he faced at home. My new friend Jaroslav from Slovakia was struggling to arrange for flights to Paris, figuring that they could make their way home more easily from the European airport. He figured that the worse-case scenario—staying on board—would still bring them closer to home. Not preferable, he admitted, as he was expected back to resume his medical practice, but not awful according to wife Eva.

Pedro, a young entrepreneur from Buenos Aires, wished to stay on board for the duration. He said that Buenos Aires had completely shut down and all work had been stopped. He could not go to his office. He had no food at home, nothing to do, and believed he could be arrested if he were found out on the streets. He was quite content to work remotely from the ship and wait it out in the Netherlands.

Most of the hotel and kitchen staff hailed from the Philippines. The servers and cleaning crews seemed quite content with the prospect of a longer cruise. When I returned to my cabin after lunch I ran into Nito, our slight, dark-haired, indefatigable cabin steward. He smiled a hello and I asked him how the change in plans affected his fellow crew members and him.

"Not too much." Nito answered.

"How so?" I queried.

Nito explained that most of the regular cruise staff had planned to stay on board anyway and they would be paid until arrival in Vlissingen. He expected that upon arrival most of his fellow crew would look for temporary housing or nearby apartment rentals until regular cruises resumed or safe travel home to the Philippines were possible. He said that he preferred staying in the Netherlands, which he assumed would be more likely to offer a safer and healthier place to quarantine than home.

Alex called us to lunch at 12:30pm on the dot. I wandered into the dining room, hit the hand sanitizer, and spotted Kathy holding two seats in our usual domain. I perused the menu with amusement, then entertained our table with a sport announcer's recitation of the inventive descriptions of the three dishes offered. Each item was constructed with the exact same components as the previous dinner—only now dressed, cut, or sauced differently. "Sorry sports fans, last night's artfully pureed white beans have been traded to start as today's navy bean soup."

"In other news, Yesterday's Mexican beef concoction is making a comeback as a Hungarian beef delicacy. But as any Budapest coach will tell you, *Paprika alone does not a Hungarian dish make.*" Nevertheless, the new offerings kept the chef's streak of delicious dishes alive and we applauded the chef's inventiveness and imaginative menu descriptions.

On the first night of our excursion Margie had asked us all to keep cellphones put away at meals and engage in conversation with one another. I appreciated the self-imposed rule and our group faithfully adhered to it throughout the journey. Until now. Jim and Bill were among the travelers who had not yet confirmed flight reservations, so their phones sat plate side while on hold for one of the few airlines still operating. Neither phone came to life during the meal. We sympathized.

After staring out at a listless sea for a while I re-entered the lounge to watch a relaxed young American male duke it out with an intense German man of similar age over the chess board in an exciting (for chess) tournament final. Low stress beat high stress. Rustyn congratulated the winner, then invited all comers to join in the final competition of the cruise—a ship wide scavenger hunt. Each two-person team was handed a sheet with a list of 25 items to locate or tasks to carry out in various places around the ship. The list contained challenges like:

- *What is the capacity of each lifeboat?*
- *What the original name of the M/V Plancius?*
- *What is Captain Artur's home country?*
- *Take a funny picture with one of the crew.*
- *Take a video of your team singing a song on the bow.*

Teams were given a two-hour time limit to complete as many tasks as possible by 4pm. I had a headache and was feeling a bit out of sorts, so Kathy and Meg teamed up for this one. Kathy will admit, under duress, that her kind-hearted husband did pitch in to help record their stirring rendition of 'Row, Row, Row Your Boat' and perhaps offered a few well-timed tips, like "You might find the lifeboat specs posted in the third deck hallway." They powered through, answered all the questions, and completed all the tasks before the deadline to finish in the top ten. Not bad.

To avoid getting trampled by stampeding teams rushing through the corridors I chose to work out in my cabin. I tend to get restless if I have not exercised for two or three days. (My cabinmate might prefer the word "irritable" but I would strenuously...not disagree.)

I had snapped at Kathy with a too sharp 'no' when she asked if I wanted to join the hunt. When I apologized my wife heartily suggested that a workout might be an exceptionally good idea. She was right, of course. (Do not tell her I said that.)

We both wanted to stay as healthy as possible for the ship-to-home gauntlet—assuming we could get off the ship sometime before Christmas. We had restarted downing Airborne tablets and other vitamins as well as kicking up the exercise. Kathy struggles on long flights, suffering extreme jet lag and 'feeling crummy' for a week or so after returning home. I am rarely bothered by either. I don't sleep much anywhere, not even at home where six hours is the maximum, so I use long flights to catch up on movies, read books and eat everything offered. Airplane calories do not count, right?

I returned to the lounge around 4:30 to sample the snack of the day and catch up on the latest rumors. I mentally placed the scattered passengers into three categories. The first group included individuals with confirmed flight reservations sprawled in window-facing chairs enjoying the late afternoon sun with books in hand. In the mid-lounge area, a surprising number of young and old sat frozen in chairs, eyes fixed at their lap, willing the internet to grant them access or for a 'flight confirmation' message to allow them to exhale.

The third group, which included Kathy and I, relaxed together with our diet cokes or wine to review completed travel plans and compare expectations. We each envisioned an altered version of the world depending on recent news from home. Margie and Kate reviewed the stricter stay-at-home guidelines already in place in California. The Florida contingent (Bill and Dottie) and the

Arizona group (Kathy, Meg, and I) had seen no such state requirements beyond store closures. Judy from Iowa had heard of no such
restrictions and neither did Jim and Wendee from Illinois.

Margie did confirm that the Sierra Club had enrolled all of us
in the State Department's Smart Traveler Enrollment Program
(STEP). STEP is a free service provided by the U.S. Government
for U.S. citizens who are traveling to, or living in, a foreign country.
According to the program, once STEP is provided with information about our trip abroad the Department of State can use it to
assist us in case of an emergency. Reportedly the traveler would
also receive the latest safety and security information for the destination country (like, perhaps, Uruguay) to make informed deci-
sions about their travel. I appreciated the Sierra Club's prompt
action on our behalf. As of that moment, no one in our group had
received any direct contact from the U.S. Embassy. In the end no
one ever did receive any direct communications, though I did have
a discussion with a U.S. Embassy official once we arrived at the
airport in Montevideo.

I continued to search for official news snippets and government updates but could find no coherent guidance from the
White House or the State Department. Quite the opposite, in
fact. Scattered reports from across the nation did align on one
point. All texts and e-mails from everyone's family and friends
warned us of massive and growing outages of toilet paper. Kathy
asked me to text Matt, her longtime friend who was house- and
dog-sitting for us. He assured us that we had an ample supply on
hand. Thank you, Matt!

The 6:30pm recap came and went with no significant news
reported from any outside source. The back-and-forth discussion

focused on the rumors of a charter flight to the U.S. routed through Sao Paulo. Most current updates seemed to originate from a 'passenger's sister's travel agent friend' or similar source.

Each potential charter passenger faced a 'chicken and egg' scenario. Supposedly the plane—if available—could not be chartered and would not take off without a sufficient number of paying passengers.

That meant that all potential charter customers would be forced to commit financially before knowing whether the flight was confirmed, and without knowing the cost per seat. For Kathy and I that would require establishing a second travel itinerary through different cities at double or triple the cost. Or not.

Skeptical flyers threw out more unanswerable questions. What airline or private charter would be flying this plane? Where would it land and what connections would be possible? Do they have authorization to fly as a repatriation flight? Since the Uruguayan government required advance documentation of our flight confirmations, how would they react to receiving multiple itineraries from the same passengers? Skepticism rose as excitement faded. By the end of the discussion I rated the likelihood of a charter rescue plane as unlikely. With our AA/LATAM bird already in hand, I opted not to consider the charter flight possibility any further.

An older woman complained about the weak air conditioning available in the cabins and the stuffy air permeating the ship. Iain explained that the Plancius was designed and fitted for polar voyages, quite unlike a luxury liner with heavy duty A/C units positioned on every deck. The system was working mightily, he said, but losing the battle to the warm Atlantic air. Although his explanation seemed plausible, a restless minority were not buying it. A surprising number of queasy passengers struggled with a recurrence of nausea brought on by the warm, cramped quarters rumbling across still rolling seas. Our writer acquaintance Rebecca had been AWOL for two days until she reappeared this afternoon, pale-faced and eager to get home.

The cleanup crew waited patiently as our post-dinner conversation ranged from memories of Antarctic highlights (was it really just a few days ago?) to the constantly shifting plans for disembarkation and the uncertain future that awaited us back in the States. One person read the now famous quote from #45, when he predicted that the virus would be gone by Easter. I recited the current numbers reported on various news sites. They indicated:

COVID cases now exceeded 50,000 in the US.

471 Americans dead from the virus.

The table quieted. Kathy took pity on the servers and herded us out just as the intercom came to life. *"Good evening, everyone, good evening. Please come to the Observation Lounge in five minutes for an update."* The latest missive had arrived from the head office.

Vlissingen, 24th March 2020, 5.30pm

Dear Passengers, Captain, Crew and Staff, and Agents

We have finally received confirmation that our vessels Plancius and Ortelius will enter the port of Montevideo this evening.

Please confirm or make your travel bookings urgently! Preferably for 25th, 26th or 27th

Our crew onboard will need this information as soon as possible.

The British embassy informed us that we have a very good chance to get everybody underway and they expect flight availability at least until the weekend.

LATAM is reacting on demand and we have informed them our needs.

You will need to make a booking as long as flights available.

Disembarkation will be through the corridor sanitaire which means the following:

- Passengers will only be allowed to disembark if they have a confirmed flight, and the Uruguayan government has confirmation that that flight is en route to Uruguay.
- Passengers will be screened as they leave by the health authority, and all passengers must wear gloves and masks. We will provide these.
- Once disembarked, passengers will be escorted straight to the airport by coach, where they will have to wait in a prepared area for their flights.

Trust to have informed you.

Michel van Gessel—CEO
Mark van der Hulst—COO
Oceanwide Expeditions

"Damn" and "not again" echoed through the corridors as efforts to secure flights home escalated from frustrated to frantic. I heard no more boasts about how someone saved money by booking through Expedia, or why they never used a travel agent. I made sympathetic noises while stair sitters and hall squatters complained about their cheap air travel sites freezing up, or how the LATAM website kicked them off when they finally progressed to the payment page, only to see the price for a seat increase as they reconnected. I would definitely send flowers to Linda when we got home.

Iain confirmed that the Plancius was approved for docking later that evening or early morning Wednesday. He cautioned, however, that despite the assurances contained in the latest letter he believed that the actual process for disembarkation at Montevideo was still evolving. He instructed all passengers who were scheduled to fly home on the next day, March 25th, to have their suitcases packed and sitting outside their cabin doors before breakfast. Everyone was instructed to remain on standby for further directions.

After six full days of 'will we or won't we' I had grown tired of oscillating between anxious anticipation and optimism. Kathy's worry meter had long since redlined.

She did pose several particularly good questions, and in fairness I think that she only repeated them EVERY THIRTY MINUTES. Were all our travel documents in order? Would the authorities let us off the ship? Will flights be cancelled? What happens when we hit U.S. Customs? Will both bags make it? Will the dog remember me?

I am a huge Jeopardy fan. I grew up watching the original show with my mother, and Jana grew up watching the Alex Trebek version with me. We both still record each episode, so we never miss a single 'Final Jeopardy" clue. As Kathy took a breath after rattling off her latest worries, I turned to her, shrugged, and said, "Unanswerable Questions for a $1000, Alex."

The next morning's travel advisory from the Embassy did not ease her mind.

NINETEEN

MAROONED AT THE DOCK

"Our worst-case scenario…"

WEDNESDAY, MARCH 25: CRUISE DAY 17

POSITION:	34°89'S / 56°19'W
WIND:	NNE 5
WEATHER:	CLEAR SKY
AIR TEMPERATURE:	+24C

I stood watch at the bow as the Plancius sailed into Montevideo harbor. We arrived dockside at 7:00am and tied up behind the other new arrival—our sister ship Ortelius. Past the docks on the port side I caught a glimpse of a larger cruise ship, its name obscured by one of many small towers of cargo containers awaiting transport. From the starboard deck I peered past a field of concrete and dirt bordering a tree-lined park, and beyond that spied a downtown portion of the Uruguayan capital. The partial view featured a mix of old and new office towers, a centuries-old stone edifice rising from a second smaller park area, and an early 20th century-looking train station that may or may not be functional.

My cellphone pinged with its "Welcome to Uruguay" greeting. I now had full service. Texts and e-mails flooded in.

March 24, 2020—Japan's Prime Minister Shinzo Abe and International Olympic Committee (IOC) president Thomas Bach agree to postpone the Olympics until 2021 amid the outbreak.

That makes sense, I thought, though I would miss watching the games while relaxing in the cool West Seattle summer, or more likely given the pandemic, an air-conditioned Tucson breeze.

The next message grabbed my full attention:

Travel Alert—U.S. Embassy, Montevideo, Uruguay (March 25, 2020)

Location: Uruguay
Event: All regularly scheduled commercial flights have been cancelled.

All regularly scheduled commercial flights departing Uruguay have been cancelled. Availability is extremely limited on intermittent commercial flights. U.S. citizens should contact their airlines if they have purchased a ticket to depart Uruguay to confirm flight status.

U.S. citizens whose flights have been cancelled and are seeking a flight to the U.S. should contact the embassy at MontevideoACS@state.gov.

For each member of your group, please include: (1) name as it appears on passport, (2) date of birth, (3) U.S. passport number, (4) telephone number and WhatsApp number, (5) current location, and (6) special medical or other considerations.

I breathed in and out once through my nose, lips tight. What does this mean, I wondered?

Are we good to go or not? Were our flights home considered "regularly scheduled commercial flights" or repatriation flights as described in previous Embassy Alerts? I felt myself getting annoyed and "prickly", as Kathy calls it. This constant, underlying state of unease expressed by many on board had infected me that morning. I wondered about our fellow Clubbers. Jason and Kathy were set to leave today for Detroit, and Jim and Wendee were also scheduled to fly home to Chicago via Sao Paulo this afternoon. Most of our group was scheduled to leave tomorrow and a few more, including Judy, were staying on board two nights before leaving on Friday, the 27th—the ship's final day in port before setting sail for the Netherlands.

Jason checked his phone. He read that their flights were still listed as confirmed through Detroit, but Jim could not get through to the airlines website to confirm their flights home to Chicago. I sent a quick note to Linda asking her to recheck our reservations— probably my 20th request since this odyssey began. Last night I did receive a confirmation that Kathy and I were checked-in for our flights to Santiago and Miami. LATAM had even sent my electronic boarding pass overnight, although Kathy had not received hers. The note accompanying the check-in confirmation instructed her to pick it up at the airport. Normally that would not be worrisome, but under the current circumstances EVERYTHING was cause for concern. Kathy is, as I mentioned, a world-class worrier. I think when everything is going fine, she worries about having nothing to worry about, so this little glitch only served to raise our collective stress level higher until we received re-confirmation of 'no change.' Thank you, U.S. Embassy, for that little scare.

Iain and Alex took turns on the intercom to call out updated instructions throughout the morning for disembarkation. They advised all exiting passengers about how to prepare for each step of the 'corridor sanitaire' as new messages were relayed from the Uruguayan officials and Embassies to Oceanwide Expeditions and the Plancius. Kathy and I wandered restlessly between the crowded, stuffy lounge and the humid, sun-drenched deck. The outside areas offered a slight breeze to offset the rising heat, but the sun grew fierce as the day progressed. Our team of eighteen had agreed that a handful of us would remain in the lounge and summon the others for each new announcement.

Passengers who were scheduled to leave that day—a total of 29 plus 3 of the expedition crew—were instructed to gather their carryon items and wait on the starboard side of the lounge; the rest of us could take up the port side of the lounge. As the day dragged on the artificial barrier disappeared. No one cared as it was replaced by constant conversations and repeated hugging.

A rotating jumble of thoughts and emotions raced through my head. I felt a bit relieved that we sat one step closer to getting home. I gained an appreciation for this small nation that I had never thought twice about—well, not even once really. In contrast to the abrupt closure of Argentinian ports, the uncaring treatment of cruise ships on the western south American coastline, and those marooned around the Caribbean and Florida, the government of Uruguay had allowed us to dock at Montevideo and were actively coordinating with multiple government and corporate officials to help get us home safely. Nevertheless, I remained apprehensive and uncertain about the next two days, fully aware that each piece of the travel puzzle could change or disappear at any moment.

We still faced the prospect of navigating through three countries, four airports, and two customs lines. I could easily foresee a last minute cancellation by American Airlines, a LATAM shutdown, a State Department snafu, or one of a hundred failures or erratic proclamations from the White House that could leave us stranded on a dock or at an airport—or on a boat bound for Europe. Oh, and we were about to re-enter a world that had fundamentally changed during our absence. I cannot say that I knew what to expect. None of us did.

Any distraction during the morning was welcome as I stood ruminating on the upper deck, so I looked down to the waterline to watch the bunkering. A bulky petrol ship pulled alongside our boat. I followed the skillful manipulations of the crew as they connected the large bibs and hoses and refueled the Plancius for a three-and-a-half-week voyage across the Atlantic. A few minutes later I moved up to the bow to observe Dragan directing the dockside workers and ship's crew as they swung the massive pallets of fruit, vegetables, and meat with boxes and boxes of canned goods and other provisions onto the lower deck. The workers then unhitched the pallets from the deck crane, attached them to the ship's crane and lowered all the items into the hold. A few of the workers were wearing masks or bandannas, but most were barefaced. One or two workers would stop from time to time and throw a wary glance up at us. During the morning briefing we had been warned by order of the Uruguayan authorities to stay on deck five or higher if we ventured outside. The crew may have likewise feared catching the virus from us, or perhaps they were just not used to an audience.

The next scheduled event was titled 'Kathy Crying Time.' After nearly three weeks at sea we were about to call our daughter. Kathy and Jana usually talked and texted at least four times a day. Kathy swears it is less than that, but I think it is more and she just doesn't tell me about all the quick hello's or check-ins. I could not be happier, though, that they have such a close relationship. I think all her purchases of 'How to Raise a Difficult Child' books during Jana's pre-school through middle school years paid off. I am not sure Kathy realized that every time she got exasperated and exclaimed "She is her father's daughter" I took it as a compliment. Jana has always been strong-willed and strong-minded, all of which led her to a challenging and successful career, marriage, and new son. I could not be prouder of what she and Brendan have accomplished.

I located the best cell signal on the forward deck. As soon as Jana's voice resonated through the phone Kathy laughed through flowing tears. Jana had stayed in touch with our travel agent Linda during the past week, and she and I had managed to exchange occasional text messages, but this was the first direct contact since we had left Ushuaia. We had been assuring each other throughout the ordeal that everything and everyone was fine, but you never believe it fully until you can hear the other person's voice tone directly. We had also learned that Jana was considered an 'essential worker' in the U.S. and we were unclear how that might have put her in harm's way.

I was greatly relieved that Jana, Brendan and 4-month-old Ryan had moved out of New York right before the massive outbreak. Brendan was able to work from home, but Jana still had to travel into the city a few times a week. I relaxed when I confirmed that the new mom and dad were healthy and that happy, noisy Ryan was doing great.

The ship's intercom buzzed to life just as I put away the phone. Iain announced that the disembarkation process would begin at 1:00pm. Anyone leaving the ship had to be in the lounge by 12:45.

The dining room opened early for lunch, each table buzzing with tense anticipation, nervousness, or impatience. Everyone was on edge. The 'go group' were eager to leave before their flight was cancelled or a random government official changed their mind. The "tomorrow crew" to which Kathy and I belonged planned to stand out on deck with hopes of observing a smooth and orderly process. Table talk wrapped up quickly. The savvy veteran travelers had already assembled mini-sandwiches and grabbed fruit from the morning breakfast offerings. Newbies grabbed the remaining cheese and crackers from the lunch leftovers. Our dining room servers proved as helpful as ever. Before anyone asked, they appeared tableside with plastic wrap and aluminum foil to help pack up the snacks.

By 12:30pm the lounge overflowed with restless humanity. Bodies circulated around the room as new friends posed for last minute selfies or traded goodbye hugs with travel buddies. The clock struck 1:00pm and…Nothing happened.

I ventured out into the bright, sticky afternoon to squint past the length of the ship along the dock. No official vehicles in sight, and not a single bus appeared. I watched a skinny, sun-darkened peddler push his ancient ice cream cart past our ship down to the opposite end of the dock where a small crew lazily unloaded a large fishing vessel. He waved hello as I and a dozen others tracked his progress. He sauntered back a few minutes later, acknowledging us with a slight nod. Nothing but the distant sounds of dockworkers moving cargo and light traffic broke through the cloudless silence.

Kathy called me back inside as Pippa descended from the bridge to deliver the latest update.

"We were told that the busses should arrive at 1:30." She relayed.

She had assumed the briefing responsibilities from Iain, who was packed and lined up to leave the Plancius with the first wave. He offered a guilty nod as he apologized for abandoning his post before all passengers had left. We smiled and told him to get off the ship. His first baby was due within the week, and the race for home was already delayed by five days.

Doctor Helleke arrived to review the specific procedures established for entering the corridor sanitaire:

1. Before stepping off the ship each passenger must be wearing the sanitary gloves and mask that would be handed to them by Helleke. The doctor proceeded to demonstrate how to put each item on. She warned everyone not to take them off at any point in the journey.
2. Passports and flight documents must be in hand.

3. As each person stepped off the gangway onto the dock the government authorities would confirm their name on the appropriate flight manifests.
4. Once confirmed each passenger must walk directly to the bus for immediate boarding.

Pippa returned to read a brief notice just received from Oceanwide headquarters.

The following message has been sent to our passengers, staff and crew on board, and our agents:

Vlissingen, 25th March 2020

Dear Passengers, Captain, Crew and Staff and Agents,

Important notice:
Now the vessels are underway to Montevideo, which is a safe port of disembarkation, with arrival early this morning passengers will *need* to book flights and disembark.

Also embassies are urging their residents to book flights and get home asap. As flights are available, staying onboard is NOT an option.

We hope you understand, as we always have stated, that we wanted to bring our passengers to a safe port and until then they could remain onboard. Now this safe port has been reached and everybody can travel home.

We would like to thank you for your patience and understanding and wish you safe travels home.

Trust to have informed you.

Michel van Gessel—CEO
Mark van der Hulst—COO
Oceanwide Expeditions

Translation: Get off our ship!

My Buenos Aires friend Carlos raced to one of the two available laptops in the library. His plan to stay onboard to enjoy a free ride to the Netherlands was not going to happen. I asked him if he could take a ferry to travel the 500 kilometers upriver to his home port.

"Nothing is running. The docks are completely shut down."

His only choice was to fly across the continent to Santiago, Chile and then hope for a connecting flight back—if there were any. He bounced back and forth between the laptop and his cell phone for hours, until finally that evening securing a seat on the only remaining flight from Santiago to Buenos Aires.

At 1:45pm I heard a shout from the outside deck. Official looking SUVs, sedans and a single pickup truck with a flashing light bar rolled toward the Plancius. The drivers emerged and shuffled unhurriedly around their vehicles. They gathered in casual groups of two or three, occasionally breaking off their conversations to glance up at the three decks full of gawkers peering down at them. above. A contingent of five men and one woman, all in black suits and ties arrived in two more SUVs—also black—and proceeded to the dockside end of the gangway. They ignored the humid afternoon heat as they traded greetings with a casually dressed man who emerged from a gray sedan, likely the local dock agent employed by Oceanwide. No American flags or embassy insignias were visible on any cars or clothing. One of the officials spoke frequently into his cellphone, but no other action took place.

Around 2:00pm I heard a faint squeaking of brakes and shifting of gears. A single bus appeared in the distance, growing larger as it drove on to the concrete dock and parked, but not at the Plancius. It settled a tantalizing 500 feet away next to the Ortelius. Was another bus on its way? No, as it turned out. We watched with growing impatience as this other lucky group trickled off their ship and one-by-one climbed up the steps and entered the bus.

An hour (seemed like ten hours) later the bus growled back to life and crawled its way forward to sit about 20 meters from the Plancius gangway. The ship's crane lifted the large net filled with suitcases and duffel bags high off the bow deck before swinging and lowering the cargo softly down next to the bus. The bus driver and dock agent removed the bags from the net and lined them up beside the vehicle.

We ducked back into the lounge as restless passengers rushed through a second round of goodbyes, but anxiety levels remained high. Nearly half of the group were scheduled to leave on the 4:30pm flight to Sao Paulo. The clock read 2:45pm. I walked back out to the starboard deck to check for any signs of progress. Still no action. I joined a group of 10 more observers to discuss all the worst-case-scenarios created by the global pandemic. One of the older men sneezed. "We didn't hear that!" I called out. It got a large, tension-relieving laugh. Timing is everything.

At 3:00pm the word came down via Pippa. Thirty-two anxious travelers shrugged on backpacks, picked up carry-ons and headed down the stairs toward the gangway corridor. I found an open spot along the starboard rail. Kathy squeezed in next to me to watch the slow parade of passengers leave the ship and march down the gangway, fully gloved and masked.

One by one, each anxious traveler stepped onto the concrete pavement and took three steps into an enveloping cloud of black suits with clipboards. It looked like a disorganized greeting line at a funeral home. I observed each passenger dutifully hand over their passport and flight documents. A name was checked off a list; the individual resumed breathing and headed toward the idling bus. As they reached the last step each turned and waved up to the horde of watchers crowding each deck. Relief washed over face after face before disappearing into the void of their escape vehicle.

I could have been viewing a suspense film where the protagonists work their way toward freedom, each step increasing the fear of having it snatched away at the last moment. We were not just watching the movie—we were all cast members. Or was it a bad reality show? We held our collective breath until each person escaped from sight.

After an agonizing forty minutes just one young woman and a married couple remained on the dock. Another five minutes passed. They remained in deep conversation with the Uruguayan officials. Iain had stood nearby to observe; he now walked up to one of the officials and grabbed the cellphone. We grew more concerned. The married couple was our friends Jim and Wendee.

"Oh oh," I grimaced. We watched in semi-horror as the three stunned passengers were escorted to the cargo hold doors of the bus. They pointed to their suitcases; two officials removed them from the hold and dropped each bag next to its owner. I heard a grinding noise to my right, stunned to see the Plancius' gangway rising up and away from the dock to be secured near the ship's stern. Iain was directed to board the bus as the Uruguayan officials escorted the threesome back toward the empty space where the gangway had disgorged them. The SUVs started up, the flashing light bars moved into position and the caravan motored down the dock and out of sight.

Kathy turned to me, her worried voice wavering: "What's happening?"

I shook my head. "I don't know." I said, too sharply.

She took my hand.

But I did know.

We had a live, unobstructed view of our nightmare.

This was the worst-case scenario. Three of 'us' stranded on the dock—trapped between worlds with no clue about what might happen next. I kept my eye on Jim. He stayed cool and kept talking to the two remaining officials and the dock agent, who remained glued to his cellphone. Wendee sat motionless atop her suitcase, unfocused eyes gazing outward, hands clenched, no doubt to hold in her rising panic.

Another ten minutes crawled by. I heard a rumbling. I looked toward the stern and saw the gangway swing back into sight and descend slowly to the dock. Wendee, Jim and the young woman grabbed their suitcases and trudged back aboard.

As much as we wished for all the details, no one wanted to swarm the couple or upset them further, so we asked Margie to check on them and learn what help might be needed. Earlier Jim had asked me if he could contact my travel agent and I did pass Linda's contact information to him, but I do not think he ever called her.

Later at dinner we crowded around a single table to hear Margie's report. Neither Jim nor Wendee were present. Margie assumed that Jim was still on the phone trying to arrange new flights. She said that Wendee was resting in their cabin, still quite shaken by the incident.

Margie relayed their story. Jim had worried all along about missing their 4:30pm flight. When he approached the Uruguayan officials at the base of the gangway he asked if the late departure would pose a problem. It would not, according to one of the black suits. He was assured that the repatriation flight would be waiting. Neither flight would leave Montevideo until all assigned passengers were aboard. They were stopped at the dock because the officials could not find their names listed on any flight manifest covering the Sao Paulo to Chicago segment. One of the Uruguayan officials called the airline directly to correctly identify the problem. The call confirmed that Jim and Wendee—and the other woman left dockside—were not listed on the manifest because there was no manifest; their second flight had been cancelled. They had never received any notification from the airline.

A reverse tug-of-war ensued dockside. Uruguayan officials wanted the trio to return to the ship. Other government representatives suggested that, since they had stepped off the ship, international regulations required them to quarantine in Montevideo for 14 days. Meanwhile, the now less-cuddly Captain Artur refused to lower the gangway. The captain insisted that once passengers had disembarked, they should stay disembarked. Jim and Wendee's frustration and fear grew as they were ping-ponged between the men in black, the local dock agent, Oceanwide Expeditions officials in the Netherlands and unseen embassy staff. A compromise was reached. All parties agreed that Jim, Wendee and the young woman had physically moved only a few meters between ship and bus. Therefore, they had 'remained within the corridor sanitaire' and had not actually crossed any international border or political barrier. They would be allowed to re-board the ship, No harm, no foul. Oceanwide HQ ordered the captain to lower the gangway and the jurisdictional crisis was averted.

I strolled out on deck after sundown for one final dose (I hoped) of cool South American night air. Around ten o'clock I headed down the inside stairs to our corridor. I found Jim sitting on the last step typing furiously on his phone, completely focused on securing two open seats on a flight home. He radiated exhaustion, his tight face and furrowed brow reflecting the effort to remain calm and in control. I just squeezed his shoulder as I went by and told him I would be awake and available for any assistance, including a call to my agent. He blew out a deep, quick breath and nodded without looking up. I said goodnight and headed to my cabin.

TWENTY

DISEMBARKATION

"How many meters apart?"

THURSDAY, MARCH 26: CRUISE DAY 18

POSITION:	34°89'S / 56°19'W
WIND:	NNE 5
WEATHER:	CLEAR SKY
AIR TEMPERATURE:	+25C

What are the three hardest words for a man? "I am sorry."

What are the three hardest words for a woman? "I am ready."

Four decades of intense marital research taught me that when a woman says she is ready—as in ready to go somewhere or do something—it does not necessarily mean that she is ready to actually walk out the door at that moment. It usually means: "I am ready. I just have to find my shoes, fix my hair and feed the dog."

Kind of like the two-minute warning in football, if the two-minute warning lasted ten minutes. Perhaps "ready" for a woman means that she is, in fact, only psychologically ready to proceed. To be fair, when my wife says 'just fifteen minutes more' she is generally on target.

It was our last morning aboard the Plancius. We had slept little that night and had been awake and about for quite some time.

"So, are you all packed and ready to go? I asked my lovely wife.

"Yes," she replied.

"Great," I said. "Let me grab your suitcase from under the bunk and I will put them both outside the door for pick-up when we head to breakfast."

"Oh, well my bag is not ready."

"What?"

"I still have stuff in the bathroom."

"But you said...." I stopped.

"Give me ten minutes."

I took a breath and grabbed my phone to check e-mails. No e-mails from American Airlines and no flight alerts. No news was good news, I hoped.

Nine and a half minutes later Kathy asked, "Are you ready to go?"

We entered the dining room and joined Margie and Meg. Margie was immediately bombarded with questions from the concerned contingent surrounding her seat.

"How is Jim?"

"Have you seen Wendee?"

"Did they get flights?"

Margie answered that she had spoken with Jim late last evening. He had struggled until nearly midnight to secure flight reservations on the same flights that Kathy and I had booked. To no one's surprise neither appeared for breakfast that morning. After everyone's curiosity was satisfied Margie handed out contact names and numbers for two Sierra Club headquarters staff who were monitoring our situation and remained available to assist us if needed until we made it home.

I stayed quiet and mentally reviewed each step of our upcoming odyssey. Getting home would be the final step. I visualized each phase. I tried to imagine each possible question, snag, or roadblock from ship to bus, bus to airport, through security and onto a plane. I thought about repeating the process at the next airport, proceeding through US customs, transiting two more American airports, and finally arranging for a ride home thirty hours later. So much was unknown; so much had changed during the past eighteen days. Just eighteen days. I faced the realization that this final voyage home signified the end of the world as we knew it. I also faced my least favorite condition. I like change; I do not like uncertainty.

At 9am I hustled up to the morning briefing. Kathy had arrived just before me and spotted Jim and Wendee nearby. We joined them.

"Are you OK?" I asked.

Jim said yes. Wendee nodded, still looking a bit shaky. Kathy and the other women did their women thing and swarmed around Wendee, dispensing hugs and sympathetic utterances. Jim walked me through the details of yesterday's fiasco on the dock. He described his utter shock as he watched the gangway lift away from the dock. That was the lowest point, he said. He felt abandoned and stranded with no immediate options in sight.

He believed that the communication from Oceanwide authorities had turned the tide in their favor. I asked if the U.S. Embassy had played any role. He said no. Jim confirmed that after spending hours on hold with two different airlines he did finally secure seats on the same flights as Kathy and me, leaving that evening at 7:21pm for Santiago and then on to Miami.

Pippa began by the briefing by categorizing yesterday's near disaster as a 'learning experience' for the Uruguayan government officials and for the cruise line. She outlined the changes made for today's process and the schedule for disembarkation and departure.

- *Bus #1 would arrive at 11am to take passengers with afternoon flight times.*
- *Bus #2 (our bus) would arrive at 1pm to take the second group with later flights. (That's us.)*
- *Each group would be called to the Observation Lounge 45 minutes in advance.*
- *Each passenger would be issued gloves and a mask, which must be worn before stepping on the gangway and not removed at any time.*
- *To avoid the delay at the end of the gangway, all documents would be re-reviewed and approved prior to exiting the ship.*
- *Each passenger would be issued a letter signed by the captain and ship's doctor confirming their healthy status with no sign of illness.*
- *The bus would proceed directly to the airport under police escort.*

Doctor Helleke stepped up and demonstrated for the second time in two days how to properly tie and wear the thin protective mask, and most important, how to identify which side was 'right-side-out.'

An exhausted Helleke soldiered through her presentation. She circled the entire room correcting upside down masks or helping folks tie them behind their head. In fairness to the struggles of one member of my immediate family, the step that did require one to manipulate four thin cloth strings behind one's ears was a wee bit tricky. Helleke calmly helped my cabinmate readjust her mask right-side-up. No surprise that the ship's doctor and expedition crew looked like they had had little sleep for the past five days—because they had not.

For the past week, when Iain or Pippa or any team member was not delivering a briefing or lecture they were likely to be found in their cramped team office on deck six, just to the left of the steps leading up to the bridge. The crew had been tasked with collecting, interpreting, and communicating the latest information from Oceanwide headquarters, transmitting passport numbers and flight confirmations for 116 passengers and several crew back to Oceanwide, distributing the correct bundles to 27 different embassies and completing a mountain of paperwork requested by the Uruguayan officials. Pippa's tired visage reflected the pressure. She admitted that they had received the message loud and clear from headquarters: No Room for Error. Despite the time crunch and shifting demands she never failed to answer a question or return a smile. She and her fellow crew members labored through the night checking and re-checking every passport and flight document.

Previously each of us had been called by name to the crew office to confirm passport numbers and flight information. We were summoned back two nights later to repeat the process when the ship's destination shifted from Buenos Aires to Montevideo. Steffi and Mal tag-teamed assisting passengers without internet access to arrange their exit flights.

Down on deck three in her compact medical office Helleke had just spent two full days assessing each passenger's state of health and medication needs, especially for those who had not brought prescription meds for an unanticipated extra week at sea. Upon arrival at Montevideo she spent several more hours producing personalized 14-day quarantine and 'clean bill of health' documents that she handed out to each of us just before we walked off the ship.

Along with managing the extra duties imposed by the response to COVID-19, crew members confronted the same challenge that we all faced: How to get home. Everyone was responsible for handling their own travel arrangements to one of four different continents. Most employment contracts for expedition team members had expired on the 20th—our original cruise completion date. Helleke was needed back at her practice near Amsterdam. Mal and Dave struggled to find flights back to New Zealand, where they faced a national requirement to arrange a place for 14 days of quarantine immediately upon landing.

Steffi had already tried and failed a few times to resolve her unique dilemma—she currently had no home. As we killed time that afternoon over diet sodas Steffi shared her situation with me. She carried a German passport and still had family in that country, but she currently declared her residence as Austria. She had rented out her Vienna apartment, though, while working in the Czech Republic, where she rented a tiny detached living space on a friend's property. I shook my head. She had always taken for granted her ability to move about the European Union freely, but now all borders were swinging shut.

Ultimately, she opted to stay aboard for the journey to the Netherlands and figure things out along the way. Tom, Adam, Felicity, Pippa and even Helleke determined that the cross-Atlantic trip offered their best route home. Rustyn, who carried a U.S. passport but lived and worked in Chile stayed aboard as well. As a guide whose work depended on travelers visiting the Patagonian region, he saw no reason to rush back.

Other members of the crew intended to continue working aboard for a few weeks longer, but that all changed when the growing pandemic forced the indefinite cancellation of all cruises. I learned on my last day aboard that the questions of additional pay or assistance with flights home for stranded crew had not yet been answered. The shortened contract periods would cause additional problems for crew members like Mal, as he would explain to me later that evening while shuffling through airport security.

One benefit of the extended voyage was the unexpected opportunity to relax and swap tales with fascinating crew members. My first impression had labeled Steffi as a stiff, competent, no-nonsense individual. I should have known better. Our conversations exposed a terrific sense of humor. I laughed at her colorful descriptions of past exploits as she compared guests from different countries.

"The Germans are too formal and less fun," she explained.

They were "not as adventuresome" as this group, she said,

referring to our Antarctic contingent, but the German company paid very well.

She expanded upon her Lying Game story about competing for a German parachuting team in Saudi Arabia and how she attracted the eye of a crown prince. Hint: She was the only female member of the team. Steffi grinned as she recounted her imagined life under wraps in a desert. She was delightful.

Steffi was called away to help an anxious couple with overloaded bags. I walked over to the window. The Oceanwide flag hung lifeless under the harsh sun; another hot and sticky afternoon awaited. I turned to greet Dave, our other New Zealand mountaineering guide. He surprised us one evening with a last-minute video presentation that showcased his work as a search and rescue specialist. The piece demonstrated how he trained dogs to find people trapped by avalanches or other disasters. His dog-in-action shots produced plenty of 'ahhhs' and endeared him to the crowd.

His subdued 'morning, mate' greeting matched his faraway look as he joined me to gaze out at the small fishing boats across the harbor. I asked him how he was doing. He answered that he was set to leave on the late afternoon bus with us, but worried about whether he had the patience needed to get through the next two weeks.

Why? I asked.

Dave replied that New Zealand had been one of the first countries to take the coronavirus threat seriously and had quickly implemented nationwide measures to stop the spread. On one day earlier the prime minister has instituted a near-total shutdown and instructed all residents to stay at home. Upon arrival in Auckland Dave would be required to find a spot to wait out a 14-day quarantine. He explained that New Zealand is comprised of two islands; Auckland sits on one island and his home and family are located on the other one. No transportation service could get him from one island to the other because none were currently running. He reviewed his options with me. His mother lived on the north island where he would be landing, but he knew that she had no space in her assisted living apartment. He sounded even less enamored with the thought of spending two weeks with his sister's family, even though they had offered a room.

I asked Dave, and later Mal, why they thought New Zealanders accepted these restrictions without significant opposition, unlike the early reports from the U.S. They offered similar answers. Mal believed that New Zealanders trusted the government because they listened to health professionals. He appreciated the clarity of his nation's four-phase plan instituted to battle the virus. Dave respected their prime minister because she communicated honestly with the public. I told him I was envious of their functional government and wished him well.

The air in the lounge grew uncomfortably hot and stuffy. Minutes became hours. I checked the time on my phone. 10:15am. The first wave of passengers rechecked and rearranged their carry-ons, checked their masks, and exchanged another round of hugs. Like everyone else I kept one eye on the doorway for any signal from Pippa or Helleke that it was time to move. Nothing.

The clock touched 11am. Pippa appeared. The room hushed and each person froze in place. New plan, she said. The first bus would leave at 12:30pm and the second bus would depart around 2:00pm. Lunch would be served by 12 noon.

We bade goodbye to the early flyers one last time and headed down for a quick meal. Food offered a welcome distraction for nervous stomachs. Half of the dining room was closed off as the kitchen crew advanced the preparations for the next phase of their journey. My mouth watered and Kathy grinned as bowls of aromatic French onion soup were placed before us, a favorite of hers. Just as she raised the first spoonful to her mouth the ship's intercom erupted with a brisk "Good afternoon, everyone, good afternoon."

Pippa continued.

"We have just received word that the busses will be traveling in one caravan to the airport, and all busses will be leaving at 1:00pm. All passengers who are leaving today please report to the Observation Lounge immediately."

"Damn," complained the anguished diner on my right as she shoved one final spoonful into her mouth and grabbed her backpack. We dashed up the stairs into the lounge, grabbed a seat, and waited....and waited.

To no one's surprise, 1:00 came and went.

"I could have finished my soup!" exclaimed my exasperated travel partner. Pippa returned, looking as frustrated as the rest of us. Keeping her cool, she reported that the plan had changed—again. There would be two different busses after all. The original '11am' bus was on its way, and the second bus was now pushed back to 3:00pm.

The first bus arrived a few minutes later. We looked on with tempered excitement as the day's first round of disembarkation began. The process proceeded without drama or further delay. We waved our goodbyes as the caravan left the dock within thirty minutes. By 2:00 pm the count of remaining passengers had shrunk considerably. The quieted lounge contained a few of the second wave of hopefuls, plus passengers like Judy and Terry and LaRae, who along with a handful of others would be spending one more night on board.

As the afternoon dragged on, I grew more and more restless. I ventured out into the glaring sun just to seek any distractions visible in the harbor or the near empty shipyard. A few minutes of humid air took its toll. I wandered back inside to let my shirt dry and read for a bit. I kept glancing up at the clock. Come on!

Rustyn returned to converse with passengers and fellow crew. He picked up the microphone to get everyone's attention.

"We have a passenger, Carrie, whose mother who is turning 90 today," he announced.

He asked if we could crowd together to sing Happy Birthday to her phone. Forty of us gathered in the center of the lounge and sang away. Everyone clapped and cheered, happy as much for the distraction as for Carrie's mother.

Kathy nudged me. She suggested that we ask people to do that for us too. I felt bad that I had not thought of it. I thought we might have missed our chance.

"You don't think people will mind doing it again?"

"No, why don't you go ask Rustyn?"

I walked over to him and shared the news that today was also our daughter Jana's 36th birthday—and that she was a new mother. Would it be OK to do it again? Did he think folks would mind singing one more time?

"No, that would be great!" he lit up instantly. "Why don't we do a video!" He grabbed the microphone and made the second request. He was right. Everyone jumped up and reassembled. Kathy had read the room right.

I handed Rustyn my phone and we recorded another joyful, tone-deaf version of "Happy Birthday." I texted it to Jana immediately with the caption 'Here's a little greeting from all our friends on the Plancius to you!'

Five minutes later my phone beeped with her response:

"Hahaha...that is incredible! I started crying! Thank you... made my day!"

I read it to the room and thanked everyone again.

I spied Carlos relaxing in a corner, so I walked over to say goodbye and wish him luck getting home to Buenos Aires. After I returned to Tucson, I learned that Carlos had taken the bus to the Montevideo airport the next day as scheduled, but he was refused boarding and supposedly arrested by Uruguayan authorities. Later I got the complete and accurate story. He had not been arrested. The local officials had simply escorted him from airport and returned him to the ship—another victim of a canceled flight. He finally managed to successfully disembark on the morning of the 28th just a few hours before the Plancius cast off for the Netherlands. I never learned exactly what route he took to get home, but I was glad to know that he made it.

I exchanged goodbye handshakes and hugs with my Slovak friends Jaroslav, Eva, and daughter Suzie. Social distancing remained an unknown concept on the Plancius. Jaroslav had managed to arrange flights on two separate itineraries to Europe. Jaroslav and wife Eva were flying out that afternoon to Sao Paulo and then on to Frankfurt. Suzie and her brother would take the same route on the following day. I asked Jaroslav if he worried about the separation. He said that the kids, mid-to-late 20s adults, were delighted. He figured that the extra day would give him time to arrange flights for the last leg of their trip from Germany to Slovakia. I asked Suzie if she felt OK about being 'abandoned' by her folks. She smiled. "No, we love the idea!" They all seemed in good spirits and equally anxious to get going. Kathy observed that three weeks of togetherness would likely last them quite a while.

The analog clock above the bar continued to mock us. Kathy read, talked with others, or napped. I continued to wander between the lounge and outer deck welcoming any hint of a breeze while checking for any sign of our 1pm-now-3pm bus. We had received the good news earlier that yesterday's travelers made it home safely, but that did little to alleviate the peak-level stress that permeated the room. I was no exception. Worst-case imaginings ran rampant.

What if today is the day LATAM shuts down? What if we are stranded in Santiago? I had already looked up the number of the U.S. embassy in Chile just in case. What if our second flight is canceled? What if we are left on the dock like Jim and Wendee? What if someone sneezes? There were enough 'what ifs' to fill a third bus.

At 4:00pm Pippa announced that our bus was within sight. We lined up and began the single-file march. As we exited the lounge Felicity and Tom stood at the doorway to return passports back to their rightful owners. Helleke handed out our personal 'clean' letters and re-checked gloves and masks one final time. Her letter stated the following:

To Whom It May Concern:

This is to state that passenger Mr. Donald Jorgensen has been onboard our vessel MV Plancius during the voyage between Ushuaia (Argentina) and Montevideo (Uruguay). Passengers have embarked in Ushuaia, Argentina on the 9th of March 2020. Disembarkation will take place in Montevideo, Uruguay on the 25th of March 2020.

During the voyage, which passage went through the Antarctic areas, no other ports have been visited. A ships health declaration stating that all onboard are in good health and no virus-like symptoms have been reported has been provided to the Uruguayan authorities prior to arrival.

We descended the three short flights of stairs to the second deck and paraded along the outside corridor. With a quick nod goodbye to the crew members standing alongside I headed down the gangway. Ten seconds later I stepped onto solid ground for the first time in over a week. The unsmiling men in black motioned us toward the bus sitting fifty feet away. I spotted our bags being loaded aboard. At 4:30pm the engine rumbled to life. Our bus lined up behind the Ortelius bus and the official vehicles, their lights flashing. As we exited the dock area six motorcycle cops pulled alongside to guide our little parade through the streets of Montevideo. The two-wheeled escorts flashed lights and sirens as they raced ahead to block intersections, flip traffic lights to green and keep us on a steady 40 mile-an-hour pace. We rode through attractive commercial areas and motored alongside a beautiful cityside ocean beach and a rich green park before turning inland to speed through the lower rent districts to the airport. The caravan never slowed or stopped until we reached the terminal doors.

As we made our way through the corridor sanitaire I stared out of the windows for my first glimpse of the coronavirus world. Business and residential streets were nearly deserted on a beautiful Thursday afternoon. I spotted a bare handful of locals walking or jogging along empty beaches. It hit me again that we had abandoned a unique, safe environment separated from civilization to enter a new reality where norms had disappeared, new rules were in constant flux, and fear and uncertainty had taken hold. Men and women stared up from the street or down from balconies as our procession passed, a mix of curiosity and fear spread across their faces.

No doubt they had spent two weeks hearing horror stories of COVID-caused cruise ship death and disease—and here we were waving at them. Only the children waved back. I turned to Kathy.

"We know something that they do not," I said.

On that day they were safer from us than we were from them— or from anyone else on earth—at least for a few more hours.

Thirty minutes later we pulled up to the front of a modern-looking terminal. The Montevideo airport seemed no larger than Tucson's. It looked small to be serving a national capital, but I guess it is a small nation. I engaged in the free-for-all of spotting and grabbing our bags as they were tossed off the bus—the drivers could not seem to leave quickly enough. We hustled into the terminal. I doubled checked my gloves and mask as uniformed officials with unsmiling faces ushered us to specific check-in lines. Our two busloads of cruise escapees were the only customers in the echoing, nearly deserted hall. I glanced at the departure screens. Our 7:30pm flight was the only flight listed.

I wheeled my large suitcase around the S-line. As we crept closer to the check-in desk I was careful to stand on one of the blue circles spaced 2 meters apart. This was my first encounter with social distancing. Three hours later we stood in the security lines in the Santiago, Chile airport on little red circles spaced just 1 meter apart 'for our safety.' We soon learned that the development of new 'COVID rules' remained a work-in-progress.

On the final curve of the check-in line I was greeted by a tall, thin, tired-looking gentleman. He looked to be in his in early 50s. Next to him stood a woman in a dark-blue business suit. Both held official-looking clipboards. Neither wore a mask.

"Hello, we are from the U.S. Embassy here in Uruguay."

"Oh, so you do actually exist." I quipped. Oops, perhaps not the best comment to make when we are so close to getting the heck out of Dodge, but I could not help it. Plus, it had already been a long day.

"Your name, sir?" he asked, expressionless.

I answered and he made a checkmark on his list before returning his eyes to me. His partner looked me over with a tired expression. He waited a beat, then smiled and introduced himself as the Assistant U.S. Consul. We engaged in a brief but friendly conversation about the behind-the-scenes work involved in getting us off the ship. I shared our experience and our group's collective frustration with the mixed messages coming from his embassy (mostly accurate, as it turned out) and from the U.S. State Department in Washington, D.C., namely the "you're on your own" missives.

As he recounted the efforts made by his team on our behalf, I thought better of the local embassy officials. I wished him well and I thanked him. I appreciated the reminder of the dedication and pride found in the work of diplomats like him posted throughout the globe. If this is #45's so-called 'deep state,' then the joke's on him. Our country is well served by these committed careerists.

We breezed through the security checkpoint and grabbed a quick sandwich before boarding. Every seat was filled as we left Uruguayan soil for an uneventful flight over stunning Andes mountain vistas at dusk. The sprawling lights of Santiago glittered below us. We landed and taxied a short distance to the terminal; a single lone airplane sitting along a row of empty gates.

We walked off the plane still fully gloved and masked and made the short trek to our next departure point. Wary health officials eyed us as passed their stations. I kept my head turned forward as we strode past without a pause. The late-night airport scene seemed almost normal, except for the quiet, darkened hallways and the lack of tired bodies sprawled in corners or across seats awaiting a red-eye flight. A uniformed gate attendant directed all international travelers down another hallway to the international security checkpoint. Our Miami-bound contingent acted as though we had done this a hundred times before—most of us had—but that did not stop anyone's heart from pounding a little faster as we approached the next hurdle. Step by step we danced our one-meter-apart shuffle toward the x-ray machines. Mal stood behind me frowning at his phone.

"Is everything OK?" I asked.

He continued to scan his messages.

"Well, as of right now I have jumped ship," he replied without moving his head.

"Excuse me?"

He looked up with a slight grin. He explained that whenever a crew member leaves his ship, whether or not his contracted tour of duty has ended, that person must have all the necessary "sign-off forms" completed and on hand. He described the forms as written letters of sea service and testimonial provided by the ship's master that confirms the time of service on board. Mal had been given permission to disembark but had not yet received his form. Without such a document he could be questioned and detained at any border.

Mal later highlighted our recent experience for his hometown newspaper, the Wanaka Sun, on April 2, 2020:

"There was a rumour that there had been a case of Covid in Ushuaia when we left. Then as we sailed, news started coming in on what was happening around the world. I felt a little bit wary- but was still comfortable we could complete the trip, and everything would be ok.

But just before the Plancius left the Antarctic Peninsula, the Argentinian government closed down the port. Heading for Ushuaia was no longer an option, Haskins said, so the ship headed for Buenos Aries. However, there were riots at the Buenos Aries airport and crowds stopping planes from arriving.

"On the morning of March 24, we arrived in Montevideo. At that point, Argentina and Chile had closed their borders completely. Uruguay and Brazil were still open."

"We were dropped at the airport, and that's where Dave and I thought we would get caught in Uruguay because one of the things you need when you get off a ship is a letter from an agent to say this is arranged and you are not jumping ship.

"We didn't have this and immigration said they couldn't let us leave. We wouldn't have been able to go back on the ship because it was now in quarantine. Thankfully, in the end, we got the document from the agent, and we got on the flight with about two minutes to spare."

"Got it." Mal grinned at me again, a little wider this time. We passed through the security gauntlet, gathered our backpacks, shook hands, and exchanged farewells. He turned toward his gate to endure his 14-hour trip home and a 14-day quarantine in an Auckland hotel.

We boarded our Santiago to Miami flight on time. Once the plane ascended and leveled off, I felt my neck muscles loosen and my shoulders relax. Next stop U.S.A. Kathy and I discussed the possibility that our Miami to Tucson flights might still be canceled. Neither of us cared. Once back on American soil we would happily rent a car to drive across the country if necessary. As the cabin lights dimmed, I shared one last thought. We were flying over the south American continent—perhaps for the last time—and headed to an unfamiliar world: COVID-19 America. I recalled every text and e-mail from the past two weeks with the same warnings; "Don't come back—you are better off on the ship." It's bad, you won't recognize it." "It's a different world."

Kathy tilted her seat back to horizontal, inserted her ear plugs and donned her eye shade. I sat back and thought about my life ahead and the decision I had reached for managing the next phase of my life. I take nothing for granted. I appreciate the more relaxed pace, the increased control over my time, and the financial security that decades of hard work on both of our parts has produced. My health is good, and I am incredibly lucky to be spending this time with the most wonderful woman I know. My incredible wife has given me more love, support, and enjoyment out of life than I could have ever expected. Still, the transition over these past few years from a challenging, non-stop, ego-boosting work life to a slower, less demanding existence has been neither comfortable nor easy. I recall an old Wall Street investment commercial that proclaimed, "The reward for hard work is...more hard work." I used to believe it. That approach matched the lessons I absorbed from my New England upbringing, aided and abetted by Catholic guilt, both giving rise to that little voice in my head that always whispered, "it's not enough, you should do more."

It is OK not to feel guilty, I told myself, trying on the idea for size.

It is OK just to enjoy life as you choose, or semi-retirement, or whatever this is. Nope, the word retirement still does not fit for me. I recognized that I must stay active and engaged... in something.

No one knows how many days or years we will spend on this earth. Our family is rife with examples of that truism. Some lived into their nineties; others had died in their forties, and our son left us at age 25. A wise old friend in his seventies once said to me, "At this stage you can get busy living or get busy dying."

Surprisingly, this trip to Antarctica plus the 'bonus' days gave me the time and perspective I needed. I now had a plan. I have always operated with a plan—I cannot stop now!

I will continue to work with CARF and speak on behalf of ShelterBox as long as they will have me. They each represent meaningful activities and I can control the time required. But that work alone is not enough. So, I will say 'Yes' to major projects that spark my interest. A project might take the form of a service-oriented endeavor. It could be a professional opportunity or a personal challenge. It could be a time-limited position or an indefinite commitment.

When such an opportunity presents itself, I will commit to full engagement with one major effort at a time. Each commitment might take six months at a time, a year at a time, perhaps even longer. I do believe that a new approach may satisfy my need to engage in other useful efforts without feeling either overcommitted or trapped in a dull or long-term obligation. I will shoot for enjoyable, but with 'meaningful' there are no guarantees. Who knows? It's worth a shot.

Kathy and I can work together on my second goal: Have more fun. It is time.

At least my first short term project is already going well—it's called "Get Us Home!"

I am rarely affected by jet lag, though I rarely sleep on long flights. It takes Kathy about a week to recover but even she was feeling less tired than expected as we endured our last two flights. We were anxious to get home and understand firsthand 'Coronavirus World.' I looked over my recent news updates for March 27, 2020:

"Nobody would ever believe a thing like that's possible. Nobody could have ever seen something like this coming..." —#45 at a task force briefing making another false claim.

Multiple news reports confirmed that #45 had been briefed on the Coronavirus threat multiple times as early as January 2020.

The latest count: Over 100,000 cases in the U.S. Over 2000 deaths and rising.

The customs officer in Miami looked us over carefully when Kathy and I stepped up to his window.

"Where are you heading?"

"Home to Tucson."

He glanced down at his screen.

"Where have you been?"

"Antarctica."

"He looked back up at us for a moment and shook his head. He grabbed his stamp and banged it on each passport.

"Should have stayed there."

I was not surprised to discover that we had been re-routed for a third time and were now heading home via Dallas. Did not matter. We found Margie sitting among colorful rocking chairs between our adjoining departure gates. Margie was bound for L.A. and Sacramento.

As we sat in the sparse and eerily quiet terminal Meg, Margie, Kathy, and I stared at a small Asian-looking female wandering by in a full space suit. That was my first impression, and my first look at someone completely decked out in an anti-virus containment suit.

"A little extreme, don't you think?" My companions concurred.

It was March 27th. None of us had experienced the level of fear and uncertainty that enveloped the country. A month later I asked Kathy if she recalled that scene.

"It makes sense now." She said. I agreed.

In the BC era (Before Covid) I would pass through the familiar terminals at DFW at least a dozen times a year. There are few options when you head east from Tucson, so I was quite familiar with the Dallas shops, restaurants, food courts and quiet corners. Now all spots were quiet. The bustling, loud terminal had morphed into rows of empty chairs, covered restaurant tables, and all but a handful of newsstands and takeout stations deserted.

My friend Randy had thoughtfully texted me earlier that day with an offer to pick us up at the Tucson airport. He punctuated the offer with a vow of cleanliness following his self-quarantine. He stood a cautious six feet away while I loaded the bags into the back of his Prius. Then naturally I sat down in the front passenger seat two feet away from him as he drove through the empty Tucson streets. How exactly is this distancing supposed to work, I wondered again? Thirty minutes later we opened our front door to an assault of huge hugs from Sienna. She was not wearing a mask, but I believe that golden retrievers are exempt.

Two days later Kathy and I adjusted to another seismic shift brought about by the coronavirus. We participated in our first Zoom meeting. The video came up and I looked upon the beautiful faces of my daughter and my laughing, amazing 5-month old grandson. Even in this strange new world, Life is good.

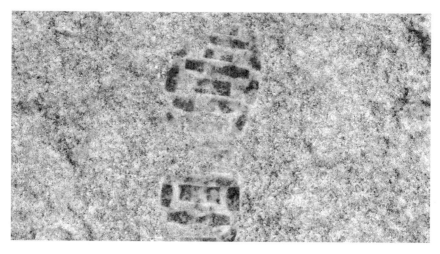

"One small step for a man...onto the seventh continent."

Kathy on a snow day.

Kathy, Margie, Meg

Nature's sculpture.

"Endless beauty."

A hungry leopard sea lurks.

"Have you been tested?"

Remains of the Deception Island whaling station.

Tommern. Hans Culliksen," 1871-1928.

"Meeting come to order." Deception Island fur seals.

"You lookin' at me?"

A lazy Weddell seal after lunch. The dark areas are blood.

Mid-polar plunge. Yes, it was that cold.

A rendezvous with the Ortelius.

Disembarkation Day 1. Jim is the large man in the center. Wendee on the left.

Unforgettable. (Photo taken by Dorette Kuipers)

EPILOGUE

The day after we returned home, we learned that all members of our Sierra Club group had arrived safely back in the U.S., and we received this eagerly awaited update from Margie:

> I have some news on Iain. I sent an e-mail to Pippa and got a response. She is on the Plancius, in the middle of the Atlantic, planning to be in the Netherlands around April 24.
>
> She got word from Iain. He made it home but had to self-isolate away from his expecting partner for two weeks, cutting it very fine for her due date. They finally reunited yesterday (she sent the e-mail April 11), lunch time....and by 10pm her waters broke!
>
> They welcomed a beautiful wee baby boy into the world in the wee hours of this morning (April 11)...So fantastic!
>
> Sally wrote to me and said she heard that the baby's name is

Struan...which means 'wee stream' in Scottish Gaelic. (Perfect.)

The more I hear about others stranded and trying to get home, the more grateful I am that we are all home safe, only extended our excursion by about a week, and we were safe, had shelter, food, and pirates!!!

I also found this final letter from Oceanwide Expeditions:

Update Coronavirus: Vessel update, 27 March 2020, 10.30pm

We are very pleased and relieved to inform, that this evening all passengers have disembarked our vessels Plancius and Ortelius in Montevideo, Uruguay.

All passengers are now on their way home!

It was an extreme expedition and we would sincerely thank our passengers for their patience and understanding, as it wasn't easy.

To all friends and families of our passengers, they will be home soon!

We want to express our appreciation to the authorities of Montevideo and Uruguay who made this possible in this very extreme situation, to provide a "corridor sanitaire" to the airport.

Lastly a special thanks to so many Embassies with whom we worked with in good cooperation over the last weeks. Their support and help were magnificent!

We wish our passengers safe travels back home.

"Difficulties are just things to overcome." —Ernest Shackleton

Michel van Gessel—CEO
Mark van der Hulst—COO
Oceanwide Expeditions

I laughed at the Shackleton quote. It might have been helpful to have expressed that in their first letter. Now it sounded like a silly pat on the back. Nevertheless, I had only good things to say about Oceanwide's handling of the entire matter. I sent a letter to the company a few days after we arrived home. It has since appeared on the Oceanwide Expeditions website (www.ocean-wide-expeditions.com.)

An Extraordinary Trip under Extraordinary Circumstances
by Don Jorgensen
Region: Antarctica
Destinations: Antarctic Peninsula
Ship: m/v Plancius

I wish to share our great respect and appreciation for the crew and staff of the Plancius during both the spectacular expedition cruise and the challenging second phase of our extended voyage— seeking a port at which to dock. I wish to single out the tireless work of the expedition leaders and staff, particularly Iain, Pippa, Steffi, Rustyn, Mal and Celine, with great support from Dorette, Felicity, Dave and Tom. At all times Iain and the team ensured that communication was swift and complete, that the passengers were fully informed and were getting the information, assistance and support they needed from the start of the trip through each challenging phase. I know that they did not consider their work complete until assured that every member had a plan to return home. Iain, as expedition leader, served as the perfect representative of Oceanwide in the demonstration of positive communication and support skills, transparency, and temperament. We would be remiss not to commend all of the hotel, dining, and cabin leaders and teams for their excellent work and positive attitudes as well from start to finish.

As you might have guessed, my first real 'project' is in your hands right now. I had not intended to write this much (and perhaps some of you wished I hadn't!), but during our self-quarantine after returning home I began putting my notes together from the trip...and this book happened. Thank you for reading it.

ACKNOWLEDGMENTS

Family, friends, and teamwork made all the difference in helping us to get home safely and avoid a South American quarantine or a slow boat to Europe. Thanks especially to Jana Jorgensen, Steve Thygersen, John Misiaszek and Randy Brooks. Thanks to Peg Gerber for her expert photo eye, and to Kathy Jorgensen for her helpful edits and ideas (and I only said, "write your own book" once!) The Most Valuable Player award must go to Linda Fugate, the world's greatest travel agent. Here is her view of our travel escapades as recorded in her log:

- *On the 5th of February when your journey started going wonky, AA answered the phone and helped me change the late schedule change time to an earlier departure.*
- *On the 6th of February I sent you your Ushuaia hotel confirmation.*
- *All was well.*

- *On March 3 I confirmed a private transfer to the Buenos Aires Hotel from the airport with the hotel concierge.*
- *On March 15 AA canceled your flight from BA to the US. I protected you in Business with an Aeromexico Flight into Mexico City and then to the US to the AA flight home.*
- *On March 16 I changed the USH flight from the 20th to the 21st. They did not answer the phone but the website gave instructions to change the dates.*
- *On March 18 USH to BA canceled*
  - Aeromexico canceled
  - First flight that showed up from USH to BA was the 26th so changed the flight to that date.
  - Searched for a new hotel since the one we used on the inbound was not available. Made the reservation for 5 nights.
- *On March 19 Canceled the non-refundable hotel.*
  - Canceled the hotel in Buenos Aries.
  - Canceled the private transfer.
  - Called the ship company and got my name put on an email list. Noted flights to them for the 26th out of BA still.
  - Started helping Meg W. with her reservations.
  - Changed AA reservation to LATAM through Santiago to Miami.
  - Updated Jana.
- *On March 20 Changed flights to leave out of Uruguay.*
- *Changed DFW AA flights to MIA DFW TUS*
- *On March 21 Flights confirmed*

- *On March 22 Watched the map as your ship steamed toward Uruguay. Loved this part. Knowing you were almost there.*
- *On March 23 Checking LATAM for confirmed flights after rumors from the ship saying otherwise.*
- *On March 26 Checked boarding procedures in Uruguay. LATAM flight delayed. Changed MIA to DFW flights to match Meg W.*
- *March 27 Success!*

SOURCES

"Protecting Whales to Protect the Planet," UN Environmental Programme Website, 2019

"The Pandemic at Sea," Rosalind S. Helderman, Hannah Sampson, Dalton Bennett and Andrew Ba Tran , Washington Post, April 25, 2020

"Whaling in Antarctica." CoolAntarctica.com

"Spotting a Royal Cypher," Georgina Tomlinson, 2016, www.postalmuseum.org

PLA32-20 Trip Log, www.oceanwide-expeditions.com

THE VOYAGE OF THE M/V PLANCIUS
(PLA32-20, Antarctic Peninsula, Basecamp)

LEFT HOME:	MARCH 6, 2020
RETURNED HOME:	MARCH 27, 2020
DAYS ON BOARD THE M/V PLANCIUS:	18 (MARCH 9-26, 2020)
TOTAL DISTANCE SAILED:	3047 NAUTICAL MILES
FURTHEST SOUTH:	64°84'S / 62°52'W
FURTHEST NORTH:	34°89'S / 56°19'W

Made in the USA
Columbia, SC
29 October 2020